NATHANIEL
HAWTHORNE

Bloom's Classic Critical Views

Jane Austen

Geoffrey Chaucer

Charles Dickens

Ralph Waldo Emerson

Nathaniel Hawthorne

Herman Melville

Edgar Allan Poe

Walt Whitman

Bloom's Classic Critical Views

NATHANIEL HAWTHORNE

Edited and with an introduction by
Harold Bloom
Sterling Professor of the Humanities
Yale University

BLOOM'S
LITERARY CRITICISM
An imprint of Infobase Publishing

Bloom's Classic Critical Views: Nathaniel Hawthorne

Copyright © 2008 Infobase Publishing

Introduction © 2008 by Harold Bloom

Bloom's Literary Criticism
An imprint of Infobase Publishing
132 West 31st Street
New York NY 10001

Library of Congress Cataloging-in-Publication Data
Nathaniel Hawthorne / [edited by] Harold Bloom.
   p. cm. — (Bloom's classic critical views)
A selection of important older literary criticism on Nathaniel Hawthorne.
Includes bibliographical references and index.
ISBN-13: 978-0-7910-9561-4 (hardcover)
ISBN-10: 0-7910-9561-4 (hardcover)
1. Hawthorne, Nathaniel, 1804–1864—Criticism and interpretation. I. Bloom, Harold.
II. Title: Bloom's classic critical views : Nathaniel Hawthorne.

PS1888.N296 2007
813'.3—dc22

                                                        2007016028

Bloom's Literary Criticism books are available at special discounts when purchased in bulk quantities for businesses, associations, institutions, or sales promotions. Please call our Special Sales Department in New York at (212) 967-8800 or (800) 322-8755.

You can find Bloom's Literary Criticism on the World Wide Web at
http://www.chelseahouse.com

Series design by Erika K. Arroyo
Cover design by Takeshi Takahashi
Printed in the United States of America
Bang EJB 10 9 8 7 6 5 4 3 2 1

This book is printed on acid-free paper.

All links and Web addresses were checked and verified to be correct at the time of publication. Because of the dynamic nature of the Web, some addresses and links may have changed since publication and may no longer be valid.

Contents

Series Introduction

Bloom's Classic Critical Views is a new series presenting a selection of the most important older literary criticism on the greatest authors commonly read in high school and college classes today. Unlike the Bloom's Modern Critical Views series, which for more than twenty years has provided the best contemporary criticism on great authors, Bloom's Classic Critical Views attempts to present the authors in the context of their time and to provide criticism that has proved over the years to be the most valuable to readers and writers. Selections range from contemporary reviews in popular magazines, which demonstrate how a work was received in its own era, to profound essays by some of the strongest critics in the British and American tradition, including Henry James, G K. Chesterton, Matthew Arnold, and many more.

Some of the critical essays and extracts presented here have appeared previously in other titles edited by Harold Bloom, such as the New Moulton's Library of Literary Criticism. Other selections appear here for the first time in any book by this publisher. All were selected under Harold Bloom's guidance.

In addition, each volume in this series contains a series of essays by a contemporary expert, who comments on the most important critical selections, putting them in context and suggesting how they might be used by a student writer to influence his or her own writing. This series is intended above all for students, to help them think more deeply and write more powerfully about great writers and their works.

Introduction by Harold Bloom

If the mythic being, "Walt Whitman," is our closest representation of the American "Adam early in the morning," then Hawthorne's Hester Prynne, besieged heroine of *The Scarlet Letter*, is still more the fictive American Eve, a worthy rival to Milton's rather English Eve in *Paradise Lost*. Hester luminously stands out against the darkening backgrounds of Hawthorne's vision of Puritan repression. Critics have remarked that Hester's tragedy was to have existed too early in American social history, a judgment I reject. Feminism and our enlightened sexual politics might not have saved the vitalistic, high-spirited Hester from the dilemma of never finding a man worthy of her sexual power and her self-reliance. The Satanic Chillingworth and the pathetic Dimmesdale would have been archaic objects for Henry James's Isabel Archer in *The Portrait of a Lady*, but the sublime Isabel, heiress of all the ages, marries the dreadful Osmond, fortune-hunter, snob, and parody of a Paterian aesthete. At seventy-seven, I meditate upon the thousands of young woman I have taught. How many of them—brilliant, beautiful, absolutely free to choose—have emulated Hester Prynne and Isabel! Shakespeare teaches us that most remarkable women have to marry down: Rosalind, Portia, Beatrice, Imogen, quite aside from Lady Macbeth in what I fear is the happiest marriage in all the plays. Both Hawthorne, and his reluctant disciple, Henry James, emulate the Shakespearean model.

I do not dispute the general judgment that James was, is, and perhaps always will be the most eminent of American novelists. Hawthorne, like his friend Melville, and like Faulkner in more recent time, composed romances rather than Balzacian novels. James's comments upon Hawthorne generally display (if I may reappropriate the phrase) the anxiety of influence. One could demonstrate that *The Wings of the Dove* is a strong creative misreading of

Hawthorne's *The Marble Faun*, just as Isabel Archer is a beguiling misprision of the superb Hester Prynne.

Aside from his two major novels, Hawthorne matters for his tales, the best of which seem to me superior to those of Melville, Mark Twain, James, Faulkner, Fitzgerald, and Hemingway. His masterpieces in this genre are extraordinarily diverse, from a historical story like "My Kinsman, Major Molineux" to fantasies like "Young Goodman Browne" and the uncanny "Wakefield" and "Feathertop." A flawless artist, Hawthorne provoked Henry James to a defensive condescension, manifested by James also in regard to George Eliot's *Middlemarch* and to much of Dickens. A marvelous critic where he felt unthreatened, as on Balzac and Turgenev, James could be rendered uneasy by genius closer to home. His most outrageous display was his review of Whitman's *Drum-Taps*, which he disowned later on, after Whitman had become the favorite poet of the James family.

Hawthorne, despite popular misconceptions, was no more a Puritan than was *his* favorite poet, Edmund Spenser. Any sensitive reader of Hawthorne would be wise to approach him without preconceptions. Emerson's "stairway of surprise" is about the only appropriate location for Hawthorne's fiction. Haunted by American history, Hawthorne nevertheless was a prophetic writer, hoping (like his Hester Prynne) for a new relation between women and men that may never transpire.

BIOGRAPHY

Nathaniel Hawthorne
(1804–1864)

Nathaniel Hawthorne was born in Salem, Massachusetts, on July 4, 1804. He was descended, on both sides, from prominent New England Puritans. In 1809, after the death of his father, Hawthorne moved, along with his mother and two sisters, into the home of his maternal grandparents. After studying at Samuel Archer's School (1819), Hawthorne attended Bowdoin College in Brunswick, Maine (1821–25), where his classmates included Henry Wadsworth Longfellow and future U.S. president Franklin Pierce whose campaign biography Hawthorne would write in 1852. Hawthorne returned to Salem in 1825 to live with his mother.

Rather than entering a trade or profession, as was expected of him, Hawthorne spent the next dozen years or so in relative isolation, concentrating on reading and writing. In 1828 he published a novel, *Fanshawe,* which drew heavily on his experiences at Bowdoin. Published anonymously and at his own expense, this book was later withdrawn by Hawthorne, who destroyed every copy he could find. Between 1830 and 1837, Hawthorne wrote tales and sketches for various periodicals, and in 1837 a collection was published as *Twice-Told Tales.* An expanded edition of the work appeared in 1842. After becoming engaged to Sophia Peabody in 1839, Hawthorne took a job as a measurer in the Boston custom house, and in 1841 he joined the Brook Farm community in West Roxbury, Massachusetts, from which he withdrew after several months. In 1842 Hawthorne and Sophia were married. They settled in Concord, where Hawthorne became a friend of Ralph Waldo Emerson, Henry David Thoreau, Margaret Fuller, and A. Bronson Alcott.

In 1846, the year in which his son, Julian, was born, Hawthorne published *Mosses for an Old Manse,* a collection of sketches and tales reprinted from a variety of periodicals. Between 1846 and 1849 he worked as a surveyor at the Salem custom house, and in 1850 he published *The Scarlet Letter,* which won him considerable fame. In this novel set in seventeenth-century New England, Hawthorne sought to explore the Puritan conscience through a drama of adultery and revenge. During 1850 and

1851 Hawthorne lived in Lenox, Massachusetts, where he became friendly with Herman Melville. In 1851, the year in which his daughter Rose was born, Hawthorne published his second novel, *The House of the Seven Gables*, a story of ancestral guilt partially based on his own family history. Also that year, a third collection of shorter pieces, *The Snow-Image and Other Twice-Told Tales*, appeared. *The Blithedale Romance*, based in large part on Hawthorne's experiences at Brook Farm, appeared in 1852, and was followed by two works for children, *A Wonder-Book for Girls and Boys* (1852) and *Tanglewood Tales* (1853), both based on Greek mythology.

In 1853 Hawthorne was appointed by President Franklin Pierce to serve as U.S. consul in Liverpool, a position he filled until 1857. He then spent from 1857 to 1859 living in Rome and Florence, an experience that inspired his novel *The Marble Faun*. This was his last completed work of fiction. In 1860 Hawthorne returned to Concord, where he spent the rest of his life. In 1863 he published *Our Old Home*, a series of essays on England and Anglo-American relations. Hawthorne traveled to New Hampshire in 1864 in an attempt to improve his failing health. On May 19 of that year he died at Plymouth, leaving four unfinished works. After his death, Sophia Hawthorne edited his English, American, and European notebooks, and several collected editions of his letters have been issued since.

PERSONAL

Accounts of Hawthorne's personal traits and qualities are not necessarily indexes to his work. However, students interested in the psychology of the author, and how this might relate to his writing, will find assessments here by some of the shrewdest judges. Hawthorne was so austere and reclusive that a cult of personality developed around him, even in his lifetime. Gossipy and legendary details about Hawthorne form a literature of their own.

As Herman Melville remarks in the letter included in this section, if Hawthorne the man was conspicuously absent, his writing was a ubiquitous presence in cultural society in the 1850s, and happily many of the foremost writers of the age had an opinion on him. Most of the great writers—an unprecedented majority—of the so-called American Renaissance (Edgar Allan Poe, Ralph Waldo Emerson, Melville, Henry David Thoreau, Emily Dickinson) have voiced in writing some view of Hawthorne, as evidenced here. A good portion of those writers had some personal acquaintance with him. Students interested in Hawthorne's relations to his contemporaries will find useful firsthand insights in these recollections.

Hawthorne lived in Concord, Massachusetts, between July 1842 and 1845 and again between 1852 and 1853. While residing there, he had considerable interaction with many of the transcendentalist writers and thinkers, particularly Emerson, Thoreau, and A. Bronson Alcott. Extracts from their journals, memoirs, and correspondences are included in this volume. Students looking at Hawthorne's philosophy and how it relates to transcendentalism (or how it does not) should consult them.

Although Hawthorne's books were everywhere in society, Hawthorne himself was not. Maria Mitchell, Bronson Alcott, George Hillard, and Charles Godfrey Leland all refer to Hawthorne's legendary shyness, an almost morbid recoil from social exchange. Students writing on the relations between self and society in Hawthorne's work—an enduring theme— should delve into those excerpts. Students discussing Hawthorne's view on the role of the writer in society will find plenty among these accounts. The author's social aloofness is significant when related to the tenor and subject of his fiction. Themes of solitude and communication, and their ethical dimension, become central.

Alcott finds Hawthorne almost strangled by his own diffidence, and relates this to Hawthorne's writing. He supposes that Hawthorne needed the pen simply to communicate with the outer world, as he was so awkward in company. Alcott believes Hawthorne is so aloof that he is even alienated from himself, a state that Alcott avers Hawthorne's "readers must feel."

Also noteworthy are the several references to Hawthorne's "feminine aspect." Writers such as James Russell Lowell, Bronson Alcott, and George S. Hillard allude almost queasily to Hawthorne's uncanny empathy with women. Alcott asks: "Was he some damsel imprisoned in that manly form?" He diagnoses Hawthorne's social reticence as similarly feminine: "as coy as a maiden." Students should consult these views when studying Hawthorne's written portrayal of women (primarily, obviously, Hester Prynne) and also when applying themes of gender and gender subversion to Hawthorne's work and the mores of his time.

George S. Hillard notes that Hawthorne was no great reader, and owned few books. This is an important distinction, and helpful to students examining questions of influence in Hawthorne's writing. Such a view is supported by George Parsons Lathrop's claim that Hawthorne was less erudite than Goethe but therefore had "less of the freezing pride of art." Andrew Preston Peabody also finds a conspicuous lack of quotation from poetry in Hawthorne: "we cannot remember a single poetic quotation in all his writings," while T.S. Eliot finds Hawthorne's mind "closed to new impressions" and complains that "Hawthorne, with his very limited culture, was not exposed to a bewildering variety of influences." This limitation was viewed as a virtue in an earlier review by Longfellow, however, when he remarked that Hawthorne "does not see by the help of other men's minds, and has evidently been more of an observer and thinker, than of a student." This remark seems somewhat ironic, since Longfellow was Hawthorne's classmate at Bowdoin College.

NATHANIEL HAWTHORNE (1821)

I have not yet concluded what profession I shall have. The being a minister is of course out of the question. I should not think that even you could desire me to choose so dull a way of life. Oh, no, mother, I was not born to vegetate forever in one place, and to live and die as calm and tranquil as—a puddle of water. As to lawyers, there are so many of them already that one half of them (upon a moderate calculation) are in a state of actual starvation. A physician, then, seems to be "Hobson's choice;" but yet I should not like to live by the diseases and infirmities of my fellow-creatures. And it would weigh very heavily on my conscience, in the course of my practice, if I should chance to send any unlucky patient "ad inferum," which being interpreted is, "to the realms below." Oh that I was rich enough to live without a profession! What do you think of my becoming an author, and relying for support upon my pen? Indeed, I think the illegibility of my handwriting is very author-like. How proud you would feel to see my works praised by the reviewers, as equal to the proudest productions of the scribbling sons of John Bull. But authors are always poor devils, and therefore Satan may take them. I am in the same predicament as the honest gentleman in *Espriella's Letters.*

> "I am an Englishman, and naked I stand here,
> A-musing in my mind what garment I shall wear."

But as the mail closes soon, I must stop the career of my pen. I will only inform you that I now write no poetry, or anything else.

—Nathaniel Hawthorne, Letter to His Mother
(March 13, 1821), cited in Julian Hawthorne,
Nathaniel Hawthorne and His Wife, 1884, Vol. 1, pp. 107–08

SOPHIA PEABODY HAWTHORNE (1842)

One afternoon Mr. Emerson and Mr. Thoreau went with him down the river. Henry Thoreau is an experienced skater, and was figuring dithyrambic dances and Bacchic leaps on the ice—very remarkable, but very ugly, methought. Next him followed Mr. Hawthorne who, wrapped in his cloak, moved like a self-impelled Greek statue, stately and grave. Mr. Emerson closed the line, evidently too weary to hold himself erect, pitching headforemost, half lying on the air.

—Sophia Peabody Hawthorne, letter to Mrs. Caleb Foote,
quoted in Rose Hawthorne Lathrop, *Memories of Hawthorne,*
Boston, 1897, p. 53

EDGAR ALLAN POE (1843)

In this letter to James Russell Lowell (see the following entry), the poet, essayist, and author of tales "grotesque and arabesque" Edgar Allan Poe seeks a contribution from Hawthorne for his projected monthly magazine *The Stylus*. Hawthorne agreed at first, even offering to procure a portrait of his likeness by his wife, but eventually had to bow out, regretfully pleading that he had "no more brains than a cabbage" at present. The letter should prove relevant to students comparing Hawthorne's work with Poe's, revealing the social tenor of the exchanges between the two writers.

When you find yourself in condition to write, I would be indebted to you if you could put me in the way of procuring a brief article (also for my opening number) from Mr. Hawthorne—whom I believe you know personally. Whatever you gave him, we should be happy to give. . . . Could you put me in possession of any likeness of yourself?—or could you do me the same favor in regard to Mr. Hawthorne?—You perceive I proceed upon the ground that you are intimate with Mr. H, and that making these inquiries would not subject you to trouble or inconvenience.

—Edgar Allan Poe, Letter to James Russell Lowell
(March 27, 1843), cited in John Ward Ostrom (ed.),
The Letters of Edgar Allan Poe, 1966, Vol. 1, pp. 232–33

JAMES RUSSELL LOWELL (1848)

James Russell Lowell was foremost a poet but also variably a Harvard professor, an essayist, a humorist, and the one-time American ambassador in London. As an editor, he published Hawthorne in *The Pioneer* and then the *Atlantic*. In his breakthrough poem "A Fable for Critics," Lowell evaluated his contemporaries—for the most part savagely. His dispatch of Poe is perhaps the most famous, and exemplifies the ambivalent tenor of the poem: "three fifths of him genius and two fifths sheer fudge." Lowell's account of Hawthorne is relatively kind in comparison, and his barbed pen was distinguished at least by candor in an age of unctuous and uncritical puffery. Bronson Alcott pronounced it the finest criticism of Hawthorne.

There is Hawthorne, with genius so shrinking and rare
That you hardly at first see the strength that is there;
A frame so robust, with a nature so sweet,

So earnest, so graceful, so solid, so fleet,
Is worth a descent from Olympus to meet;
'Tis as if a rough oak that for ages had stood,
With his gnarled bony branches like ribs of the wood,
Should bloom, after cycles of struggle and scathe,
With a single anemone trembly and rathe;
His strength is so tender, his wildness so meek,
That a suitable parallel sets one to seek,
—He's a John Bunyan Fouque, a Puritan Tieck;
When Nature was shaping him, clay was not granted
For making so full-sized a man as she wanted,
So, to fill out her model, a little she spared
From some finer-grained stuff for a woman prepared,
And she could not have hit a more excellent plan
For making him fully and perfectly man.
The success of her scheme gave her so much delight,
That she tried it again, shortly after, in Dwight;
Only, while she was kneading and shaping the clay,
She sang to her work in her sweet childish way,
And found, when she'd put the last touch to his soul,
That the music had somehow got mixed with the whole.

—James Russell Lowell, *A Fable for Critics*, 1848

HERMAN MELVILLE (1852)

Herman Melville, novelist and poet, was perhaps Hawthorne's best-known—and most eloquent—champion. Melville famously dedicated his most ambitious novel, *Moby-Dick* (1851), to Hawthorne. For more than a year, the two writers lived with their families within six miles of each other in Berkshire County, Massachusetts, and the men shared a warm friendship and correspondence. For Melville, Hawthorne seems to have come cautiously but willingly out of his social shell. They were intellectual equals and kindred spirits. One critic has called them "brothers in despair." Conversely in some ways they were very different: Hawthorne a "fatalist," Melville a "rebel."

In the period between August 1850 and November 1851, the two men shared endless conversations about "time and eternity" (Melville called them "ontological heroics") over drinks and under cigar smoke. Their correspondence continued through 1857.

Their relationship—and the correspondence—was intense. Some critics have suggested that it was *too* intense for Hawthorne. It is even claimed erroneously that he left Berkshire County out of embarrassment at Melville's ardor. Melville burned the letters he received from Hawthorne—a customary practice of his—so an adequate explanation can never be satisfactorily ascertained.

It has been further argued that Melville represented Hawthorne somewhat bleakly in his novel *The Confidence Man* in the guise of huckster Frank Goodman and as the shy pilgrim Vine in his epic poem *Clarel*.

Here, Melville describes the popular reception of *The Blithedale Romance*. His description will be useful to any student considering the social make-up of Hawthorne's readership.

———— ———— ————

My Dear Hawthorne:—This name of "*Hawthorne*" seems to be ubiquitous. I have been on something of a tour lately, and it has saluted me vocally & typographically in all sorts of places & in all sorts of ways. I was at the solitary Crusoeish island of Naushon (one of the Elisabeth group) and there, on a stately piazza, I saw it gilded on the back of a very new book, and in the hands of a clergyman.—I went to visit a gentleman in Brooklyne, and as we were sitting at our wine, in came the lady of the house, holding a beaming volume in her hand, from the city—"My Dear," to her husband, "I have brought you *Hawthorne's* new book." I entered the cars at Boston for this place. In came a lively boy "*Hawthorne's* new book!"—In good time I arrived home. Said my lady-wife "there is Mr *Hawthorne's* new book, come by mail" And this morning, lo! on my table a little note, subscribed *Hawthorne* again.—Well, the Hawthorne is a sweet flower; may it flourish in every hedge.

I am sorry, but I can not at present come to see you at Concord as you propose.—I am but just returned from a two weeks' absence; and for the last three months & more I have been an utter idler and a savage—out of doors all the time. So, the hour has come for me to sit down again.

Do send me a specimen of your sand-hill, and a sunbeam from the countenance of Mrs: Hawthorne, and a vine from the curly arbor of Master Julian.

As I am only just home, I have not yet got far into the book but enough to see that you have most admirably employed materials which are richer than I had fancied them. Especially at this day, the volume is welcome, as an antidote to the mooniness of some dreamers—who are merely dreamers—Yet who the devel aint a dreamer?

—Herman Melville, Letter to Nathaniel Hawthorne,
July 17, 1852

George W. Curtis "Hawthorne"
(1853)

George William Curtis was an American literary journalist, editor, and political reformer. He was a member of the Brook Farm community along with Hawthorne, who befriended Curtis there. As an aspiring writer and a social climber, Curtis joined Concord's salons. He here describes Hawthorne at one such salon among the transcendentalists. He provides an exclusive account of Hawthorne's private "intellectual" demeanor and its variously awestruck and amused reception among the high-thinkers of Concord.

———— ———— ————

During Hawthorne's first year's residence in Concord, I had driven up with some friends to an aesthetic tea at Mr. Emerson's. It was in the winter and a great wood-fire blazed upon the hospitable hearth. There were various men and women of note assembled, and I, who listened attentively to all the fine things that were said, was for some time scarcely aware of a man who sat upon the edge of the circle, a little withdrawn, his head slightly thrown forward upon his breast, and his bright eyes clearly burning under his black brow. As I drifted down the stream of talk, this person, who sat silent as a shadow, looked to me, as Webster might have looked had he been a poet,—a kind of poetic Webster. He rose and walked to the window, and stood quietly there for a long time, watching the dead white landscape. No appeal was made to him, nobody looked after him, the conversation flowed steadily on as if everyone understood that his silence was to be respected. It was the same thing at table. In vain the silent man imbibed aesthetic tea. Whatever fancies it inspired did not flower at his lips. But there was a light in his eye which assured me that nothing was lost. So supreme was his silence that it presently engrossed me to the exclusion of everything else. There was very brilliant discourse, but this silence was much more poetic and fascinating. Fine things were said by the philosophers, but much finer things were implied by the dumbness of this gentleman with heavy brows and black hair. When he presently rose and went, Emerson, with the "slow, wise smile" that breaks over his face, like day over the sky, said:

"Hawthorne rides well his horse of the night."

Thus he remained in my memory, a shadow, a phantom, until more than a year afterward. Then I came to live in Concord. Every day I passed his house, but when the villagers, thinking that perhaps I had some clue to the mystery, said:

"Do you know this Mr. Hawthorne?" I said: "No," and trusted to Time.

> —George W. Curtis, from "Hawthorne" (1853),
> *Homes of American Authors,* pp. 299–300

S.G. GOODRICH (1856)

Hawthorne . . . was of a rather sturdy form, his hair dark and bushy, his eye steel-gray, his brow thick, his mouth sarcastic, his complexion stony, his whole aspect cold, moody, distrustful. He stood aloof, and surveyed the world from shy and sheltered positions.

> —S.G. Goodrich, *Recollections of a Lifetime,*
> 1856, Vol. 2, pp. 269–70

MARIA MITCHELL (1857)

I sent my letter at once; from all that I had heard of Mr. Hawthorne's shyness, I thought it doubtful if he would call, and I was therefore very much pleased when his card was sent in this morning. Mr. Hawthorne was more chatty than I had expected, but not any more diffident. He remained about five minutes, during which time he took his hat from the table and put it back once a minute, brushing it each time. The engravings in the books are much like him. He is not handsome, but looks as the author of his books should look; a little strange and odd, as if not of this earth. He has large, bluish-gray eyes; his hair stands out on each side, so much so that one's thoughts naturally turn to combs and hair-brushes and toilet ceremonies as one looks at him.

> —Maria Mitchell, *Journal* (August 5, 1857), *Life, Letters, and Journals of Maria Mitchell,* ed. Phebe Mitchell Kendall, 1896, p. 89

HENRY DAVID THOREAU (1843–60)

As significant as Hawthorne's social remove was, his friendships are also revealing. That other well-known literary loner, Henry David Thoreau, did not mention Hawthorne's aloofness at all. Relevant entries from Thoreau's journal brim with fondness for, and fellowship with, Hawthorne, who is viewed as a fellow "saunterer" (a term loaded with meaning for Thoreau, evident in his essay on "Walking"). Far from gloomy, Thoreau found

Hawthorne "simple and child-like" and admired his writing (evidenced below in his appreciative reference to "The Minister's Black Veil" in his journal). Hawthorne likewise esteemed *Walden* and its author ("one of the few persons . . . with whom to hold intercourse is like hearing the wind among the boughs of a forest tree") and arranged a few lectures for Thoreau at the Salem Lyceum. However, Hawthorne found Thoreau "not an agreeable person." Thoreau, it has also been authoritatively claimed, was the basis for Donatello in *The Marble Faun*.

These excerpts demonstrate the ease with which Thoreau and Hawthorne related, and the camaraderie Thoreau felt for his friend ("Tell him not to desert"). The men traded music boxes. Students discussing Hawthorne's place among his literary peers (particularly Thoreau, of course) should read these excerpts. Perceptions of Hawthorne in a wider circle, beyond the literary salons, are voiced in Thoreau's journal entry for July 4, 1855, in which the former neighbor of Mr. Bull—Nathaniel Hawthorne—is described by a cobbler in a tavern. This is valuable to students researching perceptions of Hawthorne among a wider—even nonreading—audience.

I think I must have some muses in my pay that I know not of—for certain musical wishes of mine are answered as soon as entertained. Last summer I went to Hawthorne's suddenly for the express purpose of borrowing his music box, and almost immediately Mrs. H. proposed to lend it to me.

> —Letter to Mrs. Lucy Brown (January 24, 1843),
> Walter Harding and Carl Bode (eds.),
> *The Correspondence of Henry David Thoreau,*
> 1958, p. 76

And Hawthorne too I remember as one with whom I sauntered in old heroic times along the banks of the Scamander, amid the ruins of chariots and heroes. Tell him not to desert even after the tenth year.

> —Letter to Mr. and Mrs. Ralph Waldo Emerson,
> (July 8, 1843), *Correspondence of Thoreau*, p. 124

I thought to walk this forenoon instead of this afternoon, for I have not been in the fields and woods much of late except when surveying, but the least affair of that kind is as if you had [a] black veil drawn over your face which shut out nature, as that eccentric and melancholy minister whom I have heard of.

> —July 21, 1851, *Journal*, Vol. II, p. 326–27,
> Boston: Houghton Mifflin, 1906

Went to Gifford's Union House (the old Tailor's Inn) in Provincetown. . . . Talked with Nahum Haynes, who is making fisherman's boots there. He came into the tavern in the evening. I did not know him—only that he was a Haynes. He remembered two mud turtles caught in a seine with a shad on the Sudbury meadows forty years ago, which would weigh a hundred pounds each. Asked me, "Who was that man used to live next to Bull's,—acted as if he were crazy or out?"

> —July 4, 1855, *Journal*, Vol. VII, p. 432

I suppose that you have heard that Mr. Hawthorne has come home. I went to meet him the other evening & found that he has not altered except that he was looking pretty brown after his voyage[.] He is as simple & child-like as ever.

> —Letter to Sophia Thoreau (July 8, 1860),
> *Correspondence of Thoreau*, p. 582

FRANKLIN PIERCE (1864)

Franklin Pierce, the fourteenth president of the United States, serving from 1853 through 1857, was a friend and classmate of Hawthorne's at Bowdoin College in Brunswick, Maine. They remained friends throughout life, with Hawthorne writing Pierce's presidential campaign biography (*Life of Franklin Pierce*, 1852). As he testifies here, Pierce was also the one who discovered Hawthorne immediately after his death. The two friends had taken a trip by carriage to New Hampshire, ostensibly to rally Hawthorne's poor health. It has since been suggested that Hawthorne went with his old friend fully knowing he would die.

The poet Henry Wadsworth Longfellow—featured in the subsequent excerpt—was another classmate from Bowdoin, who here provides a eulogy.

You will have seen, with profound sorrow, the announcement of the death of the dearest and most cherished among our early friends.

You will wish to know something more of Hawthorne's last days than the articles in the newspapers furnish. . . .

We arrived at Plymouth about six o'clock. After taking a little tea and toast in his room, and sleeping for nearly an hour upon the sofa, he retired. A door opened from my room to his, and our beds were not more than five or six feet apart. I remained up an hour or two after he fell asleep. He was apparently less restless than the night before. The light was left burning in my room—the door open—and I could see him without moving from my bed. I went, however, between one and two o'clock to his bedside, and supposed him to be in a profound slumber. His eyes were closed, his position and face perfectly natural. His face was towards my bed. I awoke again between three and four o'clock, and was surprised—as he had generally been restless—to notice that his position was unchanged—exactly the same that it was two hours before. I went to his bedside, placed my hand upon his forehead and temple, and found that he was dead. He evidently had passed from natural sleep to that sleep from which there is no waking, without suffering, and without the slightest movement. . . .

The funeral is to take place at Concord, Monday, at one o'clock. I wish you could be there. I go to Lowell this afternoon, and shall drive across the country to C. to-morrow evening. I need not tell you how lonely I am, and how full of sorrow.

> —Franklin Pierce, Letter to Horatio Bridge (May 21, 1864),
> cited in Horatio Bridge, *Personal Recollections of
> Nathaniel Hawthorne,* 1893, pp. 176–79

HENRY WADSWORTH LONGFELLOW
"HAWTHORNE" (1864)

How beautiful it was, that one bright day
  In the long week of rain!
Though all its splendour could not chase away
  The omnipresent pain.
The lovely town was white with apple-blooms,
  And the great elms o'erhead

Dark shadows wove on their aerial looms
　　Shot through with golden thread.
Across the meadows, by the gray old manse,
　　The historic river flowed:
I was as one who wanders in a trance,
　　Unconscious of his road.
The faces of familiar friends seemed strange;
　　Their voices I could hear,
And yet the words they uttered seemed to change
　　Their meaning to my ear.
For the one face I looked for was not there,
　　The one low voice was mute;
Only an unseen presence filled the air,
　　And baffled my pursuit.
Now I look back, and meadow, manse, and stream
　　Dimly my thought defines;
I only see—a dream within a dream—
　　The hill-top hearsed with pines.
I only hear above his place of rest
　　Their tender undertone,
The infinite longings of a troubled breast,
　　The voice so like his own.
There in seclusion and remote from men
　　The wizard hand lies cold,
Which at its topmost speed let fall the pen,
　　And left the tale half told.
Ah! who shall lift that wand of magic power,
　　And the lost clew regain?
The unfinished window in Aladdin's tower
　　Unfinished must remain!

　　　　　—Henry Wadsworth Longfellow, "Hawthorne," 1864

RALPH WALDO EMERSON (1838–68)

Ralph Waldo Emerson, the so-called Sage of Concord, was a Unitarian minister *manqué*, a poet, essayist, and lecturer, and one of the "Representative Men" (his term, though not for himself) of nineteenth-century American letters and society. He also lived in Concord, where pilgrims, disciples, and the curious gathered to see him and speak with him. Hawthorne moved to Concord in 1842, directly after his marriage to Sophia Peabody. The couple lived for the next three years in the recently vacated Emerson family home, the Old Manse.

Hawthorne subsequently wrote about Emerson in the preface to *Notes from an Old Manse,* and his tone is slightly facetious and chiding. He was amused by Emerson. The Sage of Concord, meanwhile, was variously bemused, disappointed, and impressed by Hawthorne, as can be seen in the following excerpts from Emerson's voluminous correspondence and journal.

Although the men were friends, Emerson's references to Hawthorne in his journal are almost always critical. Only in one letter (and never in the journal) does Emerson find anything to praise (Hawthorne's allegorical tale "The Celestial Railroad"). Emerson's objections will be useful to students examining Hawthorne's relationship with the transcendentalists.

There is "no inside" to one story, Emerson grumbles. Hawthorne cannot write dialogue, he snipes elsewhere. "His writing is not good for anything," he goes on. How much validity is there to such criticisms? Students examining Hawthorne's style should look here.

Emerson provides an account of Hawthorne's funeral, which prompted Emerson to launch into a reverie concerning his own mortality. While Melville addresses Hawthorne the popular writer, mentor, and successful man of letters, Emerson looks to the one with whom he rambled through Sleepy Hollow. "I thought him a greater man than any of his works betray," he remarks after the funeral.

Elizabeth Peabody brought me yesterday Hawthorne's *Footprints on the Seashore* to read. I complained that there was no inside to it. Alcott and he together would make a man.

—*Journal,* June 13, 1838

It is no easy matter to write a dialogue. Cooper, Sterling, Dickens, and Hawthorne cannot.

—*Journal,* September 18, 1839

Nathaniel Hawthorne's reputation as a writer is a very pleasing fact, because his writing is not good for anything, and this is a tribute to the man.

—*Journal,* September 1842

Hawthorne walked with me yesterday p.m. and not until after our return did I read his "Celestial Railroad" which has a serene strength which one cannot afford not to praise,—in this low life.

—Letter to Thoreau (June 10, 1843), Walter Harding
and Carl Bode (eds.), *The Correspondence of*
Henry David Thoreau, 1958, p. 118

Hawthorne and I talked of the number of superior young men we have seen. H. said that he had seen several from whom he had expected much, but that they had not distinguished themselves; and he had inferred that he must not expect a popular success from such; he had in nowise lost his confidence in their power.

—*Journal*, June 10, 1843

Hawthorne invites his readers too much into his study, opens the process before them. As if the confectioner should say to his customers, 'Now, let us make the cake.'

—*Journal*, May 1846

Mrs. Ripley at Brook Farm, said the hard selfishness of the socialists ruined the Community. Hawthorne, I believe, sued the members for their debt to him. Howard the great philanthropist was harsh to his children., & Sterne the sentimentalist had a bad name for hardness to his mother.

—*Journal*, January–February 1861,
Porte, *Emerson in His Journals*

Yesterday, May 23, we buried Hawthorne in Sleepy Hollow, in a pomp of sunshine and verdure, and gentle winds. James Freeman Clarke read the service in the church and at the grave. Longfellow, Lowell, Holmes, Agassiz, Hoar, Dwight, Whipple, Norton, Alcott, Hillard, Fields, Judge Thomas, and I attended the hearse as pallbearers. Franklin Pierce was with the family. The church was copiously decorated with white flowers, delicately arranged. The corpse was unwillingly shown,—only a few moments to this company of his friends. But it was noble and serene in its aspect,—nothing amiss,—a calm and powerful head. A large company filled the church and the grounds of the cemetery. All was so bright and quiet that pain or mourning was hardly suggested, and Holmes said to me that it looked like a happy meeting.

Clarke in the church said that Hawthorne had done more justice than any other to the shades of life, shown a sympathy with the crime in our nature, and, like Jesus, was the friend of sinners.

I thought there was a tragic element in the event, that might be more fully rendered,—in the painful solitude of the man, which, I suppose, could not be long endured, and he died of it.

I have found in his death a surprise and disappointment. I thought him a greater man than any of his works betray, and there was still a great deal of work in him, and that he might one day show a purer power. Moreover, I have felt sure of him in his neighbourhood, and in his necessities of sympathy and intelligence,—that I could well wait his time,—his unwillingness and caprice,—and one day might conquer a friendship. It would have been a happiness, doubtless to both of us, to have come into habits of unreserved intercourse. It was easy to talk with him,—there were no barriers,—only, he said so little, that I talked too much, and stopped only because, as he gave no indications, I feared to exceed. He showed no egotism or self-assertion, rather a humility, and, at one time, a fear that he had written himself out. One day, when I found him on the top of his hill, in the woods, he paced back the path to his house, and said, '*This path is the only remembrance of me that will remain.*' Now it appears that I waited too long.

—*Journal*, May 24, 1864

In an earlier page in this book I wrote some notes touching the so called Transcendentalists of Boston in 1837. Hawthorne drew some sketches in his Blithedale Romance, but not happily, as I think: rather, I should say quite unworthy of his genius. To be sure I do not think any of his books worthy of his genius. I admired the man, who was simple, amiable, truth loving, & frank in conversation: but I never read his books with pleasure—they are too young.

—*Journal*, March 1868, Porte, p. 548

A. BRONSON ALCOTT "HAWTHORNE" (1869)

Amos Bronson Alcott was a former Connecticut Yankee peddler who transformed himself into a reformer, educationalist, philosopher, abolitionist, and vegetarian. He was renowned for his radicalism but also for his impenetrable musings. His aphoristic expressions were published as "Orphic Sayings" in *The Dial* and went understood by few and mocked by

many. Even Emerson tartly dubbed Alcott a "tedious archangel." Alcott
tried to set up his own utopian society, called Fruitlands, but it lasted
only two years and came to nothing.

Along his whimsical way, Alcott nevertheless befriended many of
the greatest thinkers of any time—Emerson, Thoreau, Hawthorne, and
Whitman. He was also the father of novelist Louisa May Alcott.

Hawthorne was of the darker temperament and tendencies. His
sensitiveness and sadness were native, and he cultivated them apparently
alike by solitude, the pursuits and studies in which he indulged, till he
became almost fated to know gayer hours only by stealth. By disposition
friendly, he seemed the victim of his temperament, as if he sought distance,
if not his pen, to put himself in communication, and possible sympathy
with others,—with his nearest friends, even. His reserve and imprisonment
were more distant and close, while the desire for conversation was livelier,
than any one I have known. There was something of strangeness even in his
cherished intimacies, as if he set himself afar from all and from himself with
the rest; the most diffident of men, as coy as a maiden, he could only be
won by some cunning artifice, his reserve was so habitual, his isolation so
entire, the solitude so vast. How distant people were from him, the world
they lived in, how he came to know so much about them, by what stratagem
he got into his own house or left it, was a marvel. Fancy fixed, he was not
to be jostled from himself for a moment, his mood was so persistent. There
he was in the twilight, there he stayed. Was he some damsel imprisoned in
that manly form pleading alway for release, sighing for the freedom and
companionships denied her? Or was he some Assyrian ill at ease afar from
the olives and the East? Had he strayed over with William the Conqueror,
and true to his Norman nature, was the baron still in republican America,
secure in his castle, secure in his tower, whence he could defy all invasion
of curious eyes? What neighbor of his ever caught him on the highway, or
ventured to approach his threshold?

> His bolted Castle gates, what man should ope,
>   Unless the Lord did will
>   To prove his skill,
> And tempt the fates hid in his horoscope?

Yet if by chance admitted, welcome in a voice that a woman might own
for its hesitancy and tenderness; his eyes telling the rest.

For such the noble language of his eye,
That when of words his lips were destitute,
Kind eyebeams spake while yet his tongue was mute.

Your intrusion was worth the courage it cost; it emboldened to future assaults to carry this fort of bashfulness. During all the time he lived near me, our estates being separated only by a gate and shaded avenue, I seldom caught sight of him; and when I did it was but to lose it the moment he suspected he was visible; oftenest seen on his hill-top screened behind the shrubbery and disappearing like a hare into the bush when surprised. I remember of his being in my house but twice, and then he was so ill at ease that he found excuse for leaving politely forthwith,—"the stove was so hot," "the clock ticked so loud." Yet he once complained to me of his wish to meet oftener, and dwelt on the delights of fellowship, regretting he had so little. . . .

He strove by disposition to be sunny and genial, traits not native to him. Constitutionally shy, recluse, melancholy, only by shafts of wit and flow of humor could he deliver himself. There was a soft sadness in his smile, a reserve in his glance, telling how isolate he was. Was he ever one of his company while in it? There was an aloofness, a *besides,* that refused to affiliate himself with himself, even. His readers must feel this, while unable to account for it, perhaps, or express it adequately. A believer in transmitted traits needs but read his pedigree to find the genesis of what characterized him distinctly, and made him and his writings their inevitable sequel. Everywhere you will find persons of his type and complexion similar in cast of character and opinions.

—A. Bronson Alcott, "Hawthorne" (July 1869),
Concord Days, 1872, pp. 193–97

Moncure Daniel Conway "Concerning Hawthorne and Brook Farm" (1869)

The Virginian Moncure Daniel Conway was a Unitarian minister as well as a literary editor and biographer. He made the pilgrimage to Concord as a young man, seeking out Emerson. That first day, as recounted in this entry, he also saw Hawthorne.

Hawthorne bristled at suggestions that he was (as Ellery Channing declared in verse) "the gentlest man that kindly Nature drew." Even Channing eventually became aware of Hawthorne's irritation at this portrait, prompting him to write a sequel in which he described Hawthorne as "sinewy and capable of action." There seemed to be a campaign to emphasize the muscular man of action over the effete, ethereal fairy tale vision of the author. (Evert Duyckinck conflated both legends, calling Hawthorne "a fine ghost in cast iron," while James Russell Lowell imagined "Nature" taking extra clay—"finer grain stuff, for a woman prepared"— to complete "so full-sized a man.") Conway's tribute to Hawthorne's "athleticism" accords with Channing's "sinewy" claims. This will be useful to students concerned with questions of Hawthorne's public persona.

Readers investigating Hawthorne's use of material from his own life in his novels, particularly *The Blithedale Romance*, should examine Conway's comments. He suggests—contrary to Rose Hawthorne Lathrop's claims in her excerpt in this volume—that Hawthorne consciously drew characters from life. Zenobia, for example, was based on Margaret Fuller. Furthermore, he claims that Hawthorne was known in literary circles as Miles Coverdale (the obnoxious, oblivious protagonist of *Blithedale*), "almost as often mentioned by that as by his real name."

Conway addresses Hawthorne's attitude to politics, specifically his unswerving loyalty to Franklin Pierce and his views on the Civil War. Students writing on Hawthorne's political commitment and his position regarding slavery (and thus, race) should read Conway's forthright account. Hawthorne's devotion to Pierce alienated him from his literary brethren, Conway says; his intense discomfort about the Civil War killed him.

—◇◇◇— —◇◇◇— —◇◇◇—

Hawthorne was among those who went out the first summer, a very graphic account of which introduces his Blithedale Romance. He chose to work on the farm, and wielded the hoe as faithfully, if not as successfully, as he before and afterwards wielded the pen. This, however, only lasted about six months; though to the last he passed a great deal of his time with his chosen friends, nearly all of whom had gone to Brook Farm, and he freely invested in it the first little earnings of his pen.

It is important to state, that these educated and refined people were gathered together at Brook Farm, with very few exceptions, solely by moral enthusiasm. They were not in pecuniary want, but meant to show the world that all its commercial and social systems were inadequate, and that the hour had struck for their transformation under the spirit of fraternity. It is also important to state, that the "radicalism" of the community was strictly confined to its commercial aspects. It is true that the members of it belonged chiefly to the more advanced schools of religious opinion which transcendentalism had evoked; but what I mean in saying that its radicalism was strictly commercial is, that those who resided there held rigidly the commonly received ideas of marriage and of the family.

Of those who made investments in Brook Farm, nearly all lost them; yet all of them, so far as I have heard, continue to regard themselves as amply rewarded by the returns they received in other than pecuniary forms. Hawthorne, who would have been the last to withhold a penny from anything that interested his intellect or heart, put, I believe, all he had in its stock; but those who have read The Blithedale Romance need not be told that he recovered it a thousand-fold in higher forms.

Of that romance it may be well to state, that while it is true, as its author has earnestly stated, that its characters and incidents are creations of his own imagination, it is also true that those personally acquainted with the Brook Farm Company are able to detect in it reminiscences of the early life that occurred there, and traits of some who lived there. As an artist takes for his ideal statue the limbs and features of many, so Hawthorne has blended the intellect and magnetism of Margaret Fuller with the beauty and passionate energy of another in the character of Zenobia. Only in honesty and homely intelligence can Silas Foster be identified with the real farmer of the community. The seamstress alluded to in this book, no doubt, suggested Priscilla; but there is another fine nature still more discernible in the character. Hollingsworth is, perhaps, more a fiction than any personage in the novel; but Miles Coverdale may be safely regarded as one of the most faithful specimens of self-portraiture ever made by any author,—indeed, Hawthorne has since been, among his literary friends, almost as often mentioned by that as by his real name.

Hawthorne, in using Brook Farm as "a theatre, little removed from the highway of ordinary travel where the creatures of his brain may play their phantasmagorical antics without exposing them to too close a comparison, with the actual events of real lives," regretted extremely that the world should have persisted in ascribing a more historical and personal design to The Blithedale Romance than was just. He particularly regretted that so many should have identified Zenobia with Margaret Fuller, or that the death of his heroine by drowning should be associated with the tragic fate of a woman who he ever held in the highest regard, and who was notably free from the morbid feelings which drove Zenobia to suicide. The terrible intensity of that picture was, indeed, justly regarded as indicating its reality; but it is referable to another case altogether. There was, at Concord, a maiden much esteemed by the literary people of the village, who was compelled by poverty to lead a life of toil so discordant with her poetic nature and aspirations that she drowned herself in Concord River. Hawthorne was called out from the Old Manse after midnight, and, with a neighbor, dragged the river until near morning, when the body of the poor girl was brought up. The scene haunted Hawthorne until he had transmuted it by his art.

I have already stated that Mr. Hawthorne had formed an intimate friendship with Franklin Pierce at college. When the latter was chosen as candidate for the presidency of the United States, Hawthorne wrote a small biography of him, which was used by the Democratic Party in the canvas; and when, after his election, Mr. Pierce appointed the novelist consul at Liverpool, there were not wanting many who regarded the proceeding as a disreputable bargain. This opinion, however, was held by none who knew Hawthorne. The truth was Hawthorne could hardly be persuaded of anything against an early friend. In vain was he afterwards told of the violent proceedings of President Pierce, taken to make Kansas a Slave State; a quiet smile and shake of the head was his only reply. There is no doubt that the influence of the President widened the gulf between him and the general opinion of his literary brothers in America; and when the controversy between the North and South waxed more fierce, and he foresaw the war, he said to a friend in Liverpool that he would "go home and die with the Republic." A most earnest patriot, the war wore deeply upon his mind, and, in connection with illness in his family during the residence in Italy, undermined his physical health. He could not share the high hopes which sustained nearly all of his friends during that terrible ordeal; he could not see beyond the black cloud a country liberated from the blight of slavery. To him the war was an overwhelming tragedy, and its inevitable end seemed to be the destruction of the Republic.

Shortly after his return from Europe, I met him at a dinner of the Literary Club in Boston. A larger number than usual had come together for the purpose of welcoming him home. But the contrast between the man I then saw and the one whom I had seen years before at the Old Manse was sad enough. He was now, indeed, more social with the persons about him. There is no doubt that residence abroad had done much toward enlarging his relations with others. Indeed, it had been noted before, by Americans who had seen and heard him on public occasions in Europe, that the silent and shy novelist had exhibited an unsuspected power of public speech and performance. He repaired, on his return, to the village he loved best, Concord; and there built him a charming modest home, which he was resolved never again to leave. Again the old shadows of New England began to weave their spells around him. Yet he was too ardent a lover of his country to be able to give himself up entirely to the repose for which he longed.

He went off to Washington while the war was still raging; and, in the absence of all faith in any great End, he walked there amid what seemed to be the ruins of his country. When he returned to Boston, I passed a night under the same roof with him, at the house of Mr. Fields, his publisher. He seemed much dejected. Mr. Fields had invited a little company; but, after the first arrivals, Hawthorne made his escape to his room, from which he did not emerge until the next morning at breakfast-time. He then came in with the amusing look of a naughty child, and pleaded that he had become lost the night before in Defoe's Ghost Stories, until it was too late to make his appearance in the company. He must, I should think, have been contemplating some phantasmal production at that time; for I remember his asking me many questions about the ghost-beliefs of the negroes, among whom I had passed my early life.

—Moncure Daniel Conway, "Concerning Hawthorne and Brook Farm," *Every Saturday*, VII, January 2, 1869, pp. 13–18

George S. Hillard "The English Note-Books of Nathaniel Hawthorne" (1870)

In him opposite qualities met, and were happily and harmoniously blended; and this was true of him physically as well as intellectually. He was tall and strongly built, with broad shoulders, deep chest, a massive head, black hair, and large dark eyes. Wherever he was he attracted attention by his imposing presence. He looked like a man who might have held the stroke-oar in a university boat. And his genius, as all the world knows, was of masculine force and sweep.

But, on the other hand, no man had more of the feminine element than he. He was feminine in his quick perceptions, his fine insight, his sensibility to beauty, his delicate reserve, his purity of feeling. No man comprehended woman more perfectly; none has painted woman with a more exquisite and ethereal pencil. And his face was as mobile and rapid in its changes of expression as is the face of a young girl. His lip and cheek heralded the word before it was spoken. His eyes would darken visibly under the touch of a passing emotion, like the waters of a fountain ruffled by the breeze of summer. So, too, he was the shyest of men. The claims and courtesies of social life were terrible to him. The thought of making a call would keep him awake in his bed. At breakfast, he could not lay a piece of butter upon a lady's plate without a little trembling of the hand: this is a fact, and not a phrase. He was so shy that in the presence of two intimate friends he would be less easy and free-spoken than in that of only one.

And yet the presence of his kind was cordial, and in some sense necessary to him. If his shyness held him back, his sympathies drew him out with a force nearly as strong. And, unlike most men who are at once intellectual and shy, he was not a lover, or a student, of books. He read books as they came in his way, or for a particular purpose, but he made no claim to the honors of learning or scholarship. A great library had no charms for him. He rarely bought a book, and the larger part of his small collection had come to him by gift. His mind did not feed upon the printed page. It will be noticed that in his writings he very seldom introduces a quotation or makes any allusion to the writings of others. The raptures of the bibliomaniac, fondling his tall copies, his wide margins, his unique specimens, his vellum pages, were as strange to him as are the movements of a violin-player's arm to the deaf man's eye.

—George S. Hillard, "The English Note-Books of
Nathaniel Hawthorne," *Atlantic,* September 1870, pp. 258–59

S.C. Hall (1883)

That most lovable of writers was also—to those who knew him intimately—one of the most lovable of men. My acquaintance with him was slight; but it has left on my mind a vivid impression of his painful shyness in general society, and the retiring—nay, morbid delicacy—with which he shrank from notice.

—S.C. Hall, *Retrospect of a Long Life,* 1883, p. 420

Julian Hawthorne
"Boyhood and Bachelorhood" (1884)

Julian Hawthorne was the only son of the novelist. After a mediocre stint at Harvard, and in opposition to his late father's hopes, Julian became an author himself. He wrote extensively, both popular fiction and bio-graphical anas—collections of sayings and expressions—relating to his father. Only the latter is valued today, and this only because Julian had unrivalled knowledge of his father's private life. Unfortunately, the products of Julian's memoir industry have been described as "anemic," and

Julian himself impressed critics much less than his father did, both as a writer and as a man.

Here, Julian discusses the contemplative and remote nature of his father; how his father could "sit down in a meditative solitude ... musing over the theories and symbols of life" at an age when "a man's blood runs warmest." Hawthorne was neither a fanatic nor a bloodless wallflower, however, and Julian is at pains to emphasize his father's physical ruggedness. Julian seems to be answering those critics who present his father as stiff and ethereal, as he describes his father as "a human being, in the widest sense." He details Hawthorne's use of liquor and cigars (moderate in both cases), but also relays an anecdote that hints at Hawthorne's revulsion at "sensuous indulgence"—in this case in his fondness for tea. Students researching Hawthorne's character will find material here to challenge the overfeminized depictions of Hawthorne.

Julian lauds the Puritan ancestry of the Hawthornes, if only for their vigor, courage, and practicality, and argues that this legacy survived well in his father. Students tracing the extent of a Puritan influence on Hawthorne the father should look here.

Finally, Julian extols his father's highly developed sense of reverence—"I do not know that too much weight can be given to this fact." Does the concept of reverence seem consistent with the Hawthorne of *The Scarlet Letter* or *The Blithedale Romance*? Students exploring Hawthorne's relations to his New England past will find much to discuss regarding this contention.

——⟨/\/\/⟩—— ——⟨/\/\/⟩—— ——⟨/\/\/⟩——

A certain mystery invests the early life of Nathaniel Hawthorne. There is a difficulty in reconciling the outward calm and uneventfulness of his young manhood with the presence of those qualities which are known to have been in him. It is not his literary or imaginative qualities that are now referred to; he found sufficient outlet for them. But here was a young man, brimming over with physical health and strength; endowed (by nature, at all events) with a strong social instinct; with a mind daring, penetrating, and independent; possessing a face and figure of striking beauty and manly grace; gifted with a stubborn will, and prone, upon occasion, to outbursts of appalling wrath;—in a word, a man fitted in every way to win and use the world, to have his own way, to live throughout the full extent of his keen senses and great faculties;—and yet we find this young engine of all possibilities and energies content (so far as appears) to sit quietly down in a meditative solitude, and spend all those years when a man's blood runs

warmest in his veins in musing over the theories and symbols of life, and
in writing cool and subtle little parables apposite to his meditations. Had he
been a fanatic or an enthusiast; had he been snatched into the current of some
narrow and overpowering preoccupation, whose interests filled each day, to
the exclusion of all other thoughts and interests; had he been a meagre and
pallid anatomy of overwrought brain and nerves,—such behavior would have
been more intelligible. But he was many-sided, unimpulsive, clear-headed;
he had the deliberation and leisureliness of a well-balanced intellect; he was
the slave of no theory and of no emotion; he always knew, so to speak, where
he was and what he was about. His forefathers, whatever their less obvious
qualities may have been, were at all events enterprising, active, practical
men, stern and courageous, accustomed to deal with and control lawless
and rugged characters; they were sea-captains, farmers, soldiers, magistrates;
and, in whatever capacity, they were used to see their own will prevail, and
to be answerable to no man. True, they were Puritans, and doubtless were
more or less under dominion to the terrible Puritan conscience; but it is
hardly reasonable to suppose that this was the only one of their traits which
they bequeathed to their successor. On the contrary, one would incline to
think that this legacy, in its transmission to a legatee of such enlightened
and unprejudiced understanding, would have been relieved of its peculiarly
virulent and tyrannical character, and become an object rather of intellectual
or imaginative curiosity than of moral awe. The fact that it figures largely in
Hawthorne's stories certainly can scarcely be said to weaken this hypothesis;
the pleasurable exercise of the imagination lies in its relieving us from the
pressure of our realities, not in repeating and dallying with them. Upon the
whole, therefore, there is no ground for assuming that, leaving out of the
question the personal or original genius of Nathaniel Hawthorne, he was not
in all other respects quite as much of a human being, in the widest sense of
the term, as old Major William himself, or Bold Daniel either. . . .

Meanwhile, however, another school of Hawthorne analysts has sprung
up, with great hopes of success. These are persons, some of whom were
acquaintances of Hawthorne during his bachelor days and for a time
afterwards, and who maintain that he not only possessed broad and even low
human sympathies and tendencies, but that he was by no means proof against
temptation, and that it was only by the kind precaution and charitable silence
of his friends that his dissolute excesses have remained so long concealed.
Singularly enough, it is as a tippler that the author of "The Scarlet Letter" most
frequently makes his appearance in the narratives of these expositors; he was
the victim of an insatiable appetite for gin, brandy, and rum, and if a bottle of

wine were put on the table, he could hardly maintain a decent self-restraint. So probable in themselves and so industriously circulated were these stories, that, when the present writer was in London, three or four years ago, Mr. Francis Bennoch, the gentleman to whom the "English Note-Books" were dedicated by Mrs. Hawthorne, related to him the following anecdote: At a dinner at which Mr. Bennoch had been present, some time before, a gentleman had got up to make some remarks, in the course of which he referred to Nathaniel Hawthorne. He spoke of him as having been, during his residence in England, a confirmed inebriate, mentioned a special occasion on which he had publicly disgraced himself at an English table, and wound up with the information that his death had been brought about by a drunken spree on which he and Franklin Pierce had gone off together. When this historian had resumed his seat, Mr. Bennoch rose and spoke nearly as follows:

> I was the friend of Nathaniel Hawthorne during many years; I knew
> him intimately: no man knew him better. . . . Whoever repeats it,
> tells a lie; and whoever repeats it after hearing what I have said, tells
> a lie knowing it to be such.

This terse little speech embodies nearly all there is to be said on this subject. Mr. Hawthorne never was a teetotaler, any more than he was an abolitionist or a thug; but he was invariably temperate. During his lifetime he smoked something like half a dozen boxes of cigars, and drank as much wine and spirits as would naturally accompany that amount of tobacco. Months and sometimes years would pass without his either drinking or smoking at all; but when he would resume those practices, it was not to "make up for lost time,"—his moderation was not influenced by his abstention. Though very tolerant of excesses in others, he never permitted them in himself; and his conduct in this respect was the result not more of moral prejudice than of temperamental aversion. He would have been sober if he had had no morality. At one time, in his younger days, he was accustomed to sup frequently at a friend's table, where the lady of the house made very excellent tea, which the guest was very fond of. One evening, in sending down to replenish his cup, she remarked, "Now, Mr. Hawthorne, I am going to play Mrs. Thrale to your Johnson. I know you are a slave to my tea." Mr. Hawthorne made no reply, but contented himself with mentally noting that he had been guilty of a personal indulgence; and during five years, dating from that evening, he never touched another cup of tea. Every aspect of his life reflects the same principle; he could not endure the thought of being in the thraldom of any selfish or sensuous habit. . . .

In Nathaniel Hawthorne the sentiment of reverence was very highly developed, and I do not know that too much weight can be given to this fact. It is the mark of a fine and lofty organization, and enables us its possessor to apprehend, to suffer, and to enjoy things which are above the sphere of other people. It exalts and refines his power of discrimination between right and wrong. It lays him open to benefits. It opens his eyes to what is above him, and thereby deepens his comprehension of what is around him and at his feet. Reverence, combined with imagination, and vivified by that faculty of divining God's meaning, which belongs to genius,—this equipment is, of itself, enough to educate a man in all the wisdom of the world, as well as in much that appertains to a higher region.

—Julian Hawthorne, "Boyhood and Bachelorhood,"
Nathaniel Hawthorne and His Wife: A Bibliography,
James R. Osgood, Boston, 1884, pp. 82–93, 119–30

Charles Godfrey Leland (1893)

Charles Godfrey Leland was a Philadelphia humorist, novelist, translator, folklorist, and editor. Bixby's was a hotel in New York City "much frequented by literary men and naval officers."

―⁓― ―⁓― ―⁓―

Hawthorne used to stay at Bixby's. He was a moody man who sat by the stove and spoke to no one.

—Charles Godfrey Leland, *Memoirs*,
New York: Appleton, 1893, p. 204

William Dean Howells
"My First Visit to New England" (1894)

William Dean Howells, punningly crowned "the dean of American letters," was a journalist first (in Columbus, Ohio), then a poet, and ultimately a prolific novelist and critic. Early on and with brave foresight, Howells heralded the coming of European realism in literature, forging his own approximation in American fiction. He was an intimate with many of the great writers of the Gilded Age, particularly Mark Twain and Henry James. His account of Hawthorne—written later in life—recalls a younger man's pilgrimage.

Fresh from Concord, Howells continued his social-climbing pilgrimage to New York, where he sought out Walt Whitman in Charles Pfaff's bar on

Broadway. En route he chanced to visit Whitman's radical friend, the New York bohemian and caustic wit, Henry Clapp Jr., editor of the *Saturday Press*. Readers studying the differing social and geographical reactions to Hawthorne will find much in these two differing excerpts.

The door was opened to my ring by a tall handsome boy whom I suppose to have been Mr. Julian Hawthorne; and the next moment I found myself in the presence of the romancer, who entered from some room beyond. He advanced carrying his head with a heavy forward droop, and with a pace for which I decided that the word would be *pondering*. It was the pace of a bulky man of fifty, and his head was that beautiful head we all know from the many pictures of it. But Hawthorne's *look* was different from that of any picture of him that I have seen. It was sombre and brooding, as the look of such a poet should have been; it was the look of a man who had dealt faithfully and therefore sorrowfully with that problem of evil which forever attracted, forever evaded Hawthorne. It was by no means troubled; it was full of a dark repose. Others who knew him better and saw him oftener were familiar with other aspects, and I remember that one night at Longfellow's table, when one of the guests happened to speak of the photograph of Hawthorne which hung in a corner of the room, Lowell said, after a glance at it, "Yes, it's good; but it hasn't his fine *accipitral* look."

In the face that confronted me, however, there was nothing of keen alertness; but only a sort of quiet, patient intelligence, for which I seek the right word in vain. It was a very regular face, with beautiful eyes; the mustache, still entirely dark, was dense over the fine mouth. Hawthorne was dressed in black, and he had a certain effect which I remember, of seeming to have on a black cravat with no visible collar. He was such a man that if I had ignorantly met him anywhere I should have instantly felt him to be a personage.

—William Dean Howells, "My First Visit to New England"
(1894), *Literary Friends and Acquaintance,* 1900

ROSE HAWTHORNE LATHROP
"MY FATHER'S LITERARY METHODS" (1894)

Rose Hawthorne Lathrop was the youngest daughter of Hawthorne. Her fate was rather different from her brother's. In later years, long after their father's death and into the early twentieth century, by the time Julian had become involved in an embezzlement scam for which he was jailed, Rose had divorced and had become a nun, caring for cancer patients in upstate New York.

The account included here anticipates the cult of the author and his or her methods of composition, familiar to contemporary literary journalism. As such, it is an excellent source for the student writing about Hawthorne's writing technique. Rose uses her incomparable knowledge to reveal her father's attitude to his own characters ("he never created a character which did not possess a soul"), the extent of his use of drafts (apparently little, Hawthorne "thinking out his plots and scenes and characters, and transcribing them rapidly without further change"), his writing regimen, as well as an exact description of when he typically wrote and the supplies he used (in the morning, on "neutral blue paper," itself an aesthetic statement). Students of Hawthorne's literary method can discern much in these small details, and these observations in turn can shed light on the texts themselves.

Rose manages to relate her father's personality to his writing, noting how his philosophy of life guided his fictional subjects. Students interested in Hawthorne's moral intent in his work should find useful matter here. Discussing her father's temperament, Rose pointedly differentiates Hawthorne from Edgar Allan Poe (citing the latter's "squandering of energy"), useful for any student comparing the two writers.

Rose continues by noting that none of Hawthorne's characters was drawn from life: "My father never imitated the men and women he met . . . and such conceptions of his way would bring us to a dense forest of mistake." Students exploring Hawthorne's creative sources and models will find relevant material here. Rose (who entered a Catholic order a year after the article was written) apparently attributes her father's inspiration to the divine, finding in his writing "material made incomprehensibly wonderful by God."

Elsewhere, Rose seems to refute the criticism that Hawthorne did not write enough (a view espoused by her husband, George Lathrop, in a subsequent entry in this volume) by detailing how he would reject and burn substandard material readily and as a matter of honor. Perhaps acknowledging the development of a literary avant garde, Rose opposes "artistic clap-trap and artistic license," and insists that Hawthorne wrote rather with a moral purpose, refusing to indulge in the "spontaneous, passionate effusions which are the substance of so much other fiction." Students gauging Hawthorne's philosophy regarding the antagonism between aestheticism and ethics in literature should take note.

I am asked to write of my father's literary methods. I wish I knew just what they were—it would be easier then to write an article pleasing to the gentle reader—I might even hope to write a romance. But as the bird on the tree bough catches here and there a glimpse of what men are about although he hardly hopes to plow the field himself or benefit by human labor until the harvest comes, so I have observed some facts and gathered some notions as to how my father thought out his literary work.

One method of obtaining his end was to work constantly at writing, whether it brought him money or not. He might not have seemed to be working all the time, but to be enjoying endless leisure in walking about the country, or the city streets. But even a bird would have had more penetration than to make such a mistake in regard to him. Another method was to choose just the right wife, whether or no she brought him money. Just the right wife let no bores reach him, if they could be diverted.

One of his methods was to love and pity mankind more than he scorned them, so that he never created a character which did not possess a soul—the only puppet he ever contrived of straw, "Feathertop," had an excellent soul until the end of the story. Still another method of gaining his success was to write with a noble respect for his own best effort, on which account he never felt satisfied with his writing unless he had exerted every muscle of his faculty; unless every word he had written seemed to his severest self-criticism absolutely true. He loved his art more than his time, more than his ease, and could thrust into the flames an armful of manuscript because he suspected the pages of weakness and exaggeration.

One of his methods of avoiding failure was to be rigorous in the care of his daily existence. A preponderance of frivolous interruption to a modicum of thorough labor at thinking was a system utterly foreign to him. He would not talk with a fool; as a usual thing he would not entertain a bore. If thrown with these common pests, he tried, I think, to study them. And they report that he did so very silently. But he did not waste his time, either by politely chattering with people whom he meant to sneer at after they had turned their backs, or in indulgences of loafing of all sorts, which leave a narcotic stupidity in their wake. He had plenty of time, therefore, for thought and he could think while walking either in the fresh air, or back and forth in his study. Men of success detest inactivity. It is a hardship for them to be as if dead for a single moment. So, when my father could not walk out-of-doors during meditation, he moved back and forth in his room, sturdily alert, his hands clasped behind him, quietly thinking, his head either bent forward or suddenly lifted upward with a light in his eager, grey eyes.

He wrote principally in the morning, with that absorption and regularity which characterize the labor of men who are remembered. When his health began to show signs of giving way, in 1861, it was suggested by a relative, whose intellect, strength of will and appetite for theories were of equally splendid proportion, that my father only needed a high desk at which to stand when writing, to be restored to all his pristine vigor. With his usual tolerance of possible wisdom he permitted such a desk to be arranged in the tower-study at "The Wayside"; but with his inexorable contempt for mistakes of judgment he never, after a brief trial, used it for writing. Upon his simple desk of walnut wood, of which he had nothing to complain, although it barely served its purpose, like most of the inexpensive objects about him, was a charming Italian bronze inkstand—over whose cover wrested the infant Hercules in the act of strangling a goose—in friendly aid, no doubt, of "drivers of the quill." My father wrote with a gold pen, and I can hear now, as it seems, the rapid rolling of his chirography over the broad page, as he formed his small, rounded, but irregular letters, when filling his journals, in Italy. He leaned very much on his left arm while writing, often holding the top of the manuscript book lovingly with his left hand quite in the attitude of a boy. At the end of a sentence or two he would sometimes unconsciously bow his head, as if bidding good-by to a thought well rid of for the present in its new garb of ink.

In writing he had little care for paper and ink. To be sure, his large, square manuscript was firmly bound into covers, and the paper was usually of a neutral blue; and when I say that he had little care for his mechanical materials I mean that he had no servile anxiety as to how they looked to another person, for I am convinced that he himself loved his manuscript books. There was a certain air about the titles, which he wrote with a flourish, as compared with the involved minuteness of the rest of the script, and the latter covers every limit of the page in a devoted way. His letters were formed obscurely, though most fascinatingly, and he was almost frolicsome in his indifference to the comfort of the compositor. Still he had none of the frantic reconsiderations of Scott or Balzac. If he made a change in a word it was while it was fresh, and no one could obliterate what he had written with a more fearless blot of the forger, or one which looked more earnest and interesting. There was no scratching nor quiddling to the mariner with which he fought for his art. Each day he thought out the problems he had set himself before beginning to write, and if a word offended him, as he recorded the result, he thrust it back into chaos before the ink had dried. I think that the manuscript of "Dr. Grimshaw's Secret" is an exception, to some extent. There are many written self-communings and changes in it. My father was declining in health while it was being evolved. But yet, in "The Dolliver

Romance," the last work of all in process of development, written while he was physically breaking down, we see the effect of will and heroic attempt. It is the most beautiful of his compositions, because his mind was greater at that time than ever and because death could not frighten him, and in its very face he desired to complete the proof of his whole power, as the dying soldier rises to the greatest act of his life, having given his life-blood for his country's cause. Though the script of this manuscript is extremely difficult to read, the speculation had evidently been done before taking up the pen. I am not sure but that my father sometimes destroyed first draughts, of which his family knew nothing. Indeed we have his own word for it that "he passed the day in writing stories and the night in burning them." Nevertheless, his tendency we know to have been that of thinking out his plots and scenes and characters, and transcribing them rapidly without further change.

Since he did not write anything wholly for the pleasure of creative writing, but had moral motives and perfect artistic harmony to consider, he could not have indulged in the spontaneous, passionate effusions which are the substance of so much other fiction. He was obliged to train his mind to reflection and judgment, and therefore he never tasted luxury of any kind. The enjoyment of historical settings in all their charm and richness, rehabilitated for their own sake or for worldly gain; the enjoyment of caricatures of the members of the human family, because they are so often so desperately funny; the enjoyment of realistic pictures of life as it is found, because life as it is found is a more absorbing study than that of geology or chemistry; the enjoyment of redundant scenes of love and intrigue, which flatter the reader like experiences of his own—these things he was not willing to admit to his art—a magic that served his literary palate with still finer food. He wrote with temperateness, and in pitying love of human nature, in the instinctive hope of helping it to know and redeem itself.

His manner was philosophy, his style forgiveness. And for this temperate and logical and laconic work—giving nothing to the world for its mere enjoyment, but going beyond all that to ennoble each reader by his perfect renunciation of artistic clap-trap and artistic license—for this aim he needed a mental method that could entirely command itself, and when necessary, weigh and gauge with the laborious fidelity of a tool surveyor, before the account was rendered with pen and ink upon paper.

But who will ever be able to weigh and gauge the genius which carries methods and philosophies and aims into an atmosphere of wonderful power, where the sunlight and the color, and the lightning and ominous thunder transfigure the familiar things of life in glorious haste and inspiration? While following his rules and habits my father was constantly attended by the rapturous spirit of such a genius, transmuting swarming reality into a few symbolic types.

Another way in which he effected telling labor was to conserve his force in the matter of wrangling. He kept his temper. He had a temper, of course. He was not without the fires of life, but he banked them. He did not permit disgust at others for the adverse destiny of the moment to absorb his vitality by throwing it off in long harangues of rage, long seasons of the sulks. There are no such good calculators as men of consummate genius. They dread the squandering of energy of an Edgar Allan Poe or of a boiling Walter Savage Landor. Temperateness implies the control of fierce elements. And as it rejoices the heart to see the graceful skill with which a Napoleon manages his mettlesome horse (says Heine), so in all subtle management of volcanic power we perceive sweetness and beauty.

When he handled sin it became uncontaminating tragedy; when he handled vulgarity, as in "The Artist of the Beautiful," it became inevitable pathos; when he handled suspicion, as in "The Birthmark" and "Rappacini's Daughter," it evolved devoted trust. When he brought within his art the personality of a human devil he honored its humanity and proved that the real devil is quite another thing. Though he dealt with romance he never gave the advantage of an inch to the wiles of bizarre witchery, the grotesque masks of wanton caprice in imagination—those elements which exhibit the intoxication of talent. His terrors were those of our own hearts; his playfulness was the merit of the sunlight, which comes from vast mysteries as dark as they are radiant. In short, he was artistically temperate, in that he guided the forces he used with the reins of truth, and he could do this unbrokenly because he governed his character with Christian fellowship.

To any one at least permeated by its atmosphere it seems strange that a truly artistic work should be thought to be an imitation of individual models. The distance of inspiration is the distance of a heavenly fair day, or of a night made luminous by mystery, giving a new quality and a new species of delight to facts about us. In reading the sympathetic merriment of the introduction to "The Scarlet Letter" and then the story itself, we perceive the difference between the charm of a Dutch-like realism and the thrill of imaginative creation, which uses material made incomprehensibly wonderful by God in order to make it comprehensibly wonderful to men. But, of course, the material thus transmuted by the distance of inspiration is only new and fine to men who have ears to hear and eyes to see. The blind puppies among books are many and noisy. My father never imitated the men and women he met, nor man nor woman, and such conceptions of his way would bring us to a dense forest of mistake.

In the afternoon my father went, if practicable, into the open spaces of nature, or at least into the fresh air, to gather inspiration for his work. I have sometimes had the pleasure of being present, always out-of-doors, while he was smoking a cigar, of which the fragrance was so exquisite that it has been a symbol of elegance to me all my life. He never, I think, smoked but one cigar a day, but it was of a quality to make up for this self-denial, and I am sure that he reserved his most puzzling literary involutions for the delicious half hour of this dainty rite. In Lenox he walked the "stately woods," as my mother calls them in a letter of that period, or lay upon his back under the trees beside the lake intervening between the "little red cottage" and Monument Mountain. Also, in Concord, a year afterward, my mother writes: "My husband at full length presented no hindrance to the tides of divine life that are ready to flow through us, if we will." She further says: "He cannot write deeply in midsummer at any rate. He can only seize the shirts of ideas, and pin them down for further investigation."

In 1861, and thereafter he traversed the wooded hilltop behind his home, which was reached by various pretty, climbing paths that crept under larches and pines and scraggy, goat-like apple trees. We could catch sight of him, going back and forth up there, with now and then a pale blue gleam of sky among the trees, against which his figure passed clear. He wore a soft brown felt hat, and looked in it like a brother to Tennyson, though with a difference. Along this path, made by his own steps only, he thought out the tragedy of "Septimius Felton," who buried the young English officer at the foot of one of the large pines my father saw at each return. At one end of the hilltop path was a thicket of birch and maple trees, and at the end toward the west and the village was the open brow of the hill sloping rapidly to the Lexington road, and overlooking meadows and distant wood-ranges, some of the cottages of humble folk, and the neighboring huge, owlet-haunted elms of Alcott's lawn.

—Rose Hawthorne Lathrop, "My Father's
Literary Methods," *The Ladies Home Journal*, March 1894

JULIAN HAWTHORNE (1900)

[Henry Clapp Jr.] was a man of such open and avowed cynicism that he may have been, for all I know, a kindly optimist at heart; some say, however, that he had really talked himself into being what he seemed. I only know that his talk, the first day I saw him, was of such a sort that if he was half as bad, he would have been too bad to be. . . .

I went to the office of the *Saturday Press* in New York . . . I had found there a bitterness against Boston as great as the bitterness against respectability, and as Boston was then rapidly becoming my second country, I could not join in the scorn thought of her and said of her by the bohemians. I fancied a conspiracy among them to shock the literary pilgrim and to minify the precious emotions he had felt in visiting other shrines; but I found no harm in that, for I knew just how much to be shocked, and I thought I knew better how to value certain things of the soul than they. Yet when their chief asked me how I got on with Hawthorne, and I began to say that he was very shy and I was rather shy, and the king of Bohemia took his pipe out to break in upon me with "Oh, a couple of shysters!" and the rest laughed, I was abashed all they could have wished and was not restored to myself till one of them said that the thought of Boston made him as ugly as sin; then I began to hope again that men who took themselves so seriously as that need not be taken very seriously by me.

—Julian Hawthorne, *Literary Friends and Acquaintance,*
New York: Harper and Brothers, 1900, pp. 69, 71

GENERAL

In the broad range of critical responses that have emerged in reference to the author, Hawthorne seems almost to be "all things to all men": simultaneously masculine and feminine, accomplished and naïve, a realist and a fantasist. Paradox and ambiguity are abiding elements in descriptions of Hawthorne, and they extend into the critical appraisals. Several accounts initially take the form of a litany of Hawthorne's shortcomings before transforming into enthusiastic approval.

In an early estimation, Horatio Bridge (a lifelong friend of Hawthorne's from their Bowdoin College days) heralds the "unequivocal evidence of talent," yet in more views than one (Edgar Allan Poe and Emily Dickinson provide obvious examples) indecision or multiple perspectives prevail, as strong praise of Hawthorne is coupled with nervous dismissal. Hawthorne's work is simultaneously attractive and repulsive, realistic and weird, clear and mystical. Poe found Hawthorne "*not* original" and "too fond of allegory" and yet praises him highly in his next paragraph.

Repeated often in the reviews and excerpts is the mention of "a national literature." When Hawthorne's writing emerged, American culture was still groping for its own national identity (see Emerson's "The American Scholar," 1837) and trying to shed the dominating influence of British writers and their styles. Even in 1883, as Alfred H. Welsh notes, Americans were "exhorted to give days and nights to Addison" (Joseph Addison, the English writer and editor of the *Spectator*, who died in 1719). Benjamin Franklin's earliest writings were brazen imitations of Addison, and this influence only became more pervasive over the next century. Hawthorne, therefore, emerged conspicuously as a possible resolution to a long-felt inferiority and debt to the English literary tradition. As Oliver Wendell Holmes remarks: "The Yankee mind has for the most part budded and flowered in pots of English earth." Understandably, then, the problem of originality obsesses critics of this period.

Not surprisingly, many of the critics notice and praise the originality and novelty of Hawthorne's work, even its experimentalism. Yet as much as certain critics extolled independence from the motherland and its canon, many others remained spellbound to those traditions and found deviation from "the norm" suspect. Of interest to students examining Hawthorne's independence from a tradition—and his anticipation of modernism—is the repeated charge of formlessness in Hawthorne's stories, how they do not rely closely on plots, do not require detail or even characterization. Hawthorne's work, it is alleged, is more fragmentary and idea driven. Yet his "experiments . . . shall satisfy his tastes and be intelligible to the outside world," writes Leslie Stephen. Hawthorne reconciles the division between artistic integrity and commerce. Students looking at Hawthorne's relation to, and resistance of, the marketplace and genre expectations will find valuable material here.

Again and again critics remark on Hawthorne's unique fictional position between verisimilitude and fantasy, between the realistic and the supernatural, and his general reconciliation of opposites in his work. Hawthorne united "the borderland between reason and insanity" (Stephen); he blurred the division between "the seen and the unseen" (Longfellow, 1842); his setting was "that delicate mean between the fanciful and the prosaic" (Stephen), "between the real world and fairyland" (Hutton, quoting from Hawthorne). Anxieties about the portrayal of reality and the lack of realism in Hawthorne's work characterize later articles. Holmes, again, finds Hawthorne's work "true as the daguerreotype" and sees his commingling of the "weird and ghostly" with "solid reality and homely truthfulness" as Hawthorne's "special difficulty."

Other writers praise Hawthorne's "guarded understatements" and "self-control" (Higginson) and his "power of condensation" (John Vance Cheney and Charles Sumner), although to George Lathrop this control, understatement, and condensation meant that Hawthorne "didn't write enough." Hawthorne's perfectionism is repeatedly mentioned—his propensity to scrap or withdraw unsatisfactory work. Poe lauds Hawthorne's clarity, purity, and brevity, noting there is "no word written of which the tendency, direct or indirect, is not to the one of the pre-established design." This same trait is distinguished also by Rose Hawthorne Lathrop and Alfred Welsh and again points to later developments in literature.

Other common topics and observations among critics include the depiction of history (and so "reality"); how well (or more often how poorly) Hawthorne reverts to historical portrayal and the ethics of such depiction. His use of Puritanism or Calvinism is challenged by several critics, while others vaunt the transformative quality of his writing—his ability to turn the previously prosaic and gray Puritan history into something "Mediterranean."

HORATIO BRIDGE (1836)

His style is classical and pure, his imagination exceedingly delicate and fanciful, and through all his writings there runs a vein of sweetest poetry.

Perhaps we have no writer so deeply imbued with the early literature of America; or who can so well portray the times and manners of the Puritans.

Hitherto Mr. Hawthorne has published no work of magnitude; but it is to be hoped that one who has shown such unequivocal evidence of talent will soon give to the world some production which shall place him in a higher rank than can be obtained by one whose efforts are confined to the sphere of magazines and annuals.

—Horatio Bridge (1836), *Personal Recollections of Nathaniel Hawthorne*, 1893, p. 71

NATHANIEL HAWTHORNE (1841)

Hawthorne wrote these two letters from Brook Farm, a working farming community outside West Roxbury, Massachusetts, that attempted to mix writers and artists with authentic sons of the earth to work together to create a better society. Brook Farm was one of many socialistic or utopian communities that were established (and that usually swiftly foundered) throughout the northeastern United States at the time.

Hawthorne's time at Brook Farm was his source for *The Blithedale Romance*, and anybody studying the novel should read these letters for Hawthorne's account of how he "attacked" a pile of manure. The pile, which Hawthorne has transformed into a "gold mine" by the second letter, became one of the most enduring symbols of the Brook Farm experiment, which failed in due course. Brook Farm was famously allied with the transcendentalists. Its founder, George Ripley, was a prominent believer in the "movement," and Margaret Fuller was a regular visitor, while Emerson made occasional well-meaning, if dubious, one-day visits. Hawthorne left the project long before its demise, and his cynical attitude toward human society and the place of the writer within that society was no doubt confirmed during this phase of his life. Students interested in Hawthorne's part in and relation to transcendentalism should inquire here.

Sweetest, I did not milk the cows last night, because Mr. Ripley was afraid to trust them to my hands, or me to their horns—I know not which. But this morning, I have done wonders. Before breakfast, I went out to the barn, and began to chop hay for the cattle; and with such "righteous vengeance" (as Mr. Ripley says) did I labor, that, in the space of ten minutes, I broke the machine. Then I brought wood and replenished the fires; and finally sat down to breakfast and ate up a huge mound of buckwheat cakes. After breakfast, Mr. Ripley put a four-pronged instrument into my hands, which he gave me to understand was called a pitch-fork; and he and Mr. Farley being armed with similar weapons, we all three commenced a gallant attack upon a heap of manure. . . . Dearest, I shall make an excellent husbandman. I feel the original Adam reviving in me.

—Letter to Sophia Peabody, April 13, 1841

I think this present life of mine gives me an antipathy to pen and ink, even more than my Custom House experience did . . . in the midst of toil, or after a hard day's work in the gold mine, my soul obstinately refuses to be poured out on paper. That abominable gold mine! Thank God we anticipate getting rid of its treasures, in the course of the next two or three days. Of all hateful places, that is the worst; and I shall never comfort myself for having spent so many days of blessed sunshine there. It is my opinion, dearest, that a man's soul may be buried and perish under a dungheap or in a furrow of the field, just as well as under a pile of money.

—Nathaniel Hawthorne, Letter to Sophia Peabody,
June 1, 1841, from Henry W. Sams, ed.,
Autobiography of Brook Farm,
Englewood Cliffs, NJ: Prentice Hall,
1958, pp. 14, 21

EDGAR ALLAN POE
"NATHANIEL HAWTHORNE" (1847)

The major critical objection to Hawthorne here seems prejudiced by Poe's own hatred of transcendentalism and New England. He sees Hawthorne's fallacious love of metaphor and allegory as a direct consequence of his time at the Brook Farm utopian community: Hawthorne's "spirit of 'metaphor run-mad'" is clearly imbibed from the phalanx and the phalanstery atmosphere." Technically, this is wrong. Brook Farm became a Fourierist phalanx only after Hawthorne had left. Poe blames Bronson Alcott for Hawthorne's "mysticism" and calls for Hawthorne to "hang (if possible) the editor of *The Dial*"—Ralph Waldo Emerson. However, even Poe's biased and wilful misreadings reveal popular cultural perceptions—and misperceptions—of the New England intelligentsia of the time.

He is peculiar and *not* original—unless in those detailed fancies and detached thoughts which his want of general originality will deprive of the appreciation due to them, in preventing them forever reaching the *public* eye. He is infinitely too fond of allegory, and can never hope for popularity so long as he persists in it. This he will not do, for allegory is at war with the whole tone of his nature, which disports itself never so well as when escaping from the mysticism of his Goodman Browns and White Old Maids into the hearty, genial, but still Indian-summer sunshine of his Wakefields and Little Annie's Rambles. Indeed, *his* spirit of "metaphor run-mad" is clearly imbibed from the phalanx and phalanstery atmosphere in which he has been so long struggling for breath. He has not half the material for the exclu-siveness of authorship that he possesses for its universality. He has the purest style, the finest taste, the most available scholarship, the most delicate humor, the most touching pathos, the most radiant imagination, the most consummate ingenuity; and with these varied good qualities he has done *well* as a mystic. But is there any one of these qualities which should prevent his doing doubly as well in a career of honest, upright, sensible, prehensible and comprehensible things? Let him mend his pen, get a bottle of visible ink, come out from the Old Manse, cut Mr. Alcott, hang (if possible) the editor of *The Dial*, and throw out of the window to the pigs all his odd numbers of *The North American Review*.

—Edgar Allan Poe, "Nathaniel Hawthorne" (1847),
Essays and Reviews, ed. G.R. Thompson, 1984, pp. 587–88

RUFUS W. GRISWOLD (1850)

The Reverend Griswold, Edgar Allan Poe's fiercest foe (and, unfortunately for Poe, also his executor and biographer) was an editor of keepsakes, journals, and the most influential literary anthologies of the antebellum period. His friendship and approval smoothed the way for writers, while his enmity could be ruinous. His estimate carried great weight. Griswold "accurately expressed the national view" (H.L. Mencken). This praise for Hawthorne says a great deal about his popular success at the time.

. . . decidedly the greatest living literary man in this country, greatest, in romance, now writing the English language.

> —Rufus W. Griswold, Letter to James T. Fields (January 24, 1850),
> *Passages from the Correspondence and Other Papers of*
> *Rufus W. Griswold*, ed. W.M. Griswold, 1898, p. 258

GEORGE ELIOT (1852)

Hawthorne is a grand favourite of mine, and I shall be sorry if he do not go on surpassing himself.

> —George Eliot, Letter to Mrs. Taylor (August 19, 1852)

ANDREW PRESTON PEABODY
"NATHANIEL HAWTHORNE" (1853)

Andrew Preston Peabody was a Unitarian minister attached to Harvard variously as its preacher, mathematics tutor, acting president, and professor of Christian morals. His central position within this New England educational institution and his religious beliefs may explain his closing indictment against Hawthorne's defamation of the New England canon.

Students investigating Hawthorne's use (and perhaps more pertinently his abuse) of history will find valuable material in this entry. Peabody examines Hawthorne's transformation of history: It is not history, he says, but "the offspring of Hawthorne's own brain, draped in Puritan costumes and baptized with ancestral names." Hawthorne mythologizes the Puritans: "Their times are his heroic age, and he has made it mythological."

Peabody's account, full of conditional but high praise, ends with a sour denunciation of the author for libeling the New England past. Hawthorne has "unwittingly defamed the fathers of New England," and "violated one of the sacred canons of literary creation." Students interested in Hawthorne's radicalism might question whether this "outraging the dead for the entertainment of the living" was really unwitting. Peabody makes a serious case against Hawthorne being labeled an ethical writer (that view espoused by Rose Hawthorne Lathrop). Students exploring Hawthorne's use of the Puritan past or the ethics of his treatment of history will also find Peabody's writing of value.

Also of interest is Peabody's claims for the failure of Hawthorne's plots. "Plain story-telling . . . is entirely beyond, or beneath, his capacity." This does not obstruct his work, Peabody claims; "if he lacks skill in the management of his plot, he is independent of it." Like Alfred H. Welsh and Richard Holt Hutton in their excerpts, Peabody presents Hawthorne in terms that seem to anticipate modernism. Hawthorne writes fragments and plot becomes irrelevant, emerging as a mere conduit for "a cluster of fancies and musings," written to "illustrate some idea or sentiment." His stories are veiled, obscure, "incapable . . . of presenting a naked thought." They challenge preconceptions of narrative. Those studying narrative form in Hawthorne's writing, or Hawthorne's relation to later literary styles, might start here.

It is difficult to refer Hawthorne to any recognized class of writers. So far as our cognizance extends, he is the only individual of his class. In the popular sense of the word, he writes no poetry. We infer his incapacity of rhyme and metre, from his having adopted prose for his Carriers' Addresses, and other similar productions, which are usually cast in metrical forms. Nor yet is his language distinguished by euphony. It never flows spontaneously in numbers, as do so many of the descriptive and pathetic passages in Dickens's stories. On the other hand, it is often crisp and harsh, betraying little sensitiveness to musical accords and cadences; and we should despair of finding a paragraph of his, in which the sound could, by the most skilful reading, be made to enhance the impression of the sense. Yet more, we cannot remember a single poetical quotation in all his writings; and, though books are occasionally referred to, mention is never, or almost never, made of a poet or a poem. His own favorite reading does not, we therefore conclude, lie in this direction, nor yet, as we apprehend, in any direction in which his fancy could borrow forms or colors, or could find nourishment homogeneous with its creations. Indeed, if we may judge from such hints as he furnishes of his own literary habits, the books with which he is chiefly familiar are the dryest of chronicles, which furnish the raw material for many of his stories.

Yet with so much that must be alleged to the discredit of his poetical affinities, Hawthorne is preeminently a poet. It belongs to his genius not merely to narrate or describe, not merely to invent characters and incidents of the same constituent elements with those in history or in real life; but to create out of nothing—to place before the imagination objects and personages which derive their verisimilitude not from their resemblance to the actual, but from their self-coherency. Plain story-telling, whether true or fictitious, is entirely beyond, or rather beneath, his capacity. He undertook, a few years ago, to write historical sketches of New England, in the Peter Parley style, for the behoof of children. He succeeded so admirably that people of mature and venerable age became children for the nonce, that they might read the legends of *Grandfather's Chair;* but it was not history; it was the offspring of Hawthorne's own brain, draped in Puritan costumes, and baptized with ancestral names. A year or two ago, he conceived the plan of reediting some of the fables of the classic mythology; but the result was a Pantheon all his own, rigidly true, indeed, to the letter of antiquity, and thus vindicating his title to genuine scholarship, while yet gods and heroes, Gorgons and Chimera, Atlas and Pegasus, all bore as close kindred to him as Minerva to Jupiter. In fine, his golden touch is as unfailing as was that of Midas, and transmutes whatever he lays hand upon. Even brutes, and homely household implements, and the motley livery of the pauper, yield to his alchemy, and are no longer coarse and sordid, yet without losing their place or their nature. In like manner, he so transforms incidents and transactions of the most trivial character, as to render them grand, pathetic, or grotesque. We may, perhaps, define more accurately this element of his power, by pressing still farther the metaphors already employed. His golden touch, we would then say, imposes no superficial glitter, but brings out upon the surface, and concentrates in luminous points, the interior gilding, which is attached to the meanest objects and the lowliest scenes by their contact with the realm of sentiment, emotion, and spiritual life. He literally transforms, draws the hidden soul of whatever he describes to the light of day, and often veils exterior phenomena from clear view by the very tissue of motives, loves, antipathies, mental and moral idiosyncrasies, which they are wont to conceal. He thus, often, when least successful in the development of a plot, gives us portraitures of character as vivid as if they were wrought in flame-colors, and transcripts of inward experience so graphic that to read them is to live them over.

But with Hawthorne's close fidelity as a painter of man's interior nature and life, there is, after all, a subtle coloring and shading derived from no model, and so characteristic as to defy imitation. His heroes, while true in thought and speech to the parts which they are made to personate, always assume a tone of discourse or sentiment which we can imagine in him and in no other, under the supposed circumstances. His stories are, in fact, like Miss Kemble's dramatic readings, in which something of the same personality must betray itself in Caliban and Juliet, in Falstaff and Hamlet, in Coriolanus and King Lear. It is this which gives a prominent, and perhaps the chief, charm of his writings. They are, in the truest sense of the word, autobiographical; and, with repeated opportunities for cultivating his acquaintance by direct intercourse, we have learned from his books immeasurably more of his mental history, tastes, tendencies, sympathies, and opinions, than we should have known had we enjoyed his daily converse for a lifetime. Diffident and reserved as to the habitudes of the outer man, yet singularly communicative and social in disposition and desire, he takes his public for his confidant, and betrays to thousands of eyes likes and dislikes, whims and reveries, veins of mirthful and of serious reflection, moods of feeling both healthful and morbid, which it would be beyond his power to disclose through the ear, even to the most intimate of friends or the dearest of kindred.

As a writer of stories, whether in the form of tales, novels, or romances, Hawthorne will not bear comparison with his contemporaries in the same department, or measurement by any conventional rule. The most paltry tale-maker for magazines and newspapers can easily excel him in what we might term the mechanical portion of his art. His plots are seldom well devised or skilfully developed. They are either too simple to excite curiosity and attract interest, or too much involved for him to clear them up to the reader's satisfaction. His conversations, too, are not such as seem natural, in the sense of being probable or possible, but natural only because they are more rigidly true to fact and feeling than speech ever is. There is also, not infrequently, an incompleteness in his choicest productions, not as if he had been careless or hurried in their execution, but as if they had been too intimately a portion of his own being for separate existence,—as if they had been too deeply rooted in their native soil to bear transplanting. But, if he lacks skill in the management of his plot, he is independent of it. Were he to eliminate every thing of a narrative character from the best of his stories, we doubt whether their currency or his reputation would suffer detriment. Indeed, he is often most successful, where he does not even attempt narration, but selects some single scene, object, or incident, as the nucleus for a cluster of fancies and musings, melancholy, grave, humorous, or gay, either by itself, each in turn, or all blending and mutually interpretating, as in actual life, in which grief has its comic, and laughter its tragic, side. Thus, of his earlier series, none impress us as more truly worthy of his genius than "The Sister Years," a sketch of the midnight interview of the worn and jaded Old Year with her blooming and sanguine successor, the New Year; "Snow Flakes," a mere series of winter fireside fantasies; and "Night Sketches beneath an Umbrella," a description of what might be seen by any eye that looked beneath the surface on a short walk in Salem on a rainy evening.

Hawthorne has written nothing more likely to survive his times than several simply, yet gorgeously, wrought and highly suggestive allegories, among which "The Celestial Railroad" holds the first place, and deserves an immortality coeval with that of the great prose-epic which furnished its theme. He represents the railroad as built, in conformity with the spirit of the times, on a route intersecting at intervals the path of Bunyan's Pilgrim, which it is designed to supersede. The old enemies of the foot-travellers have been bought over by offices on the new road, and Apollyon is engineer. Onward the cars rattle over the Slough of Despond, on a shaky causeway built of books of German rationalism and Transcendental divinity. They pass unchallenged within sight of the wicket-gate. The easy-cushioned passengers can hardly find gibes pungent enough for two determined pilgrims, whom they see trudging over the now grass-grown path, and Apollyon helps the sport by squirting steam at them. At Vanity-Fair is the chief station-house, at which they make a protracted pause for refreshment and amusement. Then, when they have satiated themselves with its gayeties, they hurry through the residue of the way, though with a dim sense of insecurity, and beset by sights and sounds of the direst omen. Arrived at the terminus, they find the black River of Death rolling angrily at their feet. No means of crossing have been provided by the projectors of the new road, or are vouchsafed to its passengers by the lord of the old way. And, as they despair of breasting the current unguided and unaided, and see its depths yawning for their utter perdition, they lift their eyes, and the despised pilgrims, who had not been ashamed of the ancient Christ-marked path, have already crossed the River, angels are leading them up the shining banks, up the crystal hills, the golden gates are opened for them, and the harps of heaven ring their welcome.

After this manner, Hawthorne's stories are generally written to illustrate some idea or sentiment, to which, and not to the personages or incidents, the author manifestly solicits his reader's heed. He is a philosopher, with a strong dash of the humorist in his composition; human life and society constitute his field of speculation; and his queries and conclusions tend, through his poetic instincts, to concrete rather than abstract forms. With him, a tale takes the place of an apophthegm; an allegory, of a homily; a romance, of an ethical treatise. He seems incapable, not from penury, but from wealth of mind, of presenting a naked thought. The outward passage of every creation of his intellect lies through the inexhaustible vestry of an imagination swarming with textures and tints strange, fantastic, sometimes sombre, sometimes radiant, always beautiful. There is thus in his writings a philosophical completeness and unity, even when, in an artistical point of view, (as is often the case,) they are fragmentary or desultory. But, while a single thought gives its pervading hue and tone to a story or a volume, and that thought is always a brilliant of faultless lustre, he abounds in lesser gems of kindred perfectness. We know of no living or recent writer, from whom it would be possible to select so many sentences that might stand alone, as conveying ideas clearly defined and vividly expressed by imagery which at once astonishes by its novelty, charms by its aptness, and dazzles by its beauty. And there are numerous single metaphors of his comprised in a word or two, that, once read, recur perpetually to the memory, and supplant ever after their more literal, yet immeasurably less significant, synonymes.

The early history of New England, more largely than any other source, has supplied Hawthorne with names, events, and incidents, for his creations. The manners, customs, beliefs, superstitions of the Puritans, and their immediate descendants, seem to have taken the strongest hold upon his fancy. Their times are his heroic age, and he has made it mythological. As illustrative of history, his stories are eminently untrustworthy; for, where he runs parallel with recorded fact in his narrative of events, the spirit that animates and pervades them is of his own creation. Thus, in the *Scarlet Letter*, he has at once depicted the exterior of early New England life with a fidelity that might shame the most accurate chronicler, and defaced it by passions too fierce and wild to have been stimulated to their desolating energy under colder skies than of Spain or Italy. At the same time, he has unwittingly defamed the fathers of New England, by locating his pictures of gross impurity and sacrilegious vice where no shadow of reproach, and no breath but of immaculate fame, had ever rested before. He thus has violated one of the most sacred canons of literary creation. A writer, who borrows nothing from history, may allow himself an unlimited range in the painting of character; but he who selects a well-known place and epoch for his fiction, is bound to adjust his fiction to the analogy of fact, and especially to refrain from outraging the memory of the dead for the entertainment of the living.

—Andrew Preston Peabody, "Nathaniel Hawthorne,"
North American Review, January 1853, pp. 227–33

NATHANIEL HAWTHORNE (1855)

In these two letters, written from Liverpool, England, to Hawthorne's American publisher and friend, William D. Ticknor, Hawthorne blasts America's literature—at least in its popular form. His focus is, famously, "a d[amne]d mob of scribbling women." This viewpoint will be extremely useful to any student writing about Hawthorne's attitude either to women or to popular literature ("trash"). He sees himself as alienated from the marketplace and perhaps also from America in general. Hawthorne also seems to be attacking the feminization of American culture, which will be significant to any student discussing Hawthorne's characterization of strong female characters such as Zenobia or Hester Prynne.

In his second letter, Hawthorne recants somewhat from his earlier statement, praising the journalist and novelist Fanny Fern (Sara Payson Willis) and her novel *Ruth Hall* (1855). Hawthorne goes on to explain his antipathy to female writers ("they write like emasculated men") and yet his words of praise ("when they throw off the restraints of decency, and come before the public stark naked . . . their books are sure to possess character and value") might equally be applied to Hawthorne's own writing. Students interested in the extent to which Hawthorne was a conservative, and to what degree he was a radical, will be rewarded here.

I shall spend a year on the Continent, and then decide whether to go back to the Wayside, or to stay abroad and write books. But I had rather hold this office two years longer; for I have not seen half enough of England, and there is the germ of a new Romance in my mind, which will be all the better for ripening slowly. Besides, America is now wholly given over to a d____d mob of scribbling women, and I should have no chance of success while the public taste is occupied with their trash—and should be ashamed of myself if I did succeed. What is the mystery of these innumerable editions of the lamplighter, and other books neither better nor worse?—worse they could not be, and better they need not be, when they sell by the 100,000.

—Letter to William D. Ticknor, January 19, 1855,
Letters of Hawthorne to William D. Ticknor, 1851–1864,
Vol. 1, Newark, N.J.: The Carteret Book Club, 1910, p. 75

In my last, I recollect I bestowed some vituperation on female authors. I have since been reading "Ruth Hall"; and I must say I enjoyed it a good deal. The woman writes as if the devil was in her; and that is the only condition under which a woman ever writes anything worth reading. Generally women write like emasculated men, and are only to be distinguished from male authors by greater feebleness and folly; but when they throw off the restraints of decency, and come before the public strk naked, as it were – then their books are sure to possess character and value. Can you tell me anything about this Fanny Fern? If you meet her, I wish you would let her know how much I admire her.

—Letter to Ticknor, February 2, 1855, *Letters of Hawthorne
to William D. Ticknor, 1851–1864,* Vol. 1, p. 78

CHARLES SUMNER (1864)

Hawthorne was a genius. As a master of prose, he will come in the first class of all who have written the English language. He had not the grand style, but who has had a delicacy of touch superior to his?

—Charles Sumner, Letter to Henry Wadsworth Longfellow (May 21, 1864), cited in Edward L. Pierce, *Memoir and Letters of Charles Sumner,* 1893, Vol. 4, p. 202

OLIVER WENDELL HOLMES "HAWTHORNE" (1864)

In a patch of sunlight, flecked by the shade of tall, murmuring pines, at the summit of a gently swelling mound where the wild-flowers had climbed to find the light and the stirring of fresh breezes, the tired poet was laid beneath the green turf. Poet let us call him, though his chants were not modulated in the rhythm of verse. The element of poetry is air: we know the poet by his atmospheric effects, by the blue of his distances, by the softening of every hard outline he touches, by the silvery mist in which he veils deformity and clothes what is common so that it changes to awe-inspiring mystery, by the clouds of gold and purple which are the drapery of his dreams. And surely we have had but one prose-writer who could be compared with him in aerial perspective, if we may use the painter's term. If Irving is the Claude of our unrhymed poetry, Hawthorne is its Poussin.

—Oliver Wendell Holmes, "Hawthorne," *Atlantic,* July 1864, pp. 100–101

GEORGE WILLIAM CURTIS "EDITOR'S EASY CHAIR" (1864)

Curtis became disillusioned by Hawthorne's apathy regarding slavery and emancipation. Two months after this obituary, he wrote in *The North American Review*: "what other man of equal power . . . could have stood merely perplexed and bewildered . . . in the vast conflict which tosses us all in its terrible vortex?" In this obituary, he chooses to laud Hawthorne's originality and his "purely American" romances. He also—perhaps significantly—emphasizes the writing Hawthorne produced before *The Scarlet Letter,* and perhaps differentiates him from the author that followed. The younger Hawthorne, Curtis suggests, thrived—even delighted—in obscurity, perhaps since it gave him the freedom to experiment.

The death of Nathaniel Hawthorne is a national event. In original creative genius no name in our literature is superior to his; and while everybody was asking whether it were impossible to write an American novel, he wrote romances that were hardly possible elsewhere, because they were so purely American. There was never, certainly, an author more utterly independent than Hawthorne of the circumstances that surrounded him. In his style, even, which, for a rich, idiomatic raciness, is unsurpassed, there was no touch of any of the schools of his time. It was as clear and simple as Thackeray's, and as felicitous; but there was a flush of color in it, sometimes, of which Thackeray has no trace. But of the literary influences of his time, and even of his personal association, there is no sign in his writings. The form in which his world was revealed, like that world itself, was entirely his own.

Nor was there any foreign flavor whatever in his genius. It was not a growth of the English, or the German, or the French; nor was it eclectic. It was American. It was almost New England, except for that universality which belongs to such genius, and which made the *Marble Faun* no less a characteristic work of Hawthorne's than the *Scarlet Letter*. Yet in both there is the same general quality, although one is a story of old Puritan days in Boston, and the other of modern life in Rome.

It is remarkable that Hawthorne was an author, and a copious one, long before he was generally recognized. His delight, in former days, was to insist that no writer was so obscure as he; and it is one evidence of the vitality of his power that he still wrote on. He piped, and the world would not sing; he played, and it would not dance. But he was sent to be a piper, and so he piped until the world paused, charmed by the rare melody, and acknowledged the master. His place in our literature he took at once when the *Scarlet Letter* was published, and in that place he was never disturbed, and will always remain. . . .

The charm of his writings is imperishable. The fresh glow of genius which pervades them, apart from the essential interest of the stories, is indescribable. They have an individual pungency which does not always mark the works of our authors of an equal fame. The sparkle of humor which glitters every where upon his page, often weird but never dull, and a certain steadiness and self-possession of tone, equally free from rhetoric or baldness, certify a manly vigor and character which does not necessarily distinguish so subtle and poetic a nature.

—George William Curtis, "Editor's Easy Chair,"
Harper's New Monthly Magazine, August 1864, p. 405

James Russell Lowell "Thoreau" (1865)

In this excerpt from a famously unkind essay on Thoreau, Lowell casts Hawthorne as an "unwilling" poet of Puritanism. Several times Lowell had boasted that New England Puritans and Yankees were closer to Shakespeare than their English contemporaries, since they had been less changed in the time since. Perhaps this is why he finds in Hawthorne the creative heir to Shakespeare.

Lowell continues on in the same passage (not included here) locating the "Puritanism that made New England what it is, and is destined to make America what it should be," in Emerson.

~~~~~~~

The Puritanism of the past found its unwilling poet in Hawthorne, the rarest creative imagination of the century, the rarest in some ideal respects since Shakespeare.

—James Russell Lowell, "Thoreau" (1865), *Works,*
Riverside ed., Vol. 1, p. 365

Noah Porter (1870)

The devotee of Hawthorne is unrelenting in certain moody prejudices, Epicurean in his tastes and aspirations, and dreamy and uncertain in his theory of this life and the next.

—Noah Porter, *Books and Reading,* 1870, p. 230

Richard Holt Hutton
"Nathaniel Hawthorne" (1871)

Richard Holt Hutton was an English writer, editor, and theologian. In this essay, he discusses the disparity between Hawthorne's written world and the actuality of the "cold, inquisitive and shrewd" nineteenth-century Yankee. Hutton focuses on the idea of ghosts and haunting in Hawthorne's writing.

Hawthorne's subject is this transformation from Puritan to Yankee, and the lack of communication between the two ages and types. Hawthorne himself, Hutton argues, is "a sign to New England of the divorce . . . between its people's spiritual and earthly nature." Like a "ghost of New England," Hawthorne revisits the Puritan past on a Yankee nation: "They are ghostly writings." Students interested in Hawthorne's literary motivation in writing on New England's past should find plenty of note here.

Hutton meditates on the "mind-body problem" in Hawthorne's work and life, and finds that Hawthorne's "spirit haunted rather than ruled his body; his body hampered his spirit." Students can contrast this view with Moncure Daniel Conway's portrayal of Hawthorne as a vigorous athlete. Readers studying the contrast between the body and the spirit in Hawthorne's work should focus particularly on this essay.

Hutton discusses Hawthorne's practical employment (his "external career") as a customs house officer and then as a consul, but argues that Hawthorne—by his own repeated admission in his prefaces—could not transfer these experiences to his writing, to chronicle "the actual events of real lives."

Taking a phrase of Hawthorne's ("the moonlight of romance"), Hutton demonstrates how Hawthorne's "creative imagination" sits between "purely ideal" romances "made out of moonshine" at one extreme and those fictions that depict "actual life as it has existed, or still exists" at the other. Hawthorne portrays a quotidian reality, but through the lens of twilight: "moonlight in a familiar room." The effect is the defamiliarization of the everyday, and students exploring Hawthorne's literary style should take note.

Like Peabody, Hutton finds that the form Hawthorne adopts for his novels defies customary novelistic practice: Hawthorne "barely has *room* for a novel in the ordinary sense of the word. . . . Accordingly, his novels are not novels in the ordinary sense." Narrowly populated, at a remove from the humdrum world, ideas and situations are played out in the loose form of a novel. Hutton, like Peabody and Welsh, seems to hint at a proto-modernist Hawthorne, and students interested in Hawthorne's anticipation of later literature may find this excerpt of particular value.

Finally, Hutton compares Hawthorne to Edgar Allan Poe, and finds Hawthorne's advantage to be that he presents a "healthy, simple, natural" world into which "sin and disease" can intrude, and from which they draw their horror, while Poe simply gives the reader "terrors." Any student comparing Hawthorne and Poe should consult Hutton's essay.

⸺◈⸺　⸺◈⸺　⸺◈⸺

Hawthorne has been called a mystic, which he was not,—and a psychological dreamer, which he was in very slight degree. He was really the ghost of New England,—I do not mean the "spirit," nor the "phantom," but the ghost in the older sense in which that term is used, the thin, rarefied essence which is supposed to be found somewhere behind the physical organisation: embodied, indeed, and not at all in a shadowy or diminutive earthly tabernacle, but yet only half embodied in it, endowed with a certain painful sense of the gulf between his nature and its organisation, always recognising the gulf, always trying to bridge it over, and always more or less unsuccessful in the attempt. His writings are not exactly spiritual writings, for there is no dominating spirit in them. They are ghostly writings. Hawthorne was, to my mind, a sort of sign to New England of the divorce that has been going on there (and not less perhaps in old England) between its people's spiritual and earthly nature, and of the difficulty which they will soon feel, if they are to be absorbed more and more in that shrewd hard common sense which is one of their most striking characteristics, in even *communicating* with their former self. Hawthorne, with all his shyness, and tenderness, and literary reticence, shows very distinct traces also of understanding well the cold, inquisitive, and shrewd spirit which besets the Yankees even more than other commercial peoples. His heroes have usually not a little of this hardness in them. Coverdale, for instance, in *The Blithedale Romance,* and Holgrave, in *The House of the Seven Gables,* are of this class of shrewd, cold inquisitive heroes. Indeed there are few of his tales without a character of this type. But though Hawthorne had a deep sympathy with the practical as well as the literary genius of New England, it was always in a ghostly kind of way, as though he were stricken by some spell which half-paralysed him, and so prevented him from communicating with the life around him, as though he saw it only by a reflected light. His spirit haunted rather than ruled his body; his body hampered his spirit.

Yet his external career was not only not romantic, but identified with all the dullest routine of commercial duties. That a man who consciously *telegraphed,* as it were, with the world, transmitting meagre messages through his material organisation, should have been first a custom-house officer in Massachusetts, and then the consul in Liverpool, brings out into the strongest possible relief the curiously representative character in which he stood to New England as its literary or intellectual ghost. There is nothing more ghostly in his writings than his account of the consulship in Liverpool,—how he began by trying to communicate frankly with his fellow-countrymen, how he found the task more and more difficult, and gradually drew back into the twilight of his reserve, how he shrewdly and somewhat coldly watched "the dim shadows as they go and come," speculated idly on their fate, and all the time discharged the regular routine of consular business, witnessing the usual depositions, giving captains to captainless crews, affording meagrely doled-out advice or assistance to Yankees when in need of a friend, listening to them when they were only anxious to offer, not ask, assistance, and generally observing them from that distant and speculative outpost of the universe whence all common things looked strange.

Hawthorne, who was a delicate critic of himself, was well aware of the shadowy character of his own genius, though hardly aware that precisely here lay its curious and thrilling power. In the preface to *Twice-told Tales* he tells us frankly, "The book, if you would see anything in it, requires to be read in the clear brown twilight atmosphere in which it was written; if opened in the sunshine, it is apt to look exceedingly like a volume of blank pages."

It is one of his favourite theories that there must be a vague, remote, and shadowy element in the subject-matter of any narrative with which his own imagination can successfully deal. Sometimes he apologises for this idealistic limitation to his artistic aims. "It was a folly," he says in his preface to *The Scarlet Letter*, "with the materiality of this daily life pressing so intrusively upon me, to attempt to fling myself back into another age, or to insist on creating the semblance of a world out of airy matter, when at every moment the impalpable beauty of my soap-bubble was broken by the rude contact of some actual circumstance. The wiser effort would have been to diffuse thought and imagination through the opaque substance of to-day, and thus to make it a bright transparency; to spiritualise the burden that began to weigh so heavily; to seek resolutely the true and indestructible value that lay hidden in the petty and wearisome incidents and ordinary characters with which I was now conversant. The fault was mine. The page of life that was spread out before me was so dull and commonplace only because I had not fathomed its deeper import. A better book than I shall ever write was there; leaf after leaf presenting itself to me just as it was written out by the reality of the flitting hour, and vanishing as fast as written, only because my brain wanted the insight and my hand the cunning to transcribe it. At some future day, it may be, I shall remember a few scattered fragments and broken paragraphs and write them down, and find the letters turn to gold upon the page."

And yet that dissatisfaction with his own idealism which Hawthorne here expresses never actually sufficed to divert his efforts into the channel indicated. In *The Blithedale Romance* he tells us that he chose the external scenery of the Socialist community at Brook Farm "merely to establish a theatre, a little removed from the highway of ordinary travel, where the creatures of his brain may play their phantasmagorical antics without exposing them to too close a comparison with the actual events of real lives. In the old countries with which fiction has long been conversant, a certain conventional privilege seems to be awarded to the romancer; his work is not put exactly side by side with nature; and he is allowed a license with regard to every-day probability, in view of the improved effects which he is bound to produce thereby. Among ourselves, on the contrary, there is as yet no such Fairy Land so like the real world that, in a suitable remoteness, one cannot well tell the difference, but with an atmosphere of strange enchantment, beheld through which the inhabitants have a propriety of their own. This atmosphere is what the American romancer wants. In its absence, the beings of imagination are compelled to show themselves in the same category as actually living mortals,—a necessity that generally renders the paint and pasteboard of their composition but too painfully discernible." And once more, in the preface to his last novel, *Transformation,* he reiterates as his excuse for laying the scene in Italy, that "no author without a trial can conceive of the difficulty of writing a romance about a country where there is no shadow, no antiquity, no mystery, no picturesque and gloomy wrong, nor anything but a commonplace prosperity in broad and simple daylight, as is happily the case with my dear native land. It will be very long, I trust, before romance writers may find congenial and easily-handled themes either in the annals of our stalwart republic, or in any characteristic and probable event of our individual lives. Romance and poetry, ivy, lichens, and wall-flowers, need ruin to make them grow." These passages throw much light on the secret affinities of Hawthorne's genius. But it would be a mistake to conclude from them, as he himself would apparently have us, that he is a mere romantic idealist, in the sense in which these words are commonly used,—that he is one all whose dramatic conceptions are but the unreal kaleidoscopic combinations of fancies in his own brain.

I may, perhaps, accept a phrase of which Hawthorne himself was fond,—"the moonlight of romance,"—and compel it to explain something of the secret of his characteristic genius. There are writers—chiefly poets, but also occasionally writers of fanciful romances like Longfellow's *Hyperion*— whose productions are purely ideal, are not only seen by the light of their own imagination but constituted out of it,—made of moonshine,—and rendered vivid and beautiful, so far as they are vivid and beautiful, with the vividness and beauty merely of the poet's own mind. In these cases there is no distinction between the delineating power and the delineated object; the dream is indistinguishable from the mind of the dreamer, and varies wholly with its laws. Again, at the opposite extreme, there is a kind of creative imagination which has its origin in a deep sympathy with, and knowledge of, the real world. That which it deals with is actual life as it has existed, or still exists, in forms so innumerable that it is scarcely possible to assert that its range is more limited than life itself. Of course the only adequate example of such an imagination is Shakespeare's, and this kind of imaginative power resembles sunlight, not only in its brilliancy, but especially in this, that it casts a light so full and equable over the universe it reveals, that we never think of its source at all. We forget altogether, as we do by common daylight, that the light by which we see is not part and parcel of the world which it presents to us. The sunlight is so efficient that we forget the sun. We find so rich and various a world before us, dressed in its own proper colours, that no one is reminded that the medium by which those proper colours are seen is uniform and from a single source. We merge the delineative magic by which the scene is illuminated, in the details of the scene itself.

Between these two kinds of creative imagination there is another, which also shows a real world, but shows it so dimly in comparison with the last as to keep constantly before our minds the unique character of the light by which we see. The ideal light itself becomes a more prominent element in the picture than even the objects on which it shines; and yet is made so chiefly by the very fact of shining on those objects which we are accustomed to think of as they are seen in their own familiar details in full daylight. If the objects illuminated were not real and familiar, the light would not seem so mysterious; it is the pale uniform tint, the loss of colour and detail, and yet the vivid familiar outline and the strong shadow, which produce what Hawthorne calls the "moonlight of romance." "Moonlight in a familiar room," he says, in his preface to *The Scarlet Letter,* "falling so white upon the carpet, and showing all its figures so distinctly, making every object so minutely visible, yet so unlike a morning or noontide visibility,—is a medium the most suitable for a romance writer to get acquainted with his illusive guests. There is the little domestic scenery of the well-known apartment; the chairs, with each its separate individuality; the centre table, sustaining a work-basket, a volume or two, and an extinguished lamp; the sofa, the bookcase, the picture on the wall;—all these details, so completely seen, are so spiritualised by the unusual light, that they seem to lose their actual substance and become things of intellect. Nothing is too small or too trifling to undergo this change and acquire dignity thereby. A child's shoe, the doll seated in her little wicker carriage, the hobby-horse,—whatever, in a word, has been used or played with during the day, is now invested with a quality of strangeness and remoteness, though still almost as vividly present as by daylight. Thus, therefore, the floor of our familiar room has become a neutral territory, somewhere between the real world and fairyland, where the Actual and the

Imaginary may meet, and each imbue itself with the nature of the other." Sir Walter Scott's delineative power partakes both of this moonlight imagination and of the other more powerful, brilliant, and realistic kind. Often it is a wide genial sunshine, of which we quite forget the source in the vividness of the common life which it irradiates. At other times, again, when Scott is in his Black Douglas mood, as I may call it, it has all the uniformity of tint and the exciting pallor of what Hawthorne terms the moonlight of romance.

At all events, there is no writer to whose creations the phrase applies more closely than to Hawthorne's own. His characters are by no means such unreal webs of moonshine as the idealists proper constitute into the figures of their romance. They are real and definitely outlined, but they are all seen in a single light,—the contemplative light of the particular idea which has floated before him in each of his stories,—and they are seen, not fully and in their integrity, as things are seen by daylight, but like things touched by moonlight,—only so far as they are lighted up by the idea of the story. The thread of unity which connects his tales is always some pervading thought of his own; they are not written mainly to display character, still less for the mere narrative interest, but for the illustration they cast on some idea or conviction of their author's. Amongst English writers of fiction, we have many besides Shakespeare whose stories are merely appropriate instruments for the portraiture of character, and who therefore never conceive themselves bound to confine themselves scrupulously to the one aspect most naturally developed by the tale. Once introduced, their characters are given in full,—both that side of them which is, so to say, turned *towards* the story, and others which are not. Other writers, again, make the characters quite subsidiary to the epical interest of the plot, using them only to heighten the colouring of the action it describes. Hawthorne's tales belong to neither of these classes. Their unity is ideal. His characters are often real and distinct, but they are illuminated only from one centre of thought. So strictly is this true of them that he has barely *room* for a novel in the ordinary sense of the word. If he were to take his characters through as many phases of life as are ordinarily comprised in a novel, he could not keep the ideal unity of his tales unbroken; he would be obliged to delineate them from many different points of view. Accordingly his novels are not novels in the ordinary sense; they are ideal situations, expanded by minute study and trains of clear, pale thought into the dimensions of novels. A very small group of figures is presented to the reader in some marked ideal relation; or if it be in consequence of some critical event, then it must be some event which has struck the author as rich in ideal or spiritual suggestion. But it is not usually in his way—though his last complete novel gives us one remarkable exception to this observation—to seize any glowing crisis of action where the passion is lit or the blow is struck that gives a new mould to life, for his delineation; he prefers to assume the crisis past, and to delineate as fully as he can the ideal situation to which it has given rise; when it is beginning to assume a fainter and more chronic character. . . .

His power over his readers always arises from much the same cause as that of his own fanciful creation,—the minister who wore the black veil as a symbol of the veil which is on all hearts, and who startled men less because he was hidden from their view than because he made them aware of their own solitude. "Why do you tremble at *me alone?*" says the mild old man on his deathbed, from beneath his black veil, and with the glimmering smile on his half-hidden lips; "tremble also at each other! Have men avoided me, and women shown no pity, and children screamed and fled only from my black veil? What but the mystery which it obscurely typifies has made this piece of crape so awful? When the friend shows his inmost heart to his friend, the lover to his best beloved, when man does not vainly shrink from the eye of his Creator, loathsomely treasuring up the secret of his sin, then deem me a monster for the symbol beneath which I have lived and died! I look around me, and lo! on every visage a black veil?" Hawthorne, with the pale melancholy smile that seems to be always on his lips, speaks from a somewhat similar solitude. Indeed I suspect the story was a kind of parable of his own experience.

But, though Hawthorne's imagination was a solitary and twilight one, there was nothing allegorical about his genius. If we want to find his power at the very highest, we must look to his instinctive knowledge of what we may call the laws, not exactly of *discordant* emotions, but of emotions which *ought* to be mutually exclusive, and which combine with the thrill and the shudder of disease. This is almost the antithesis of Allegory. And he makes his delineation of such "unblest unions" the more striking, because it stands out from a background of healthy life, of genial scenes and simple beauties, which renders the contrast the more thrilling. I have often heard the term "cobweby" applied to his romances; and their most marking passages certainly cause the same sense of unwelcome shrinking to the spirit which a line of unexpected cobweb suddenly drawn across the face causes physically when one enters a deserted but familiar room. Edgar Poe, indeed, is much fuller of uncanny terrors; but then there is nothing in his writings of the healthy, simple, and natural background which gives sin and disease all its horror. It is the pure and severe New

England simplicity which Hawthorne paints so delicately that brings out in full relief the adulterous mixture of emotions on which he spends his main strength. I might almost say that he has carried into human affairs the old Calvinistic type of imagination. The same strange combination of clear simplicity, high faith, and reverential realism, with a reluctant, but for that very reason intense and devouring, conviction of the large comprehensiveness of the Divine Damnation which that grim creed taught its most honest believers to consider as the true trust in God's providence, Hawthorne copies into his pictures of human life. He presents us with a scene of pale severe beauty, full of truthful goodness, and then he uncovers in some one point of it a plague-spot, that, half-concealed as he keeps it, yet runs away with the imagination till one is scarcely conscious of anything else. Just as Calvinism, with all its noble features, can never keep its eyes off that one fact, as it thinks it, of God's calm foreknowledge of a widespread damnation; and this gradually encroaches on the attention till the mind is utterly absorbed in the fascinating terror of the problem how to combine the clashing emotions of love and horror which its image of Him inspires;—so Hawthorne's finest tales, with all the simplicity of their general outline, never detain you long from some uneasy mixture of emotions which only disease can combine in the same subject, until at last you ask for nothing but the brushing clean away of the infected web.

—Richard Holt Hutton, "Nathaniel Hawthorne,"
Literary Essays, 1871, pp. 437–58

EDWARD FITZGERALD (1872)

Hawthorne seems to me the most of a Man of Genius America has produced in the way of Imagination: yet I have never found an Appetite for his Books.

—Edward FitzGerald, Letter to W.F. Pollock (November 1872)

SIR LESLIE STEPHEN
"NATHANIEL HAWTHORNE" (1875)

Sir Leslie Stephen was a noted Victorian English essayist and critic. He was the son-in-law of the novelist William Makepeace Thackeray and the father of Virginia Woolf. As an Englishman, Stephen inevitably and painstakingly compares Hawthorne to British writers including John Bunyan, Thomas Carlyle, Charlotte Brontë, Oliver Goldsmith, and Walter Scott.

Considering several of the works in turn, Stephen explores Hawthorne's "antipathy to John Bull," or the way he resists, differs, or breaks from the English tradition.

Stephen remarks that *The Marble Faun* (called *Transformation* in England) veers from the narrative into travelogue writing. He especially faults an apparently needless aside by the author about Italian bread. Students examining Hawthorne's lauded "clarity" and "brevity" can contrast this with Rose Lathrop Hawthorne's claim that her father never wrote "superfluous" matter. Stephen adds that such a gratuitous description would not blight Hawthorne's fiction set in America. Such a contention should interest students concerned with Hawthorne's treatment of Europe in fiction, or those comparing Hawthorne's Italian novel with his American ones.

Stephen next compares Hawthorne's treatment of New England with Charlotte Brontë's depiction of the "bleak Yorkshire moors," finding a "decided family resemblance." He finds Hawthorne's style "more graceful and flexible," but less moving or sympathetic than Brontë's. Several times he notes Hawthorne's passionless style. He continues by comparing *The Scarlet Letter* to John Bunyan's *Pilgrim's Progress*. The English, he decides, crave substantiality, which is why Hawthorne kept John Bull "at arm's length."

Next Stephen contrasts Hawthorne with "his rival" Poe, who "seems to have had recourse to strong stimulants to rouse a flagging imagination." What is "fanciful and airy" in Hawthorne becomes "dabblings in the charnel-house" in Poe. Students comparing the two writers will find relevant material here. Discussing *Twice-Told Tales*, Stephen portrays a pluralist Hawthorne, whose "fragments" partake of various genres: historical romance, allegory, the "domestic piece," the "pure *diablerie*" (tales of the devil), and the psychological problem. Hawthorne's presiding subject is the "borderland between reason and insanity."

Turning to the subject of Puritanism, Stephen argues that had Hawthorne lived in colonial times he would have been a believer in witchcraft. His thoughts "delight to dwell in the same regions where the daring speculations of his theological ancestors took their origin." Stephen compares the hero of Hawthorne's last (unfinished and rarely noticed) novel, *Septimius Felton*, to its author. Both "sought refuge from the hard facts of commonplace life by retiring into a visionary world."

The story which perhaps generally passes for his masterpiece is *Transformation*, for most readers assume that a writer's longest book must necessarily be his best. In the present case, I think that this method, which has its conveniences, has not led to a perfectly just conclusion. In *Transformation,* Hawthorne has for once the advantage of placing his characters in a land where "a sort of poetic or fairy precinct," as he calls it, is naturally provided for them. The very stones of the streets are full of romance, and he cannot mention a name that has not a musical ring. Hawthorne, moreover, shows his usual tact in confining his aims to the possible. He does not attempt to paint Italian life and manners; his actors belong by birth, or by a kind of naturalisation, to the colony of the American artists in Rome; and he therefore does not labour under the difficulty of being in imperfect sympathy with his creatures. Rome is a mere background, and surely a most felicitous background, to the little group of persons who are effectually detached from all such vulgarising associations with the mechanism of daily life in less poetical countries. The centre of the group, too, who embodies one of Hawthorne's most delicate fancies, could have breathed no atmosphere less richly perfumed with old romance. In New York he would certainly have been in danger of a Barnum's museum, beside Washington's nurse and the woolly horse. It is a triumph of art that a being whose nature trembles on the very verge of the grotesque should walk through Hawthorne's pages with such undeviating grace. In the Roman dreamland he is in little danger of such prying curiosity, though even there he can only be kept out of harm's way by the admirable skill of his creator. Perhaps it may be thought by some severe critics that, with all his merits, Donatello stands on the very outside verge of the province permitted to the romancer. But without cavilling at what is indisputably charming, and without dwelling upon certain defects of construction which slightly mar the general beauty of the story, it has another weakness which it is impossible quite to overlook. Hawthorne himself remarks that he was surprised, in re-writing his story, to see the extent to which he had introduced descriptions of various Italian objects. "Yet these things," he adds, "fill the mind everywhere in Italy, and especially in Rome, and cannot be kept from flowing out upon the page when one writes freely and with self-enjoyment." The associations which they called up in England were so pleasant that he could not find it in his heart to cancel. Doubtless that is the precise truth, and yet it is equally true that they are artistically out of place. There are passages which recall the guide-book. To take one instance—and, certainly, it is about the worst—the whole party is going to the Coliseum, where a very striking scene takes place. On the way they pass a baker's shop.

'The baker is drawing his loaves out of the oven,' remarked Kenyon. 'Do you smell how sour they are? I should fancy that Minerva (in revenge for the desecration of her temples) had slyly poured vinegar into the batch, if I did not know that the modern Romans prefer their bread in the acetous fermentation.'

The instance is trivial, but it is characteristic. Hawthorne had doubtless remarked the smell of the sour bread, and to him it called up a vivid recollection of some stroll in Rome; for, of all our senses, the smell is notoriously the most powerful in awakening associations. But then what do we who read him care about the Roman taste for bread "in acetous fermentation"? When the high-spirited girl is on the way to meet her tormenter, and to receive the provocation which leads to his murder, why should we be worried by a gratuitous remark up about Roman baking? It somehow jars upon our taste, and we are certain that, in describing a New England village, Hawthorne would never have admitted a touch which has no conceivable bearing upon the situation. There is almost a superabundance of minute local colour in his American Romances, as, for example, in the *House of the Seven Gables;* but still, every touch, however minute, is steeped in the sentiment and contributes to the general effect. In Rome the smell of a loaf is sacred to his imagination, and intrudes itself upon its own merits, and, so far as we can discover, without reference to the central purpose. If a baker's shop impresses him unduly because it is Roman, the influence of ancient ruins and glorious works of art is of course still more distracting. The mysterious Donatello, and the strange psychological problem which he is destined to illustrate, are put aside for an interval, whilst we are called upon to listen to descriptions and meditations, always graceful, and often of great beauty in themselves, but yet, in a strict sense, irrelevant. Hawthorne's want of familiarity with the scenery is of course responsible for part of this failing. Had he been a native Roman, he would not have been so preoccupied with the wonders of Rome. But it seems that for a romance bearing upon a spiritual problem, the scenery, however tempting, is not really so serviceable as the less prepossessing surroundings of America. The objects have too great an intrinsic interest. A counter-attraction distorts the symmetry of the system. In the shadow of the Coliseum and St. Peter's you cannot pay much attention to the troubles of a young lady whose existence is painfully ephemeral. Those mighty objects will not be relegated to the background, and condescend to act as mere scenery. They are, in fact, too romantic for a romance. The fountain of Trevi, with all its allegorical marbles, may be a

very picturesque object to describe, but for Hawthorne's purposes it is really
not equal to the town-pump at Salem; and Hilda's poetical tower, with the
perpetual light before the Virgin's image, and the doves floating up to her
from the street, and the column of Antoninus looking at her from the heart
of the city, somehow appeals less to our sympathies than the quaint garret in
the House of the Seven Gables, from which Phoebe Pyncheon watched the
singular idiosyncracies of the superannuated breed of fowls in the garden.
The garret and the pump are designed in strict subordination to the human
figures: the tower and the fountain have a distinctive purpose of their own.
Hawthorne, at any rate, seems to have been mastered by his too powerful
auxiliaries. A human soul, even in America, is more interesting to us than all
the churches and picture-galleries in the world; and, therefore, it is as well
that Hawthorne should not be tempted to the too easy method of putting
fine description in place of sentiment.

But how was the task to be performed? How was the imaginative glow to be
shed over the American scenery, so provokingly raw and deficient in harmony?
A similar problem was successfully solved by a writer whose development, in
proportion to her means of cultivation, is about the most remarkable of
recent literary phenomena. Miss Bronte's bleak Yorkshire moors, with their
uncompromising stone walls, and the valleys invaded by factories, are at
first sight as little suited to romance as New England itself, to which, indeed,
both the inhabitants and the country have a decided family resemblance.
Now that she has discovered for us the fountains of poetic interest, we can
all see that the region is not a mere stony wilderness; but it is well worth while
to make a pilgrimage to Haworth, if only to discover how little the country
corresponds to our preconceived impressions, or, in other words, how
much depends upon the eye which sees it, and how little upon its intrinsic
merits. Miss Bronte's marvellous effects are obtained by the process which
enables an "intense and glowing mind" to see everything through its own
atmosphere. The ugliest and most trivial objects seem, like objects heated
by the sun, to radiate back the glow of passion with which she has regarded
them. Perhaps this singular power is still more conspicuous in *Villette*,
where she had even less of the raw material of poetry. An odd parallel may
be found between one of the most striking passages in *Villette* and one in
Transformation. Lucy Snowe in one novel, and Hilda in the other, are left to
pass a summer vacation, the one in Brussels and the other in pestiferous
Rome. Miss Snowe has no external cause of suffering but the natural effect
of solitude upon a homeless and helpless governess. Hilda has to bear about
with her the weight of a terrible secret, affecting, it may be, even the life of

her dearest friend. Each of them wanders into a Roman Catholic church, and each, though they have both been brought up in a Protestant home, seeks relief at the confessional. So far the cases are alike, though Hilda, one might have fancied, has by far the strongest cause for emotion. And yet, after reading the two descriptions—both excellent in their way—one might fancy that the two young ladies had exchanged burdens. Lucy Snowe is as tragic as the innocent confidante of a murderess; Hilda's feelings never seem to rise above that weary sense of melancholy isolation which besieges us in a deserted city. It is needless to ask which is the best bit of work artistically considered. Hawthorne's style is more graceful and flexible; his descriptions of the Roman Catholic ceremonial and its influence upon an imaginative mind in distress are far more sympathetic, and imply wider range of intellect. But Hilda scarcely moves us like Lucy. There is too much delicate artistic description of picture-galleries and of the glories of St. Peter's to allow the poor little American girl to come prominently to the surface. We have been indulging with her in some sad but charming speculations, and not witnessing the tragedy of a deserted soul. Lucy Snowe has very inferior materials at her command; but somehow we are moved by a sympathetic thrill: we taste the bitterness of the awful cup of despair which, as she tells us, is forced to her lips in the night-watches; and are not startled when so prosaic an object as the row of beds in the dormitory of a French school suggests to her images worthy of rather stately tombs in the aisles of a vast cathedral, and recalls dead dreams of an elder world and a mightier race long frozen in death. Comparisons of this kind are almost inevitably unfair; but the difference between the two illustrates one characteristic—we need not regard it as a defect—of Hawthorne. His idealism does not consist in conferring grandeur upon vulgar objects by tinging them with the reflection of deep emotion. He rather shrinks than otherwise from describing the strongest passions, or shows their working by indirect touches and under a side-light. An excellent example of his peculiar method occurs in what is in some respects the most perfect of his works, the *Scarlet Letter*. There, again, we have the spectacle of a man tortured by a life-long repentance. The Puritan Clergyman, reverenced as a saint by all his flock, conscious of a sin which, once revealed, will crush him to the earth, watched with a malignant purpose by the husband whom he has injured, unable to summon up the moral courage to tear off the veil, and make the only atonement in his power, is a singularly striking figure, powerfully conceived and most delicately described. He yields under terrible pressure to the temptation of escaping from the scene of his prolonged torture with the partner of his guilt. And then, as he is returning homewards after

yielding a reluctant consent to the flight, we are invited to contemplate the
agony of his soul. The form which it takes is curiously characteristic. No
vehement pangs of remorse, or desperate hopes of escape overpower his
faculties in any simple and straightforward fashion. The poor minister is
seized with a strange hallucination. He meets a venerable deacon, and can
scarcely restrain himself from uttering blasphemies about the Communion-
supper. Next appears an aged widow, and he longs to assail her with what
appears to him to be an unanswerable argument against the immortality of
the soul. Then follows an impulse to whisper impure suggestions to a fair
young maiden, whom he has recently converted. And, finally, he longs
to greet a rough sailor with a "volley of good, round, solid, satisfactory, and
heaven-defying oaths." The minister, in short, is in that state of mind which
gives birth in its victim to a belief in diabolical possession; and the meaning
is pointed by an encounter with an old lady, who, in the popular belief,
was one of Satan's miserable slaves and dupes, the witches, and is said—for
Hawthorne never introduces the supernatural without toning it down by a
supposed legendary transmission—to have invited him to meet her at the
blasphemous Sabbath in the forest. The sin of endeavouring to escape from
the punishment of his sins had brought him into sympathy with wicked
mortals and perverted spirits.

This mode of setting forth the agony of a pure mind tainted by one
irremovable blot, is undoubtedly impressive to the imagination in a high
degree; far more impressive, we may safely say, than any quantity of such
rant as very inferior writers could have poured out with the utmost facility
on such an occasion. Yet it might possibly be mentioned that a poet of the
highest order would have produced the effect by more direct means. Remorse
overpowering and absorbing does not embody itself in these recondite and,
one may almost say, over-ingenious fancies. Hawthorne does not give us
so much the pure passion as some of its collateral effects. He is still more
interested in the curious psychological problem than moved by sympathy
with the torture of the soul. We pity poor Mr. Dimmesdale profoundly, but
we are also interested in him as the subject of an experiment in analytical
psychology. We do not care so much for his emotions as for the strange
phantoms which are raised in his intellect by the disturbance of his natural
functions. The man is placed upon the rack, but our compassion is aroused,
not by feeling our own nerves and sinews twitching in sympathy, but by
remarking the strange confusion of ideas produced in his mind, the singularly
distorted aspect of things in general introduced by such an experience, and
hence, if we please, inferring the keenest of the pangs which have produced

them. This turn of thought explains the real meaning of Hawthorne's antipathy to poor John Bull. That worthy gentleman, we will admit, is in a sense more gross and beefy than his American cousin. His nerves are stronger, for we need not decide whether they should be called coarser or less morbid. He is not, in the proper sense of the word, less imaginative, for a vigorous grasp of realities is rather a proof of a powerful than a defective imagination. But he is less accessible to those delicate impulses which are to the ordinary passions as electricity to heat. His imagination is more intense and less mobile. The devils which haunt the two races partake of the national characteristics. John Bunyan, Dimmesdale's contemporary, suffered under the pangs of a remorse equally acute, though with apparently far less cause. The devils who tormented him whispered blasphemies in his ears; they pulled at his clothes; they persuaded him that he had committed the unpardonable sin. They caused the very stones in the streets and tiles on the houses, as he says, to band themselves together against him. But they had not the refined and humorous ingenuity of the American fiends. They tempted him, as their fellows tempted Dimmesdale, to sell his soul; but they were too much in earnest to insist upon queer breaches of decorum. They did not indulge in that quaint play of fancy which tempts us to believe that the devils in New England had seduced the "tricksy spirit," Ariel, to indulge in practical jokes at the expense of a nobler victim than Stephano or Caliban. They were too terribly diabolical to care whether Bunyan blasphemed in solitude or in the presence of human respectabilities. Bunyan's sufferings were as poetical, but less conducive to refined speculation. His were the fiends that haunt the valley of the shadow of death; whereas Hawthorne's are to be encountered in the dim regions of twilight, where realities blend inextricably with mere phantoms, and the mind confers only a kind of provisional existence upon the "airy nothings" of its creation. Apollyon does not appear armed to the teeth and throwing fiery darts, but comes as an unsubstantial shadow threatening vague and undefined dangers, and only half-detaching himself from the background of darkness. He is as intangible as Milton's Death, not the vivid reality which presented itself to mediaeval imaginations.

This special attitude of mind is probably easier to the American than to the English imagination. The craving for something substantial, whether in cookery or in poetry, was that which induced Hawthorne to keep John Bull rather at arm's length. We may trace the working of similar tendencies in other American peculiarities. Spiritualism and its attendant superstitions are the gross and vulgar form of the same phase of thought as it occurs in men of highly-strung nerves but defective cultivation. Hawthorne always speaks of these modern goblins with the contempt they deserve, for they shocked his imagination as much as his reason; but he likes to play with fancies which are not altogether dissimilar, though his refined taste warns him that they become disgusting when grossly translated into tangible symbols. Mesmerism, for example, plays an important part in the *Blithedale Romance* and the *House of the Seven Gables,* though judiciously softened and kept in the background. An example of the danger of such tendencies may be found in those works of Edgar Poe, in which he seems to have had recourse to strong stimulants to rouse a flagging imagination. What is exquisitely fanciful and airy in Hawthorne is too often replaced in his rival by an attempt to overpower us by dabblings in the charnel-house and prurient appeals to our fears of the horribly revolting. After reading some of Poe's stories one feels a kind of shock to one's modesty. We require some kind of spiritual ablution to cleanse our minds of his disgusting images; whereas Hawthorne's pure and delightful fancies, though at times they may have led us too far from the healthy contact of everyday interests, never leave a stain upon the imagination, and generally succeed in throwing a harmonious colouring upon some objects in which we had previously failed to recognise the beautiful. To perform that duty effectually is perhaps the highest of artistic merits; and though we may complain of Hawthorne's colouring as too evanescent, its charm grows upon us the more we study it.

Hawthorne seems to have been slow in discovering the secret of his own power. The *Twice-Told Tales,* he tells us, are only a fragmentary selection from a great number which had an ephemeral existence in long-forgotten magazines, and were sentenced to extinction by their author. Though many of the survivors are very striking, no wise reader will regret that sentence. It could be wished that other authors were as ready to bury their innocents, and that injudicious admirers might always abstain from acting as resurrection-men. The fragments, which remain with all their merits, are chiefly interesting as illustrating the intellectual development of their author. Hawthorne, in his preface to the collected edition (all Hawthorne's prefaces are remarkably instructive) tells us what to think of them. The book, he says, "requires to be read in the clear brown twilight atmosphere in which it was written; if opened in the sunshine it is apt to look exceedingly like a volume of blank pages." The remark, with deductions on the score of modesty, is more or less applicable to all his writings. But he explains, and with perfect truth, that though written in solitude, the book has not the abstruse tone which marks the written communications of a solitary mind with itself. The reason is that the sketches "are not the talk of a secluded man with his own mind and heart, but his attempts to open an intercourse with the world." They may, in fact, be compared to Brummel's failures; and, though they do not display the perfect grace and fitness which would justify him in presenting himself to society, they were well worth taking up to illustrate the skill of the master's manipulation. We see him trying various experiments to hit off that delicate mean between the fanciful and the prosaic, which shall satisfy his taste and be intelligible to the outside world. Sometimes he gives us a fragment of historical romance, as in the story of the stern old regicide who suddenly appears from the woods to head the colonists of Massachusetts in a critical emergency; then he tries his hand at a bit of allegory, and describes the search for the mythical carbuncle which blazes by its inherent splendour on the face of a mysterious cliff in the depths of the untrodden wilderness, and lures old and young, the worldly and the romantic, to waste their lives in the vain effort to discover it—for the carbuncle is the ideal which mocks our pursuit, and may be our curse or our blessing. Then perhaps we have a domestic piece—a quiet description of a New England country scene, touched with a grace which reminds us of the creators of Sir Roger de Coverley or the Vicar of Wakefield. Occasionally there is a fragment of pure *diablerie,* as in the story of the lady who consults the witch in the hollow of the three hills; and more frequently he tries to work out one of those strange psychological problems which he afterwards treated with more fulness of power. The minister who, for an unexplained reason, puts on a black veil one morning in his youth, and wears it until he is laid with it in his grave—a kind of symbolic prophecy of Dimmesdale; the eccentric Wakefield (whose original, if I remember rightly, is to be found in *King's Anecdotes),* who leaves his house one morning for no particular reason, and though living in the next street, does not reveal his existence to his wife for twenty years; and the hero of the "Wedding Knell" the elderly bridegroom whose early love has jilted him, but agrees to marry him when she is an elderly widow and he an old bachelor, and who appals the marriage party by coming to the church in his shroud, with the bell tolling as for a funeral—all these bear the unmistakable stamp of Hawthorne's mint, and each is a study of his favourite subject, the borderland between reason and insanity. In many of these stories appears the element of interest, to which Hawthorne clung the more closely both from early associations and because it is the one undeniable poetical element in the American character. Shallow-minded people fancy Puritanism to be prosaic, because the laces and ruffles of the Cavaliers are a more picturesque costume at a masked ball than the dress of the Roundheads. The Puritan has become a grim and ugly scarecrow, on whom every buffoon may break his jest. But the genuine old Puritan spirit ceases to be picturesque only because of its sublimity: its poetry is sublimed into religion. The great poet of the Puritans fails, as far as he fails, when he tries to transcend the limits of mortal imagination—

> The living throne, the sapphire blaze,
> Where angels tremble as they gaze,
> He saw: but blasted with excess of light,
> Closed his eyes in endless night.

To represent the Puritan from within was not, indeed, a task suitable to Hawthorne's powers. Carlyle has done that for us with more congenial sentiment than could have been well felt by the gentle romancer. Hawthorne fancies the grey shadow of a stern old forefather wondering at his degenerate son. "A writer of story-books! What kind of business in life, what mode of glorifying God, or being serviceable to mankind in his day and generation, may that be? Why, the degenerate fellow might as well have been a fiddler!" And yet the old strain remains, though strangely modified by time and circumstance. In Hawthorne it would seem that the peddling element of the old Puritans had been reduced to its lowest point; the more spiritual element had been refined till it is probable enough that the ancestral shadow would have refused to recognise the connection. The old dogmatical framework to which he attached such vast importance had dropped out of his descendant's mind, and had been replaced by dreamy speculation, obeying no laws save those imposed by its own sense of artistic propriety. But we may often recognise, even where we cannot express in words, the strange family likeness which exists in characteristics which are superficially antagonistic. The man of action may be bound by subtilities to the speculative metaphysician; and Hawthorne's mind, amidst the most obvious differences, had still an affinity to his remote forefathers. Their bugbears had become his playthings; but the witches, though they have no reality, have still a fascination for him. The interest which he feels in them, even in their now shadowy state, is a proof that he would have believed in them in good earnest a century and a half earlier. The imagination, working in a different intellectual atmosphere, is unable to project its images upon the external world; but it still forms them in the old shape. His solitary musings necessarily employ a modern dialect, but they often turn on the same topics which occurred to Jonathan Edwards in the woods of Connecticut. Instead of the old Puritan speculations about predestination and free-will, he dwells upon the transmission by natural laws of an hereditary curse, and upon the strange blending of good and evil, which may cause sin to be an awakening impulse in a human soul. The change which takes place in Donatello in consequence of his crime is a modern symbol of the fall of man and the eating the fruit of the knowledge of good and evil. As an artist he gives concrete images instead of abstract theories; but his thoughts evidently delight to dwell in the same regions where the daring speculations of his theological ancestors took their origin. Septimius, the rather disagreeable hero of his last romance, is a peculiar example of a similar change. Brought up under the strict discipline of New England, he has retained the love of musing upon insoluble mysteries, though he has abandoned the old dogmatic guide-posts. When such a man finds that the orthodox scheme of the universe provided by his official pastors has somehow broken down with him, he forms some audacious theory of his own, and is perhaps plunged into an unhallowed revolt against the divine order. Septimius, under such circumstances, develops into a kind of morbid and sullen Hawthorne. He considers—as other people have done—that death is a disagreeable fact, but refuses to admit that it is inevitable. The romance tends to show that such a state of mind is unhealthy and dangerous, and Septimius is contrasted unfavourably with the vigorous natures who preserve their moral balance by plunging into the stream of practical life. Yet Hawthorne necessarily sympathises with the abnormal being whom he creates. Septimius illustrates the dangers of the musing temperament, but the dangers are produced by a combination of an essentially selfish nature with the meditative tendency. Hawthorne, like his hero, sought refuge from the hard facts of commonplace life by retiring into a visionary world. He delights in propounding much the same questions as those which tormented poor Septimius, though for obvious reasons, he did not try to compound an elixir of life by means of a recipe handed down from Indian ancestors. The strange mysteries in which the world and our nature are shrouded are always present to his imagination; he catches dim glimpses of the laws which bring out strange harmonies, but, on the whole, tend rather to deepen than to clear the mysteries. He loves the marvellous, not in the vulgar sense of the word, but as a symbol of perplexity which encounters every thoughtful man in his journey through life. Similar tenants at an earlier period might, with almost equal probability, have led him to the stake as a dabbler in forbidden sciences, or have caused him to be revered as one to whom a deep spiritual instinct had been granted.

Meanwhile, as it was his calling to tell stories to readers of the English language in the nineteenth century, his power is exercised in a different sphere. No modern writer has the same skill in so using the marvellous as to interest without unduly exciting our incredulity. He makes, indeed, no positive demands on our credulity. The strange influences which are suggested rather than obtruded upon us are kept in the background, so as not to invite, nor indeed to render possible, the application of scientific tests. We may compare him once more to Miss Bronte, who introduces, in *Villette,* a haunted garden. She shows us a ghost who is for a moment a very terrible spectre indeed, and then, very much to our annoyance, rationalises him into a flesh-and-blood lover. Hawthorne would neither have allowed the ghost to intrude so forcibly, nor have expelled him so decisively. The garden in his hands would have been haunted by a shadowy terror of which we could render no precise account to ourselves. It would have refrained from actual contact with professors and governesses; and as it would never have taken bodily form, it would never have been quite dispelled. His ghosts are confined to their proper sphere, the twilight of the mind, and never venture into the broad glare of daylight. We can see them so long as we do not gaze directly at them; when we turn to examine them they are gone, and we are left in doubt whether they were realities or an ocular delusion generated in our fancy by some accidental collocation of half-seen objects. So in the *House of the Seven Gables* we may hold what opinion we please as to the reality of the curse which hangs over the Pyncheons and the strange connection between them and their hereditary antagonists; in the *Scarlet Letter* we may, if we like, hold that there was really more truth in the witch legends which colour the imaginations of the actors than we are apt to dream of in our philosophy; and in *Transformation* we are left finally in doubt as to the great question of Donatello's ears, and the mysterious influence which he retains over the animal world so long as he is unstained by bloodshed. In *Septimius* alone, it seems to me that the supernatural is left in rather too obtrusive a shape in spite of the final explanations; though it might possibly have been toned down had the story received the last touches of the author. The artifice, if so it may be called, by which this is effected—and the romance is just sufficiently dipped in the shadow of the marvellous to be heightened without becoming offensive—sounds, like other things, tolerably easy when it is explained; and yet the difficulty is enormous, as may appear on reflection as well as from the extreme rarity of any satisfactory work in the same style by other artists. With the exception of a touch or two in Scott's stories, such as the impressive Bodach Glas, in *Waverley,* and the apparition in the exquisite *Bride of Lammermoor,* it would be difficult to discover any parallel.

In fact Hawthorne was able to tread in that magic circle only by an exquisite refinement of taste, and by a delicate sense of humour, which is the best preservative against all extravagance. Both qualities combine in that tender delineation of character which is, after all, one of his greatest charms.

His Puritan blood shows itself in sympathy, not with the stern side of the ancestral creed, but with the feebler characters upon whom it weighed as an oppressive terror. He resembles, in some degree, poor Clifford Pyncheon, whose love of the beautiful makes him suffer under the stronger will of his relatives and the prim stiffness of their home. He exhibits the suffering of such a character all the more effectively because, with his kindly compassion there is mixed a delicate flavour of irony. The more tragic scenes affect us, perhaps, with less sense of power; the playful, though melancholy, fancy seems to be less at home when the more powerful emotions are to be excited; and yet once, at least, he draws one of those pictures which engrave themselves instantaneously on the memory. The grimmest or most passionate of writers could hardly have improved the scene where the body of the magnificent Zenobia is discovered in the river. Every touch goes straight to the mark. The narrator of the story, accompanied by the man whose coolness has caused the suicide, and the shrewd, unimaginative Yankee farmer, who interprets into coarse, downright language the suspicions which they fear to confess to themselves, are sounding the depths of the river by night in a leaky punt with a long pole. Silas Foster represents the brutal, commonplace comments of the outside world, which jar so terribly on the more sensitive and closely intersected actors in the tragedy.

> Heigho! [he soliloquises, with offensive loud-ness], life and death together make sad work for us all. Then I was a boy, bobbing for fish; and now I'm getting to be an old fellow, and here I be, groping for a dead body! I tell you what lads, if I thought anything had really happened to Zenobia, I should feel kind o' sorrowful.

That is the discordant chorus of the gravediggers in *Hamlet*. At length the body is found, and poor Zenobia is brought to the shore with her knees still bent in the attitude of prayer, and her hands clenched in immitigable defiance. Foster tries in vain to straighten the dead limbs. As the teller of the story gazes at her, the grimly ludicrous reflection occurs to him that if Zenobia had foreseen all "the ugly circumstances of death—how ill it would become her, the altogether unseemly aspect which she must put on, and especially old Silas Foster's efforts to improve the matter—she would no more have committed the dreadful act than have exhibited herself to a public assembly in a badly-fitting garment."

—Sir Leslie Stephen, "Nathaniel Hawthorne" (1875),
Hours in a Library (1874–79), 1904, Vol. 1, pp. 244–70

GEORGE PARSONS LATHROP (1876)

Lathrop was Hawthorne's son-in-law, marrying Rose Hawthorne seven years after the author's death and, as a result, breaking the heart of her older sister, Una. Students exploring Hawthorne's characterizations should read Lathrop's opinion. He finds a prevailing homogeneity of characters, which he calls a "monotone." He relates this to Hawthorne's genius, however, reasoning that the author is so in control of his fictional worlds that he allows his characters to utter no loose or ungrammatical language. There is no realism, then, although the writing seeks to portray a truth; Hawthorne's is a "new species of fiction," aiming rather at "what is most beautiful, and this he finds only in moral truth."

Lathrop finds in Hawthorne the "embodiment of the youth of this country," because he points to and will influence a future literature rather than looking back to literary antecedents. Lathrop finds Hawthorne to be a radical: "though turning on the axis of conservatism, the radicalism of his mind is irresistible." Students concerned with the degree of Hawthorne's radicalism will find useful material in this entry.

———————

Hawthorne, it is true, expanded so constantly, that however many works he might have produced, it seems unlikely that any one of them would have failed to record some large movement in his growth; and therefore it is perhaps to be regretted that his life could not have been made to solely serve his genius, so that we might have had the whole sweep of his imagination clearly exposed. As it is, he has not given us a large variety of characters; and Hester, Zenobia, and Miriam bear a certain general likeness one to another. Phoebe, however, is quite at the opposite pole of womanhood; Hilda is as unlike any of them as it is easy to conceive of her being; and Priscilla, again, is a feminine nature of unique calibre, as weird but not so warm as Goethe's Mignon, and at the same time a distinctly American type, in her nervous yet captivating fragility. In Priscilla and Phoebe are embodied two widely opposed classes of New England women. The male characters, with the exception of Donatello and Hollingsworth, are not so remarkable as the feminine ones: Coverdale and Kenyon come very close together, both being artistic and both reflectors for the persons that surround them; and Dimmesdale is to some extent the same character,—with the artistic escape closed upon his passions, so that they turn within and ravage his heart,—arrested and altered by Puritan influences. Chillingworth is perhaps too devilish a shape of revenge to be discussed as a human individual. Septimius, again, is distinct; and the characterization of

Westervelt, in *Blithedale,* slight as it is, is very stimulating. Perhaps, after all, what leads us to pronounce upon the whole fictitious company a stricture of homogeneity is the fact that the author, though presenting us each time with a set of persons sufficiently separate from his previous ones, does not emphasize their differences with the same amount of external description that we habitually depend upon from a novelist. The similarity is more in the author's mode of presentation than in the creations themselves.

This monotone in which all the personages of his dramas share is nearly related with some special distinctions of his genius. He is so fastidious in his desire for perfection, that he can scarcely permit his actors to speak loosely or ungrammatically: though retaining their essential individuality, they are endowed with the author's own delightful power of expression. This outward phasis of his work separates it at once from that of the simple novelist, and leads us to consider the special applicability to it of the term "romance." He had not the realistic tendency, as we usually understand that, but he possessed the power to create a new species of fiction. For the kind of romance that he has left us differs from all compositions previously so called. It is not romance in the sense of D'Urfe's or Scuderi's; it is very far from coming within the scope of Fielding's "romances"; and it is entirely unconnected with the tales of the German Romantic school. It is not the romance of sentiment; nor that of incident, adventure, and character viewed under a worldly coloring: it has not the mystic and melodramatic bent belonging to Tieck and Novalis and Fouque. There are two things which radically isolate it from all these. The first is its quality of revived belief. Hawthorne, as has been urged already, is a great believer, a man who has faith; his belief goes out toward what is most beautiful, and this he finds only in moral truth. With him, poetry and moral insight are sacredly and indivisibly wedded, and their progeny is perfect beauty. This unsparingly conscientious pursuit of the highest truth, this metaphysical instinct, found in conjunction with a varied and tender appreciation of all forms of human or other life, is what makes him so decidedly the representative of a wholly new order of novelists. Belief, however, is not what he has usually been credited with, so much as incredulity. But the appearance of doubt is superficial, and arises from his fondness for illuminating fine but only half-perceptible traces of truth with the torch of superstition. Speaking of the supernatural, he says in his English journal: "It is remarkable that Scott should have felt interested in such subjects, being such a worldly and earthly man as he was; but then, indeed, almost all forms of popular superstition do clothe the ethereal with earthly attributes, and so make it grossly perceptible." This observation has a still greater value when applied to Hawthorne himself. And out of this questioning belief and transmutation of superstition into truth—for such is more exactly his method—proceeds also that quality of value and rarity and awe-enriched significance, with which he irradiates real life until it is sublimed to a delicate cloud-image of the eternal verities.

If these things are limitations, they are also foundations of a vast originality. Every greatness must have an outline. So that, although he is removed from the list of novelists proper, although his spiritual inspiration scares away a large class of sympathies, and although his strictly New England atmosphere seems to chill and restrain his dramatic fervor, sometimes to his disadvantage, these facts, on the other hand, are so many trenches dug around him, fortifying his fair eminence. Isolation and a certain degree of limitation, in some such sense as this, belong peculiarly to American originality. But Hawthorne is the embodiment of the youth of this country; and though he will doubtless furnish inspiration to a long line of poets and novelists, it must be hoped that they, likewise, will stand for other phases of its development, to be illustrated in other ways. No tribute to Hawthorne is less in accord with the biddings of his genius than that which would merely make a school of followers.

It is too early to say what position Hawthorne will take in the literature of the world; but as his influence gains the ascendant in America, by prompting new and un-Hawthornesque originalities, it is likely also that it will be made manifest in England, according to some unspecifiable ratio. Not that any period is to be distinctly colored by the peculiar dye in which his own pages are dipped; but the renewed tradition of a highly organized yet simple style, and still more the masculine tenderness and delicacy of thought and the fine adjustment of aesthetic and ethical obligations, the omnipresent truthfulness which he carries with him, may be expected to become a constituent part of very many minds widely opposed among themselves. I believe there is no fictionist who penetrates so far into individual consciences as Hawthorne; that many persons will be found who derive a profoundly religious aid from his unobtrusive but commanding sympathy. In the same way, his sway over the literary mind is destined to be one of no secondary degree. "Deeds are the offspring of words," says Heine; "Goethe's pretty words are childless." Not so with Hawthorne's. Hawthorne's repose is the acme of motion; and though turning on an axis of conservatism, the radicalism of his mind is irresistible; he is one of the most powerful because most unsuspected revolutionists of the world. Therefore, not only is he an incalculable factor in private character, but in addition his unnoticed leverage for the thought of the age is prodigious. These great abilities, subsisting with a temper so modest and unaffected, and never unhumanized by the abstract enthusiasm for art, place him on a plane between Shakespere and Goethe. With the universality of the first only just budding within his mind, he has not so clear a response to all the varying tones of lusty human life, and the individuality in his utterance amounts, at particular instants, to constraint. With less erudition than Goethe, but also less of the freezing pride of art, he is infinitely more humane, sympathetic, holy. His creations are statuesquely moulded like Goethe's, but they have the same quick music of heart-throbs that Shakespere's have. Hawthorne is at the same moment ancient and modern, plastic and picturesque.

—George Parsons Lathrop,
A Study of Hawthorne, 1876, pp. 326–31

HENRY ADAMS (1876)

Henry Adams was the historian, novelist, and autobiographical author of *The Education of Henry Adams*. He does not treat Hawthorne directly in this excerpt, it being a review of George Parsons Lathrop's study of his father-in-law, but Adams's feelings about Hawthorne (and *"intuitional* biography" generally) can readily be inferred from his tone and his objections.

Like Sir Leslie Stephen, Adams sympathizes with Hawthorne's wish for his juvenilia and inferior works to be left alone by "resurrection men" (Stephen's term), and with his desire to remain private (even in death). Students investigating Hawthorne's influence on subsequent authors will detect a lineage linking Hawthorne to Adams. There is a clear identification; like Hawthorne, Adams—another scion of New England aristocracy—venerates Italy, execrates New England Puritanism, and advocates dignified privacy.

Aside from exposing several of Lathrop's more florid excesses, Adams shows the shortcomings of those sycophantic and pedantic literary biographies that were popular at this time ("Mr. Lathrop . . . tells us the length of Mr. Hawthorne's foot"). Students interested in examining the varying public perceptions of Hawthorne would do well to consult this review.

We remember to have read that in some of the ancient churches on the eastern coast of England a special petition was inserted in their litany against the incursions of the Danes. Mr. Lathrop's book may well lead the next man of genius whom New England produces to pray, "From plague, pestilence, and *intuitional* biographers, good Lord, deliver us." Mr. Hawthorne did what he could, by strongly expressed wishes, and by what Mr. Lathrop describes, as "vigilant suppression" of early imperfect compositions, to prevent any such book being written; but in vain! Mr. Lathrop writes from "a consciousness of sympathy with the subject;" which he considers "a sort of inspiration," and says, "my guide has been intuition." He claims also a peculiar fitness for his work, founded on the fact that he had never even seen Mr. Hawthorne, and strong in such armor, writes with a detail wholly opposed to Mr. Hawthorne's shy personal reserve, and an exaggeration utterly repugnant to the delicate sense of proportion which was so marked a characteristic of Mr. Hawthorne's writings.

Mr. Lathrop, having begun his book, has neither hesitation nor relenting; he perpetuates (so far as in him lies) every possible coincidence of publicity (see page 123), every scrap of youthful verse, though he owns to the difficulties he finds in his sway, "so successful was Hawthorne in his attempt to exterminate" what Mr. Lathrop is determined to preserve. Not satisfied with thwarting the wishes of Mr. Hawthorne, and cleft into the "natural piety" which leads us to regard the lightest desire of the dead, Mr. Lathrop elaborates so unmercifully and exaggerates so injuriously, that the reader can hardly refrain from pleading in Mr. Hawthorne's behalf, "Good friend, for Jesus' sake, forbear!"

We regret our inability to praise Mr. Lathrop's method any more than sympathize with his intention. He tells us that "the history of Hawthorne's genius is in some sense a summary of all New England history" (*sic*) that "when Hawthorne came, his utterance was a culmination of two preceding centuries" and goes on to point out the likeness between Salem and Florence, apropos (as far we can see) to the equivalency of Hawthorne and Dante! Certainly, as the excellent Fluellen tells us, "There be rivers to Monmouth, and rivers in Macedon," but it is difficult to find greater similarity between "the flower-crowned city," where the gifts of climate, of race, and of art made life beautiful that its boisterous politics and its bloody feuds seemed of small account, and the bleak, maritime, Calvinistic town whose *festas* were witch-trials, and where a theocracy far more effective than any Israelitish ruler's kept its grip unloosed for scores of years. Crabbe has described the sort of rigid quiet that reigned in Salem:—

"It was that which one superior will
Decrees by making all inferior still,
Which bids all murmur, all objection, cease,
And in imperious voice announces—Peace!"

Fundamental granite underlying many good New England qualities but not much like the turbulent loveliness of Florence.

Mr. Lathrop finds that Hawthorne was a more fortunate mixture of Bunyan and Milton, having "the same positive unrelenting grasp of allegory" as Bunyan, and "the same delight in art for art's sake, that added such a grace to Milton's sinewy and large-limbed port"; and further, that "Bunyan's characters being moods," Milton's "were traits," and that if one were to "pour the *ebullient undulating* prose style of the poet into the allegorist's firm leather-jerkined English," "the result would not be alien to Hawthorne"!

Ebullient undulations in a leather-jerkined style is not a pretty picture; but we pass on to the description of Salem, where Mr. Lathrop mentions with interest that he has heard that "persons have gone mad from no other cause than inherited insanity,"—a singularity manifestly peculiar to Salem, which Dr. Maudaley should note in his next edition. Mr. Hawthorne's ancestry, of a good New England sort, is described with some detail; the early death of his father, and Hawthorne's removal with his mother to Cumberland County in Maine, where he remained till 1821, when he entered Bowdoin College at the same time with Longfellow. Extracts from a mysterious note-book relating to this time given by Mr. Lathrop, but his investigations into their authenticity amount only to this,—that either Hawthorne did write there or he did not; that if he did, they have a certain interest; if he did not, they are of no value; but Mr. Lathrop has not arrived at a conclusion.

Mr. Lathrop notes the remarkable fact that, being blamed while at Bowdoin for the fault of another person, Hawthorne did not denounce his classmate; he tells us the length of Mr. Hawthorne's foot; he draws youthful verses from their appropriate oblivion; he tells us that Mr. Hawthorne's inability to distinguish one tune from another was owing "*merely* to the absence of any musical instinct"; that his genius had "a pensive perfume," and at the same time "a perfume of surprise," and bids us "be grateful that Hawthorne does not so covet the applause of the clever club-man, or of the unconscious vulgarian, as to junket about in caravan, carrying the passions with him in gaudy cages and feeding them with raw flesh." Strewing his way with such flowers of style, Mr. Lathrop finally lands his subject "on a plane between Shakespeare and Goethe," and, to borrow the tag of an old story, "I There—my lord—I leave you."

—Henry Adams, *North American Review,*
from a review of Lathrop's *Study of Hawthorne,* October 1876

OLIVER WENDELL HOLMES (1876)

Oliver Wendell Holmes was a New England humorist, essayist, and poet, best remembered for writing *The Autocrat of the Breakfast Table.* The genteel Holmes recognizes in a private letter what he could not say in the public press, and what could only properly be acknowledged by later critics such as Frederick Crews, that Hawthorne's fiction is sexually charged, and that "there is rich red blood in Hester." This direct and carnal reading was antithetical to the more usual praise of Hawthorne as an ethical and feminized recluse. It is probably significant that Holmes was also a professor of anatomy, first at Dartmouth College and then at Harvard University.

I think we have no romancer but yourself, nor have had any for this long time. I had become so set in this feeling, that but for your last two stories I should have given up hoping, and believed that all we were to look for in the way of spontaneous growth were such languid, lifeless, sexless creations as in the view of certain people constitute the chief triumphs of a sister art as manifested among us. But there is rich red blood in Hester, and the flavor of the sweet-fern and the bayberry are not truer to the soil than the native sweetness of our little Phoebe! The Yankee mind has for the most part budded and flowered in pots of English earth, but you have fairly raised yours as a seedling in the natural soil. My criticism has to stop here; the moment a fresh mind takes in the elements of the common life about us and transfigures them, I am contented to enjoy and admire, and let others analyze. Otherwise I should be tempted to display my appreciating sagacity in pointing out a hundred touches, transcriptions of nature, of character, of sentiment, true as the daguerreotype, free as crayon sketching, which arrested me even in the midst of the palpitating story. Only one word, then this: that the solid reality and homely truthfulness of the actual and present part of the story are blended with its weird and ghostly shadows with consummate skill and effect; this was perhaps the special difficulty of the story.

—Oliver Wendell Holmes, Letter to Nathaniel Hawthorne
(April 9, 1851), cited in George Parsons Lathrop,
A Study of Hawthorne, 1876, p. 232

Edmund Clarence Stedman (1877)

But he whose quickened eye
Saw through New England's life her inmost spirit,—
    Her heart, and all the stays on which it leant,—
Returns not, since he laid the pencil by
Whose mystic touch none other shall inherit!

—Edmund Clarence Stedman, "Hawthorne," 1877

Emily Dickinson (1879)

Emily Dickinson was the Amherst, Massachusetts, poetess whose removal from society exceeded even Hawthorne's. Dickinson was sparing in her commentary on other writers; yet her analysis of Hawthorne, while comprising only three words, captures well the ambivalent draw of his writing, noticed time and again by critics who find his works simultaneously attracting and repelling.

Hawthorne appalls—entices.

—Emily Dickinson, Letter to
Thomas Wentworth Higginson (1879)

Anthony Trollope
"The Genius of Nathaniel Hawthorne" (1879)

Anthony Trollope was the prolific English novelist whose works include the series of Palliser novels and the series often referred to as the Chronicles of Barsetshire. In this essay, he draws on his own considerable career to compare (or rather contrast) his experiences and views with Hawthorne's. He responds with modesty to Hawthorne's earlier evaluation of his own work ("written on the strength of beef and through the inspiration of ale"—a faintly stinging remark Trollope alludes to several times here).

Trollope adeptly discusses *The Scarlet Letter, The House of the Seven Gables, The Marble Faun,* and several of the tales. Like Henry James, Trollope finds Hawthorne's work starkly removed from everyday life and the qualities associated with realism. Hawthorne's characters and incidents, Trollope avers, are "often but barely within the bounds of possibility . . . sometimes altogether without those bounds." Unlike

James, though, Trollope praises the dreamy weirdness he detects in the writing, and rather feels indicted by his own "beef and ale" realism.

Trollope also emphasizes the vein of humor running even through Hawthorne's darkest passages—the "ghastly spirit of drollery" here and the "touch of burlesque" there. Despite the considerable suffering in Hawthorne's work—which Trollope praises—he insists that "there is never a page written by Hawthorne not tinged by satire." Students examining Hawthorne's narrative tenor might investigate this juxtaposition of the harrowing with the humorous.

Students focusing on Hawthorne's narrative structure will appreciate Trollope's critique of Hawthorne's structural formlessness and the way Trollope faults Hawthorne's "lop-sided" thinking and his tendency to be vague and meandering (particularly in The Marble Faun and The House of the Seven Gables). Trollope finds fault with the contrived and inapt ending of Seven Gables—"quite unlike Hawthorne," as if "added by some every-day, beef-and-ale, realistic novelist, into whose hands the unfinished story had unfortunately fallen."

***

There never surely was a powerful, active, continually effective mind less round, more lop-sided, than that of Nathaniel Hawthorne. . . . I have been specially driven to think of this by the strong divergence between Hawthorne and myself. It has always been my object to draw my little pictures as like to life as possible, so that my readers should feel that they were dealing with people whom they might probably have known, but so to do it that the every-day good to be found among them should allure, and the every-day evil repel; and this I have attempted, believing that such ordinary good and ordinary evil would be more powerful in repelling or alluring than great and glowing incidents which, though they might interest, would not come home to the minds of readers. Hawthorne, on the other hand, has dealt with persons and incidents which were often but barely within the bounds of possibility,—which were sometimes altogether without those bounds,—and has determined that his readers should be carried out of their own little mundane ways, and brought into a world of imagination in which their intelligence might be raised, if only for a time, to something higher than the common needs of common life. . . .

Hawthorne is severe, but his severity is never of a nature to form laws for life. His is a mixture of romance and austerity, quite as far removed from the realities of Puritanism as it is from the sentimentalism of poetry. He creates a melancholy which amounts almost to remorse in the minds of his readers.

There falls upon them a conviction of some unutterable woe which is not altogether dispelled till other books and other incidents have had their effects. The woe is of course fictitious, and therefore endurable,—and therefore alluring. And woe itself has its charm. It is a fact that the really miserable will pity the comfortable insignificance of those who are not unhappy, and that they are apt even to boast of their own sufferings. There is a sublimity in mental and even in corporal torment which will sometimes make the position of Lucifer almost enviable. "All is not lost" with him! Prometheus chained, with the bird at his liver, had wherewithal to console himself in the magnificence of his thoughts. And so in the world of melancholy romance, of agony more realistic than melancholy, to which Hawthorne brings his readers, there is compensation to the reader in the feeling that, in having submitted himself to such sublime affliction, he has proved himself capable of sublimity. The bird that feeds upon your vitals would not have gorged himself with common flesh. You are beyond measure depressed by the weird tale that is told to you, but you become conscious of a certain grandness of nature in being susceptible to such suffering. When you hear what Hawthorne has done to others, you long to search his volumes. When he has operated upon you, you would not for the world have foregone it. You have been ennobled by that familiarity with sorrow. You have been, as it were, sent through the fire and purged of so much of your dross. For a time, at least, you have been free from the mundane touch of that beef and ale with which novelists of a meaner school will certainly bring you in contact. No one will feel himself ennobled at once by having read one of my novels. But Hawthorne, when you have studied him, will be very precious to you. He will have plunged you into melancholy, he will have overshadowed you with black forebodings, he will almost have crushed you with imaginary sorrows; but he will have enabled you to feel yourself an inch taller during the process. Something of the sublimity of the transcendent, something of the mystery of the unfathomable, something of the brightness of the celestial, will have attached itself to you, and you will all but think that you too might live to be sublime, and revel in mingled light and mystery.

The creations of American literature generally are no doubt more given to the speculative,—less given to the realistic,—than are those of English literature. On our side of the water we deal more with beef and ale, and less with dreams. Even with the broad humor of Bret Harte, even with the broader humor of Artemus Ward and Mark Twain, there is generally present an undercurrent of melancholy, in which pathos and satire are intermingled. There was a touch of it even with the simple-going Cooper and the kindly

Washington Irving. Melancholy and pathos, without the humor, are the springs on which all Longfellow's lines are set moving. But in no American writer is to be found the same predominance of weird imagination as in Hawthorne. There was something of it in M. G. Lewis—our Monk Lewis as he came to be called, from the name of a tale which he wrote; but with him, as with many others, we feel that they have been weird because they have desired to be so. They have struggled to achieve the tone with which their works are pervaded. With Hawthorne we are made to think that he could not have been anything else if he would. It is as though he could certainly have been nothing else in his own inner life. We know that such was not actually the case. Though a man singularly reticent,—what we generally call shy,—he could, when things went well with him, be argumentative, social, and cheery. I have seen him very happy over canvas-back ducks, and have heard him discuss, almost with violence, the superiority of American vegetables. Indeed, he once withered me with a scorn which was anything but mystic or melancholy because I expressed a patriotic preference for English peas. And yet his imagination was such that the creations of his brain could not have been other than such as I have described. Oliver Wendell Holmes has written a well-known story, weird and witch-like also, and has displayed much genius in the picture which he has given us of Elsie Venner. But the reader is at once aware that Holmes compelled himself to the construction of *Elsie Venner*, and feels equally sure that Hawthorne wrote "The Marble Faun" because he could not help himself.

I will take a few of his novels,—those which I believe to be the best known,— and will endeavor to illustrate my idea of his genius by describing the manner in which his stories have been told.

The Scarlet Letter is, on the English side of the water, perhaps the best known. It is so terrible in its pictures of diseased human nature as to produce most questionable delight. The reader's interest never flags for a moment. There is nothing of episode or digression. The author is always telling his one story with a concentration of energy which, as we can understand, must have made it impossible for him to deviate. The reader will certainly go on with it to the end very quickly, entranced, excited, shuddering, and at times almost wretched. His consolation will be that he too has been able to see into these black deeps of the human heart. The story is one of jealousy,—of love and jealousy,—in which love is allowed but little scope, but full play is given to the hatred that can spring from injured love. A woman has been taken in adultery,—among the Puritans of Boston some two centuries since,—and is brought upon the stage that she may be punished by a public stigma. She was beautiful and young, and had been married to an old husband who had wandered away from her for a time. Then she has sinned, and the partner of her sin, though not of her punishment, is the young minister of the church to which she is attached. It is her doom to wear the Scarlet Letter, the letter A, always worked on her dress,—always there on her bosom, to be seen by all men. The first hour of her punishment has to be endured, in the middle of the town, on the public scaffold, under the gaze of all men. As she stands there, her husband comes by chance into the town and sees her, and she sees him, and they know each other. But no one else in Boston knows that they are man and wife. Then they meet, and she refuses to tell him who has been her fellow sinner. She makes no excuse for herself. She will bear her doom and acknowledge its justice, but to no one will she tell the name of him who is the father of her baby. For her disgrace has borne its fruit, and she has a child. The injured husband is at once aware that he need deal no further with the woman who has been false to him. Her punishment is sure. But it is necessary for his revenge that the man too shall be punished,—and to punish him he must know him. He goes to work to find him out, and he finds him out. Then he does punish him with a vengeance and brings him to death,— does it by the very stress of mental misery. After a while the woman turns and rebels against the atrocity of fate,—not on her own account, but for the sake of that man the sight of whose sufferings she can not bear. They meet once again, the two sinful lovers, and a hope of escape comes upon them,—and another gleam of love. But fate in the shape of the old man is too strong for them. He finds them out, and, not stopping to hinder their flight, merely declares his purpose of accompanying them! Then the lover succumbs and dies, and the woman is left to her solitude. That is the story.

The personages in it with whom the reader will interest himself are four,—the husband, the minister who has been the sinful lover, the woman, and the child. The reader is expected to sympathize only with the woman,—and will sympathize only with her. The husband, an old man who has knowingly married a young woman who did not love him, is a personification of that feeling of injury which is supposed to fall upon a man when his honor has been stained by the falseness of a wife. He has left her and has wandered away, not even telling her of his whereabout. He comes back to her without a sign. The author tells us that he had looked to find his happiness in her solicitude and care for him. The reader, however, gives him credit for no love. But the woman was his wife, and he comes back and finds that she had gone astray. Her he despises, and is content to leave to the ascetic cruelty of the town magistrates; but to find the man out and bring the man to his grave by slow torture is enough of employment for what is left to him of life and energy.

With the man, the minister, the lover, the reader finds that he can have nothing in common, though he is compelled to pity his sufferings. The woman has held her peace when she was discovered and reviled and exposed. She will never whisper his name, never call on him for any comfort or support in her misery; but he, though the very shame is eating into his soul, lives through the seven years of the story, a witness of her misery and solitude, while he himself is surrounded by the very glory of sanctity. Of the two, indeed, he is the greater sufferer. While shame only deals with her, conscience is at work with him. But there can be no sympathy, because he looks on and holds his peace. Her child says to him,—her child, not knowing that he is her father, not knowing what she says, but in answer to him when he would fain take her little hand in his during the darkness of night,—"Wilt thou stand here with mother and me to-morrow noontide"? He can not bring himself to do that, though he struggles hard to do it, and therefore we despise him. He can not do it till the hand of death is upon him, and then the time is too late for reparation in the reader's judgment. Could we have sympathized with a pair of lovers, the human element would have prevailed too strongly for the author's purpose.

He seems hardly to have wished that we should sympathize even with her; or, at any rate, he has not bid us in so many words to do so, as is common with authors. Of course, he has wished it. He has intended that the reader's heart should run over with ruth for the undeserved fate of that wretched woman. And it does. She is pure as undriven snow. We know that at some time far back she loved and sinned, but it was done when we did not know her. We are not told so, but come to understand, by the wonderful power of the writer in conveying that which he never tells, that there has been no taint of foulness in her love, though there has been deep sin. He never even tells us why that letter A has been used, though the abominable word is burning in our ears from first to last. We merely see her with her child, bearing her lot with patience, seeking no comfort, doing what good she can in her humble solitude by the work of her hands, pointed at from all by the finger of scorn, but the purest, the cleanest, the fairest also among women. She never dreams of supposing that she ought not to be regarded as vile, while the reader's heart glows with a longing to take her soft hand and lead her into some pleasant place where the world shall be pleasant and honest and kind to her. I can fancy a reader so loving the image of Hester Prynne as to find himself on the verge of treachery to the real Hester of flesh and blood who may have a claim upon him. Sympathy can not go beyond that; and yet the author deals with her in a spirit of assumed hardness, almost as though he assented to the judgment and the manner in which it was carried out. In this, however, there is a streak of that satire with which Hawthorne always speaks of the peculiar institutions of his own country. The worthy magistrates of Massachusetts are under his lash throughout the story, and so is the virtue of her citizens and the chastity of her matrons, which can take delight in the open shame of a woman whose sin has been discovered. Indeed, there is never a page written by Hawthorne not tinged by satire.

The fourth character is that of the child, Pearl. Here the author has, I think, given way to a temptation, and in doing so has not increased the power of his story. The temptation was, that Pearl should add a picturesque element by being an elf and also a charming child. Elf she is, but, being so, is incongruous with all else in the story, in which, unhuman as it is, there is nothing of the ghost-like, nothing of the unnatural. The old man becomes a fiend, so to say, during the process of the tale; but he is a man-fiend. And Hester becomes sublimated almost to divine purity; but she is still simply a woman. The minister is tortured beyond the power of human endurance; but neither do his sufferings nor his failure of strength adequate to support them come to him from any miraculous agency. But Pearl is miraculous,—speaking, acting, and thinking like an elf,—and is therefore, I think, a drawback rather than an aid. The desolation of the woman, too, would have been more perfect without the child. It seems as though the author's heart had not been hard enough to make her live alone;—as sometimes when you punish a child you can not drive from your face that gleam of love which shoots across your frown and mars its salutary effect.

Hatred, fear, and shame are the passions which revel through the book. To show how a man may so hate as to be content to sacrifice everything to his hatred; how another may fear so that, even though it be for the rescue of his soul, he can not bring himself to face the reproaches of the world; how a woman may bear her load of infamy openly before the eyes of all men,—this has been Hawthorne's object. And surely no author was ever more successful. The relentless purpose of the man, in which is exhibited no passion, in which there is hardly a touch of anger, is as fixed as the hand of Fate. No one in the town knew that the woman was his wife. She had never loved him. He had left her alone in the world. But she was his wife; and, as the injury had been done to him, the punishment should follow from his hands! When he finds out who the sinner was, he does not proclaim him and hold him up to disgrace; he does not crush the almost adored minister of the gospel by declaring the sinner's trespass. He simply lives with his enemy in the same house, attacking not the man's body,—to which, indeed, he acts as a wise physician,—but his conscience, till we see the wretch writhing beneath the treatment.

Hester sees it too, and her strength, which suffices for the bearing of her own misery, fails her almost to fainting as she understands the condition of the man she has loved. Then there is a scene, the one graceful and pretty scene in the book, in which the two meet,—the two who were lovers,—and dare for a moment to think that they can escape. They come together in a wood, and she flings away, but for a moment, the badge of her shame, and lets down the long hair which has been hidden under her cap, and shines out before the reader for once,—just for that once,—as a lovely woman. She counsels him to fly, to go back across the waters to the old home whence he had come, and seek for rest away from the cruelty of his tyrant. When he pleads that he has no strength left to him for such action, then she declares that she will go with him and protect him and minister to him and watch over him with her strength. Yes; this woman proposes that she will then elope with the partner of her former sin. But no idea comes across the reader's mind of sinful love. The poor wretch can not live without service, and she will serve him. Were it herself that was concerned, she would remain there in her solitude, with the brand of her shame still open upon her bosom. But he can not go alone, and she too will therefore go.

As I have said before, the old man discovers the plot, and crushes their hopes simply by declaring that he will also be their companion. Whether there should have been this gleam of sunshine in the story the critic will doubt. The parent who would be altogether like Solomon should not soften the sternness of his frown by any glimmer of parental softness. The extreme pain of the chronicle is mitigated for a moment. The reader almost fears that he is again about to enjoy the satisfaction of a happy ending. When the blackness and the rumbling thunder-claps and the beating hailstones of a mountain storm have burst with all their fearful glories on the wanderer among the Alps, though he trembles and is awestruck and crouches with the cold, he is disappointed rather than gratified when a little space of blue sky shows itself for a moment through the clouds. But soon a blacker mantle covers the gap, louder and nearer comes the crash, heavier fall the big drops till they seem to strike him to the bone. The storm is awful, majestic, beautiful;—but is it not too pitiless? So it is with the storm which bursts over that minister's head when the little space of blue has vanished from the sky.

But through all this intensity of suffering, through this blackness of narrative, there is ever running a vein of drollery. As Hawthorne himself says, "a lively sense of the humorous again stole in among the solemn phantoms of her thought." He is always laughing at something with his weird, mocking spirit. The very children when they see Hester in the streets are supposed to speak of her in this wise: "Behold, verily, there is the woman of the scarlet letter. Come, therefore, and let us fling mud at her." Of some religious book he says, "It must have been a work of vast ability in the somniferous school of literature." "We must not always talk in the market-place of what happens to us in the forest," says even the sad mother to her child. Through it all there is a touch of burlesque,—not as to the suffering of the sufferers, but as to the great question whether it signifies much in what way we suffer, whether by crushing sorrows or little stings. Who would not sooner be Prometheus than a yesterday's tipsy man with this morning's sick-headache? In this way Hawthorne seems to ridicule the very woes which he expends himself in depicting.

As a novel *The House of the Seven Gables* is very inferior to *The Scarlet Letter*. The cause of this inferiority would, I think, be plain to any one who had himself been concerned in the writing of novels. When Hawthorne proposed to himself to write *The Scarlet Letter*, the plot of his story was clear to his mind. He wrote the book because he had the story strongly, lucidly manifest to his own imagination. In composing the other he was driven to search for a plot, and to make a story. *The Scarlet Letter* was written because he had it to write, and the other because he had to write it. The novelist will often find himself in the latter position. He has characters to draw, lessons to teach, philosophy perhaps which he wishes to expose, satire to express, humor to scatter abroad. These he can employ gracefully and easily if he have a story to tell. If he have none, he must concoct something of a story laboriously, when his lesson, his characters, his philosophy, his satire, and his humor will be less graceful and less easy. All the good things I have named are there in *The House of the Seven Gables*; but they are brought in with less artistic skill, because the author has labored over his plot, and never had it clear to his own mind.

There is a mystery attached to the house. That is a matter of course. A rich man obtained the ground on which it was built by fraud from a poor man, and the poor man's curse falls on the rich man's descendants, and the rich man with his rich descendants are abnormally bad, though very respectable. They not only cheat but murder. The original poor man was hung for witchcraft,—only because he had endeavored to hold his own against the original rich man. The rich men in consequence die when they come to advanced age, without any apparent cause of death, sitting probably upright in their chairs, to the great astonishment of the world at large, and with awful signs of blood about their mouths and shirt-fronts. And each man as he dies is in the act of perpetrating some terrible enormity against some poor member of his own family. The respectable rich man with whom we become personally acquainted in the story,—for as to some of the important characters we hear of them only by the records which are given of past times,—begins by getting a cousin convicted of a murder of which he knew that his kinsman was not guilty, and is preparing to have the same kinsman fraudulently and unnecessarily put into a lunatic asylum, when he succumbs to the fate of his family and dies in his chair, all covered with blood. The unraveling of these mysteries is vague, and, as I think, inartistic. The reader is not carried on by any intense interest in the story itself, and comes at last not much to care whether he does or does not understand the unraveling. He finds that his interest in the book lies elsewhere,—that he must seek it in the characters, lessons, philosophy, satire, and humor, and not in the plot. With *The Scarlet Letter* the plot comes first, and the others follow as accessories.

Two or three of the characters here drawn are very good. The wicked and respectable gentleman who *drees* the doom of his family, and dies in his chair all covered with blood, is one Judge Pyncheon. The persistent, unbending, cruel villainy of this man,—whose heart is as hard as a millstone, who knows not the meaning of conscience, to whom money and respectability are everything,—was dear to Hawthorne's heart. He likes to revel in an excess of impossible wickedness, and has done so with the Judge. Though we do not care much for the mysteries of the Judge's family, we like the Judge himself, and we like to feel that the author is pouring out his scorn on the padded respectables of his New England world. No man had a stronger belief than Hawthorne in the superiority of his own country; no man could be more sarcastic as to the deficiencies of another,—as I had reason to discover in that affair of the peas; but, nevertheless, he is always throwing out some satire as to the assumed virtues of his own immediate countrymen. It comes from him in little touches as to every incident he handles. In truth, he can not write without satire; and, as in these novels he writes of his own country, his shafts fall necessarily on that.

But the personage we like best in the book is certainly Miss Hepzibah Pyncheon. She is a cousin of the Judge, and has become, by some family arrangement, the life-possessor of the house with seven gables. She is sister also of the man who had been wrongly convicted of murder, and who, when released after a thirty-years' term of imprisonment, comes also to live at the house. Miss Hepzibah, under a peculiarly ill-grained exterior, possesses an affectionate heart and high principles. Driven by poverty, she keeps a shop,—a cent-shop, a term which is no doubt familiar enough in New England, and by which it would be presumed that all her articles were to be bought for a cent each, did it not appear by the story that she dealt also in goods of greater value. She is a lady by birth, and can not keep her cent-shop without some feeling of degradation; but that is preferable to the receiving of charity from that odious cousin the Judge. Her timidity, her affection, her true appreciation of herself, her ugliness, her hopelessness, and general incapacity for everything,—cent-shop-keeping included,—are wonderfully drawn. There are characters in novels who walk about on their feet, who stand upright and move, so that readers can look behind them, as one seems to be able to do in looking at a well-painted figure on the canvas. There are others, again, so wooden that no reader expects to find in them any appearance of movement. They are blocks roughly hewed into some more or less imperfect forms of humanity, which are put into their places and which there lie. Miss Hepzibah is one of the former. The reader sees all round her, and is sure that she is alive,—though she is so incapable.

Then there is her brother Clifford, who was supposed to have committed the murder, and who, in the course of the chronicle, comes home to live with his sister. There are morsels in his story, bits of telling in the description of him, which are charming, but he is not so good as his sister, being less intelligible. Hawthorne himself had not realized the half-fatuous, dreamy, ill-used brother, as he had the sister. In painting a figure it is essential that the artist should himself know the figure he means to paint.

There is yet another Pyncheon,—Phoebe Pyncheon, who comes from a distance, Heaven knows why, to live with her far-away cousin. She is intended as a ray of sunlight,—as was Pearl in *The Scarlet Letter*,—and is more successful. As the old maid Pyncheon is capable of nothing, so is the young maid Pyncheon capable of everything. She is, however, hardly wanted in the story, unless it be that the ray of sunlight was necessary. And there is a young "daguerreotypist,"—as the photographer of the day used to be called,—who falls in love with the ray of sunlight, and marries her at the end; and who is indeed the lineal descendant of the original ill-used poor man who was hung as a witch. There is just one love-scene in the novel, most ghastly in its details; for the young man offers his love, and the girl accepts it, while they are aware that the wicked, respectable old Judge is sitting, all smeared with blood, and dead, in the next room to them. The love-scene, and the hurrying up of the marriage, and all the dollars which they inherit from the wicked Judge, and the "handsome dark-green barouche" prepared for their departure, which is altogether unfitted to the ideas which the reader has formed respecting them, are quite unlike Hawthorne, and would seem almost to have been added by some every-day, beef-and-ale, realistic novelist, into whose hands the unfinished story had unfortunately fallen.

But no one should read *The House of the Seven Gables* for the sake of the story, or neglect to read it because of such faults as I have described. It is for the humor, the satire, and what I may perhaps call the philosophy which permeates it, that its pages should be turned. Its pages may be turned on any day, and under any circumstances. To *The Scarlet Letter* you have got to adhere till you have done with it; but you may take this volume by bits, here and there, now and again, just as you like it. There is a description of a few poultry, melancholy, unproductive birds, running over four or five pages, and written as no one but Hawthorne could have written it. There are a dozen pages or more in which the author pretends to ask why the busy Judge does not move from his chair,—the Judge the while having dree'd his doom and died as he sat. There is a ghastly spirit of drollery about this which would put the reader into full communion with Hawthorne if he had not read a page before, and did not intend to read a page after. To those who can make literary food of such passages as these, *The House of the Seven Gables* may be recommended. To others it will be caviare.

Mosses from an Old Manse will be caviare to many. By this I intend no slight to the intelligence of the many readers who may not find themselves charmed by such narratives. In the true enjoyment of Hawthorne's work there is required a peculiar mood of mind. The reader should take a delight in looking round corners, and in seeing how places and things may be approached by other than the direct and obvious route. No writer impresses himself more strongly on the reader who will submit to him; but the reader must consent to put himself altogether under his author's guidance, and to travel by queer passages, the direction of which he will not perceive till, perhaps, he has got quite to the end of them. In *The Scarlet Letter,* though there are many side paths, there is a direct road, so open that the obstinately straightforward traveler will find his way, though he will not, perhaps, see all that there is to be seen. In *The House of the Seven Gables* a kind of thoroughfare does at last make itself visible, though covered over with many tangles. In the volume of which I am now speaking there is no pathway at all. The reader must go where the writer may choose to take him, and must consent to change not only his ground, but the nature of his ground, every minute. This, as the name implies, is a collection of short stories,—and of course no thread or general plot is expected in such a compilation. But here the short narratives are altogether various in their style, no one of them giving any clew as to what may be expected to follow. They are, rather than tales, the jottings down of the author's own fancies, on matters which have subjected themselves to his brain, one after the other, in that promiscuous disorder in which his manner of thinking permitted him to indulge. He conceives a lovely woman, who has on her cheek a "birth-mark," so trifling as to be no flaw to her beauty. But her husband sees it, and, seeing it, can not rid himself of the remembrance of it. He is a man of science, concerned with the secrets of chemistry, and goes to work to concoct some ichor by which the mark may be eradicated. Just as success is being accomplished, the lady dies under the experiment. "You have aimed loftily," she says to her husband, at her last gasp; "you have done nobly. Do not repent." Whether the husband does repent we are not told; but the idea left is that, seeking something more than mortal perfection, he had thrown away the happiness which, as a mortal, he might have enjoyed. This is transcendental enough; but it is followed, a few pages on, by the record of Mrs. Bullfrog, who had got herself married to Mr. Bullfrog, as the natural possessor of all feminine loveliness, and then turns out to be a hideous virago, with false hair and false teeth, but who is at last accepted graciously by Bullfrog, because her money is real. The satire is intelligible, and is Hawthornean, but why Hawthorne should have brought himself to surround himself with objects so disagreeable the reader does not understand.

"The Select Party" is pleasant enough. It is held in a castle in the air, made magnificent with all architectural details, and there the Man of Fancy, who is its owner, entertains the Oldest Inhabitant, Nobody, M. Ondit, the Clerk of the Weather, Mother Carey, the Master Genius of his Age,—a young American, of course,—and sundry others, who among them have a good deal to say which is worth hearing. The student of Hawthorne will understand what quips and quirks will come from this mottled company.

Then there is an Italian, one Rappacini, and his daughter, weird, ghostlike, and I must own very unintelligible. The young lady, however, has learned under the teaching of her father, who is part doctor, part gardener, and part conjurer, to exist on the essence of a flower which is fatal to everybody else. She becomes very detrimental to her lover, who has no such gifts, and the story ends as a tragedy. There is a very pretty prose pastoral called "Buds and Bird-Voices," which is simply the indulgence of a poetic voice in the expression of its love of nature. "The Hall of Fantasy" is a mansion in which some unfortunates make their whole abode and business, and "contract habits which unfit them for all the real employments of life. Others,—but these are few,—possess the faculty, in their occasional visits, of discovering a purer truth than the world can impart." The reader can imagine to himself those who, under Hawthorne's guidance, would succeed and those who would fail by wandering into this hall. "The Procession of Life" is perhaps the strongest piece in the book,—the one most suggestive and most satisfactory. Hawthorne imagines that, by the blowing of some trumpet such as has never yet been heard, the inhabitants of the world shall be brought together under other circumstances than those which at present combine them. The poor now associate with the poor, the rich with the rich, the learned with the learned, the idle with the idle, the orthodox with the orthodox, and so on. By this new amalgamation the sick shall associate with the sick, the strong-bodied with the strong, the weak-bodied with the weak, the gifted with the gifted, the sorrowful with the sorrowful, the wicked with the wicked, and the good with the good. Here is a specimen of Hawthorne's manner in bringing the wicked together: "The hideous appeal has swept round the globe. Come all ye guilty ones, and rank yourselves in accordance with the brotherhood of crime. This, indeed, is an awful summons. I almost tremble to look at the strange partnerships that begin to be formed, reluctantly, but by the invincible necessity of like to like, in this part of the procession. A forger from the State prison seizes the arm of a distinguished financier . . . Here comes a murderer with his clanking chain, and pairs himself,—horrible to tell!—with as pure and upright a man, in all observable respects, as ever partook of the consecrated bread and wine. Why do that pair of flaunting girls, with the pert, affected laugh, and the sly leer at the bystander, intrude themselves into the same rank with yonder decorous matron and that somewhat prudish maiden?" The scope for irony and satire which Hawthorne could get from such a marshaling as this was unbounded.

There is a droll story, with a half-hidden meaning, called "Drowne's Wooden Image," in which Copley the painter is brought upon the scene, so that I am led to suppose that there was a Drowne who carved head-pieces for ships in Boston, and who, by some masterpiece in his trade, and by the help of Hawthorne, has achieved a sort of immortality. Here the man, by dint of special energy on this special job,—he is supposed to be making a figure-head for a ship,—hews out of the wood a female Frankenstein, all alone, but lovely as was the other one hideous. The old idea, too, is conveyed that, as within every block of marble, so within every log of wood, there is a perfection of symmetry and beauty, to be reached by any one who may have the gift of properly stripping off the outlying matter.

"P's Correspondence" is the last I will mention. P. is a madman, who, in writing to his friend in Boston from his madhouse chamber, imagines himself to have met in London Byron, Burns, Scott, and a score of other literary worthies, still alive as he supposes, but who by the stress of years have been changed in all their peculiarities, as men are changed when they live long. Byron becomes very religious, and professes excessive high-church tendencies,—as certain excellent and over-liberal friends of mine have in their old age become more timid and more conservative than they who were to the manner born. Hawthorne adds to this the joke that all his own American literary contemporaries,—men whom he knew to be alive, and with whom he probably was intimate,—are, alas! dead and gone. The madman weeps over Bryant, Whittier, and Longfellow, while he has been associating with Keats, Canning, and John Kemble.

Such is the nature of the Mosses from the old Manse each morsel of moss damp, tawny, and soft, as it ought to be, but each with enough of virus to give a sting to the tender hand that touches it.

I have space to mention but one other of our author's works; *The Marble Faun*, as it is called in America, and published in England under the name of *Transformation; or, The Romance of Monte Beni*. The double name, which has given rise to some confusion, was, I think, adopted with the view of avoiding the injustice to which American and English authors are subjected by the want of international copyright. Whether the object was attained, or was in any degree attainable by such means, I do not know.

In speaking *of The Marble Faun*, as I will call the story, I hardly know whether, as a just critic, to speak first of its faults or of its virtues. As one always likes to keep the sweetest bits for the end of the banquet, I will give priority of place to my caviling. The great fault of the book lies in the absence of arranged plot. The author, in giving the form of a novel to the beautiful pictures and images which his fancy has enabled him to draw, and in describing Rome and Italian scenes as few others have described them, has in fact been too idle to carry out his own purpose of constructing a tale. We will grant that a novelist may be natural or supernatural. Let us grant, for the occasion, that the latter manner, if well handled, is the better and the more efficacious. And we must grant also that he who soars into the supernatural need not bind himself by any of the ordinary trammels of life. His men may fly, his birds may speak. His women may make angelic music without instruments. His cherubs may sit at the piano. This wide latitude, while its adequate management is much too difficult for ordinary hands, gives facility for the working of a plot. But there must be some plot, some arrangement of circumstances, with an intelligible conclusion, or the reader will not be satisfied. If, then, a ghost, who,—or shall I say which?—is made on all occasions to act as a *Deus ex machina,* and to create and to solve every interest, we should know something of the ghost's antecedents, something of the causes which have induced him, or it, to meddle in the matter under discussion. The ghost of Hamlet's father had a manifest object, and the ghost of Banquo a recognized cause. In *The Marble Faun* there is no ghost, but the heroine of the story is driven to connive at murder, and the hero to commit murder, by the disagreeable intrusion of a personage whose *raison d'etre* is left altogether in the dark. "The gentle reader," says our author as he ends his narrative, "would not thank us for one of those minute elucidations which are so tedious and after all so unsatisfactory in clearing up the romantic mysteries of a story." There our author is, I think, in error. His readers will hardly be so gentle as not to require from him some explanation of the causes which have produced the romantic details to which they have given their attention, and will be inclined to say that it should have been the author's business to give an explanation neither tedious nor unsatisfactory. The critic is disposed to think that Hawthorne, as he continued his narrative, postponed his plot till it was too late, and then escaped from his difficulty by the ingenious excuse above given. As a writer of novels, I am bound to say that the excuse can not be altogether accepted.

But the fault, when once admitted, may be well pardoned on account of the beauty of the narrative. There are four persons,—or five, including the mysterious intruder who is only, I think, seen and never heard, but who is thrown down the Tarpeian rock and murdered. Three of them are artists,—a lady named Miriam, who is haunted by the mysterious one and is an assenting party to his murder; another lady named Hilda, an American from New England, who lives alone in a tower surrounded by doves; and a sculptor, one Kenyon, also from the States, who is in love with Hilda. The fourth person is the Faun, as to whom the reader is left in doubt whether he be man or Satyr,—human, or half god half animal. As to this doubt the critic makes no complaint. The author was within his right in creating a creature partaking of these different attributes, and it has to be acknowledged on his behalf that the mystery which he has thrown over this offspring of his brain has been handled by him, a writer of prose, not only with profound skill but with true poetic feeling. This faun, who is Count of Monte Beni,—be he most god, or man, or beast; let him have come from the hills and the woods and the brooks like a Satyr of old, or as any other count from his noble ancestors and ancestral towers,—attaches himself to Miriam, as a dog does to a man, not with an expressed human love in which there is a longing for kisses and a hope for marriage, but with a devotion half doglike as I have said, but in its other half godlike and heavenly pure. He scampers round her in his joy, and is made happy simply by her presence, her influence, and her breath. He is happy, except when the intruder intrudes, and then his jealousy is that as of a dog against an intruding hound. There comes a moment in which the intrusion of the intruder is unbearable. Then he looks into Miriam's eyes, and, obtaining the assent for which he seeks, he hurls the intruder down the Tarpeian rock into eternity. After that the light-hearted creature, overwhelmed by the weight of his sin, becomes miserable, despondent, and unable to bear the presence of her who had so lately been all the world to him. In the end light-hearted joy returns to him; but the reason for this second change is not so apparent.

The lives of Kenyon and Hilda are more commonplace, but, though they are commonplace between man and woman, the manner in which they are told is very beautiful. She is intended to represent perfect innocence, and he manly honesty. The two characters are well conceived and admirably expressed.

In *The Marble Faun*, as in all Hawthorne's tales written after *The Scarlet Letter*, the reader must look rather for a series of pictures than for a novel. It would, perhaps, almost be well that a fastidious reader should cease to read when he comes within that border, toward the end, in which it might be natural to expect that the strings of a story should be gathered together and tied into an intelligible knot. This would be peculiarly desirable in regard to *The Marble Faun*, in which the delight of that fastidious reader, as derived from pictures of character and scenery, will be so extreme that it should not be marred by a sense of failure in other respects.

In speaking of this work in conjunction with Hawthorne's former tales, I should be wrong not to mention the wonderful change which he effected in his own manner of writing when he had traveled out from Massachusetts into Italy. As every word in his earlier volumes savors of New England, so in *The Marble Faun* is the flavor entirely that of Rome and of Italian scenery. His receptive imagination took an impress from what was around him, and then gave it forth again with that wonderful power of expression which belonged to him. Many modern writers have sought to give an interest to their writings by what is called local coloring; but it will too often happen that the reader is made to see the laying on of the colors. In Hawthorne's Roman chronicle the tone of the telling is just as natural,—seems to belong as peculiarly to the author,—as it does with *The Scarlet Letter* or *The House of the Seven Gables.*

—Anthony Trollope, "The Genius of Nathaniel Hawthorne,"
North American Review, September 1879, pp. 204–22

THOMAS WENTWORTH HIGGINSON "HAWTHORNE" (1880)

In addition to being a man of letters in his own right, Higginson was best known as being Emily Dickinson's foremost literary correspondent and her first champion. He compares Hawthorne favorably to James Russell Lowell, and emphasizes Hawthorne's "marvelous self-control." Like Rose Hawthorne Lathrop, Higginson finds in Hawthorne a precision and lack of undue flamboyance that is unique to him. "Hawthorne never needed italic letters to distribute his emphasis," Higginson writes, "never a footnote for assistance."

One of the most characteristic of Hawthorne's literary methods is his habitual use of guarded under-statements and veiled hints. It is not a sign of weakness, but of conscious strength, when he surrounds each delineation with a sort of penumbra, takes you into his counsels, offers hypotheses, as, "May it not have been?" or, "Shall we not rather say?" and sometimes, like a conjurer, urges particularly upon you the card he does not intend you to accept. He seems not quite to know whether Arthur Dimmesdale really had a fiery scar on his breast, or what finally became of Miriam and her lover. He will gladly share with you any information he possesses, and, indeed, has several valuable hints to offer; but that is all. The result is, that you place yourself by his side to look with him at his characters, and gradually share with him the conviction that they must be real. Then, when he has you thus in possession, he calls your attention to the profound ethics involved in the tale, and yet does it so gently that you never think of the moral as being obtrusive.

All this involved a trait which was always supreme in him,—a marvellous self-control. He had by nature that gift which the musical composer Jomelli went to a teacher to seek,—"the art of not being embarrassed by his own ideas." Mrs. Hawthorne told me that her husband grappled alone all winter with *The Scarlet Letter,* and came daily from his study with a knot in his forehead; and yet his self-mastery was so complete that every sentence would seem to have crystallized in an atmosphere of perfect calm. We see the value of this element in his literary execution, when we turn from it to that of an author so great as Lowell, for instance, and see him often entangled and weighed down by his own rich thoughts, his style being overcrowded by the very wealth it bears. Hawthorne never needed Italic letters to distribute his emphasis, never a footnote for assistance. There was no conception so daring that he shrank from attempting it; and none that he could not so master as to state it, if he pleased, in terms of monosyllables.

—Thomas Wentworth Higginson, "Hawthorne,"
Short Studies of American Authors, 1880, pp. 8–9

ALFRED H. WELSH (1883)

Like Higginson, Welsh singles out Hawthorne's clarity of language and his ability to find the right word or phrase. Welsh also believes Hawthorne's stories are "deficient in converging unity," his characters seldom revealing of themselves, and his narratives depending little on plot or incident. Despite these drawbacks, he contends that *The Scarlet Letter* is perhaps unparalleled in the English language. Hawthorne's fiction is a new form, undaunted by prevailing models. What Welsh hints at seems to point to literary modernism: a precise, untrammeled language and a subversion of customary forms.

Welsh pointedly takes issue (even while cribbing the terms) with Henry James's famous extolling of England in his study of Hawthorne, when Welsh dismisses the "worn-out paraphernalia of abbeys, castles, courts." Students familiar with James's criticism should be aware of Welsh's counterargument.

Simpler, clearer, more elegant English has never—even by Swift, Addison, or Goldsmith—been made the vehicle of thought and emotion equally profound, delicate, variant, and tortuous. Singularly choice and appropriate in diction; flowing and placid in movement, always sweet and pellucid, giving to objects a subtle ethereal aspect. His pen is a magician's wand, 'creating the semblance of a world out of airy matter, with the impalpable beauty of a soap-bubble.' We have all been exhorted to give days and nights to Addison. Rather, let us give days and nights to Macaulay, Carlyle and Hawthorne.

Standing aloof from common interests, looking at the present with shaded eyes, into the past with a half-wistful gaze, attracted by the remote, strange, and unusual, with a style admirably adapted to produce the effect of weird-like mystery,—Hawthorne is not a novelist. His fictions, in conception and performance, are always and essentially romances. Yet have they a character of fundamental trueness to spiritual laws, of harmony with time, place, and circumstance,—of realism existing in an ideal atmosphere, or invested with the halo of a poetic medium. We have not the worn-out paraphernalia of abbeys, castles, courts, gentry, aristocracy, and sovereigns; but we have types, mental conditions,—beyond the sphere of habitual experience, indeed, yet belonging profoundly to spirit and to man. No civilization has produced a romantic genius at all comparable in power to his. Other writers have been more learned, more dramatic, more versatile, more comprehensive. His stories are generally deficient in converging unity. His personages seldom reveal themselves; but, as in the *Marble Faun,* we are told what they are, in page upon page of description, keen, minute, finished,—marvellous workmanship. No one ever depended so little upon plot or incident. Facts are subordinated to the influences with which they are charged. He is not a portrait-painter who sets forth a complete individuality. His forte is not in adventure, not in movement; but in the depicture of the rare and the occult, in the operation and results of involved and conflicting motives, feelings, and tendencies. He is here a solitary original in English letters. It may be questioned whether the *Scarlet Letter,* as an example of imaginative writing, has its parallel in any literature.

—Alfred H. Welsh, *Development of English*
Literature and Language, 1883, Vol. 2, pp. 512–13

Henry Cabot Lodge (1884)

Lodge, formerly a student of Henry Adams's at Harvard University, was later the editor of *The North American Review* and eventually a conservative Republican, serving first in the U.S. Congress and then in the Senate. As a historian, Lodge inevitably examines the relation of Hawthorne's work to history: "One cannot help looking on every page of New England history for the characters of Hawthorne." Students exploring Hawthorne's use of history, and the extent to which he uses history, may find this entry a valuable resource.

In New England, the history with which we are most familiar is that according to Nathaniel Hawthorne. Now dark and sombre, now warm and full of sunlight, always picturesque and imaginative, the story of the past, disconnected and uncertain, but yet vivid and real, has been woven by the hand of the enchanter to charm and fascinate all who listen. In Hawthorne's pages the ancient Puritan society, austere and rigid, and the later colonial aristocracy, laced and powdered, live and move, a delight to the present generation. But over all alike, over grave and gay, over the forbidding and the attractive, the delicate and morbid genius of the novelist has cast an air of mystery. In these stories we live in an atmosphere of half-told secrets, which are withal so real that we cannot help believing that somewhere, in some musty records or in letters yellow with time, we shall find answers to the questionings with which they fill our minds. Surely there must have been some one who had peeped beneath the black veil, who had known Maule and the Pyncheons, who had seen the prophetic pictures, who could tell us what the little world of Boston said about Hester Prynne and little Pearl, about Arthur Dimmesdale and Roger Chillingworth. One cannot help looking on every page of New England history for the characters of Hawthorne, and for an explanation of their lives. Disappointment always ensues, but hope is revived with each old manuscript that finds its way into print.

—Henry Cabot Lodge,
Studies in History, 1884, pp. 21–22

Andrew Lang
"To Edgar Allan Poe" (1886)

He was a great writer—the greatest writer in prose fiction whom America has produced.

—Andrew Lang, "To Edgar Allan Poe,"
Letters to Dead Authors, 1886, p. 149

Edward P. Roe
"The Element of Life in Fiction" (1888)

The people are gaining upon Nathaniel Hawthorne's works. A century hence, when the most popular authors of to-day are forgotten, he will probably be more widely read than ever.

—Edward P. Roe, "The Element of Life in Fiction,"
Forum, April 1888, p. 229

WALT WHITMAN (1889)

The "Old Gray Poet" Walt Whitman was the author of the ever-evolving autobiographical epic poem *Leaves of Grass*. In New York, in the taverns, among the bohemians and the Broadway stagecoach drivers, Whitman was seemingly Hawthorne's opposite, at some remove from Concord's genteel and insular society. The poet was in many ways Hawthorne's opposite. While Whitman was popularly viewed as sensuous and licentious, Hawthorne was seen as cold and puritanical.

Whitman was an admirer of Hawthorne's *Twice-Told Tales*, resenting the fact that Hawthorne received "a paltry seventy-five dollars for a two volume work" ("shall real American genius shiver with neglect—while the public run after this foreign trash?") Whitman's opinion seems to have lessened in later years, however. In one of his many conversations recorded by Horace Traubel, Whitman came to doubt whether Hawthorne was "immortal" but, when challenged, conceded that he was a "master." Whitman initially agreed with Hawthorne's politics, both being Democrats, but this changed with the Civil War. Whitman came to view Hawthorne as a Copperhead—a Northern supporter of the Confederacy—in other words, a traitor. Yet there is also detectable admiration for Hawthorne's steadfastly felt beliefs ("somehow we take to such characters"), and if Whitman places Hawthorne alongside Aaron Burr, he also places him by Robert Burns and "(perhaps)" Shakespeare.

<hr />

[H]ave been looking (2d time) again at the *Hawthorne* in Fields's "Yesterdays"— H seems to have been quite a good deal what we Unionists & Anti-Slaveryites call'd a *copperhead*—yet somehow we take to such characters—not pure silver or gold—quite mixed, even questionable—like Burns, Mary Stuart, Aaron Burr, (perhaps Shakspere)[.]

—Walt Whitman, Letter to Richard Maurice Bucke
(November 9, 1889), in Edward Haviland Miller (ed.), *Walt Whitman: The Correspondence*, Vol. 4, New York University Press, 1969, p. 396

JOHN VANCE CHENEY "HAWTHORNE" (1891)

It is hardly necessary to add that success, such as Hawthorne's, implies the happiest expression. Not to dwell on Hawthorne's style, simple mention may be made of his power of condensation, his exquisite application of the law of contrast, his repose, his judgment or taste; and, over and above all, his poet's skill in suggestiveness and in the creation of atmosphere, his primal power of pure, bold, sustained imagination—imagination which, for purity and subtilty has been equalled in English literature perhaps not more than once before since the robe fell from the shoulders of the unapproachable Elizabethan.

> —John Vance Cheney, "Hawthorne," *The Golden Guess:*
> *Essays on Poetry and the Poets,* 1891, pp. 291–92

Barrett Wendell
"American Literature" (1893)

Wendell, a Harvard professor of literature and an early biographer of the Puritan minister Cotton Mather, makes an informed and original interpretation of Hawthorne's use of Puritan materials. He finds that Hawthorne articulates a "strange, morbid" Other which "underlay the intense idealism of the emigrant Puritans."

To men of our time, beyond doubt, his work seems generally not fantastic but imaginative, and surely not meretricious but in its own way beautiful. Nor is this the whole story: almost alone among our writers, we may say, Hawthorne has a lasting native significance. For this there are surely two good reasons. In the first place, he is almost the solitary American artist who has phrased his meaning in words of which the beauty seems sure to grow with the years. In the second place, what marks him as most impregnably American is this: when we look close to see what his meaning really was, we find it a thing that in the old days, at last finally dead and gone, had been the great motive power of his race. What Hawthorne really voices is that strange, morbid, haunting sense of other things that we see or hear, which underlay the intense idealism of the emigrant Puritans, and which remains perhaps the most inalienable emotional heritage of their children. It is Hawthorne, in brief, who finally phrases the meaning of such a life as Theophilus Eaton lived and Cotton Mather recorded.

> —Barrett Wendell, "American Literature," *Stelligeri and*
> *Other Essays Concerning America,* 1893, p. 139

Camilla Toulmin Crosland (1893)

I suppose there are few English readers of fiction, having a taste for better things than the merely sensational novel, who are not acquainted with *The Scarlet Letter, The House of the Seven Gables,* and other works of Nathaniel Hawthorne, though I am afraid they are now less read'—and, may I add, appreciated—than they were thirty years ago. Perhaps there is a reason for this; Hawthorne's works remind us of the laborious, patient, and delicate art of the fine gem-cutter, and to "taste" them thoroughly every detail has to be noticed and dwelt upon, and its suggestiveness remembered. A writer who produces this sort of work cannot be extremely voluminous, and, nowadays, for an author to retain his popularity he must be constantly producing some new thing—constantly, as it were, keeping himself "in evidence."

—Camilla Toulmin Crosland, *Landmarks of a Literary Life,*
1893, pp. 210–11

Hamilton W. Mabie "The Most Popular Novels in America" (1893)

The Scarlet Letter is beyond doubt the foremost story yet written on this continent, and the fact that it holds the third place in this long list is both suggestive and encouraging. *The Marble Faun* follows close upon its greater companion; for, however fascinating the later book in its subtle psychologic insight and however beautiful its art, it remains true that the earlier story surpasses it in closeness of construction and in depth and intensity of human interest. That a book of such quality finds so wide a reading shows that the finest art does not fail to charm when it allies itself with the deepest life.

—Hamilton W. Mabie, "The Most Popular Novels in America,"
Forum, December 1893, p. 512

Henry A. Beers (1895)

Hawthorne was no transcendentalist. He dwelt much in a world of ideas, and he sometimes doubted whether the tree on the bank or its image in the stream were the more real. But this had little in common with the philosophical idealism of his neighbors. He reverenced Emerson, and he held kindly intercourse—albeit a silent man and easily bored—with Thoreau and Ellery Channing, and even with Margaret Fuller. But his sharp eyes saw whatever was whimsical or weak in the apostles of the new faith. He had little enthusiasm for causes or reforms, and among so many abolitionists he remained a Democrat, and even wrote a campaign life of his friend Pierce.

—Henry A. Beers, *Initial Studies in
American Letters*, 1895, p. 123

CHARLES F. JOHNSON (1898)

Of the moderns, Hawthorne possesses in a remarkable degree the power of impressing unity on his creations. His hand is firm. He never wavers in style, stand-point, aim, or subject by a hair's-breadth. His plots are simple, his motives more so; in fact, no people ever were dominated by so few impulses as are the characters in Hawthorne's romances. There is something Greek in their simplicity, although they are as unlike a Greek conception of humanity as are Caliban or Ariel. But they never waver. Such as the author conceived them in the first chapter, they remain to the end. There is no growth or development of character. This gives his tales an atmosphere which is never blown away by any nineteenth-century wind, and a unity which insures them a place in the literature which endures. There is a certain sameness about his style which might become monotonous in spite of its wonderful charm, and a limited experience of life which might become uninteresting, and an impress of a poverty-stricken and repellent external world which might become disheartening, but the unity is so thoroughly artistic that the pleasure received far outweighs the annoyance which is caused by the depressing and fatalistic atmosphere which envelops some of his romances.

—Charles F. Johnson, *Elements of Literary Criticism*, 1898, pp. 34–35

WILBUR L. CROSS (1899)

Nearly all the Gothic machinery of Walpole, Mrs. Radcliffe, and Godwin is to be found in this Puritan: high winds, slamming doors, moonlight and starlight, magic and witchcraft, mysterious portraits, transformations, malignant beings, the elixir of life, the skeleton, the funeral, and the corpse in its shroud. To these sources of excitement were added, as time went on, mesmerism and clairvoyance. The novelty of Hawthorne's work is in his treatment. Like Shakespeare, he offers only a partial explanation of his unusual phemonena or none at all. Most unconventional is his use of witchcraft, as was pointed out by Poe, in 'The Hollow of Three Hills,' where to the imagination of the woman of sin, as she lays her head upon the witch's knees beneath the magic cloak, distant scenes of sorrow for which she is responsible are conveyed, not by viewing them in a magic mirror, but by the subtle sense of sound. And almost equally novel is the use made of the fountain of youth in 'Dr. Heidegger's Experiment.' The persecuting demon of romance, when he appears in Hawthorne's pages under the name of Roger Chillingworth, or the Spectre of the Catacomb, is a personification of the mistakes, misfortunes, and sins of our past life, which will not out of our imagination. The transformations—Pearl from a capricious, elfish being into a sober woman, and Donatello from a thoughtless, voluptuous animal into a man who feels the sad weight of humanity—have their analogies in real life. The supernatural world was with Hawthorne but the inner world of the conscience.

The ethical import of his narrative is always conveyed by means of a fanciful symbolism. The embroidered A that is hung about Hester Prynne's neck, the red stigma over Arthur Dimmesdale's heart, and Pearl in scarlet dress, are obviously symbolical. The black veil with which a Puritan minister conceals his face is the shadow of a dark deed. Donatello's hair-tipped ears are suggestions of his animalism. Moreover, Hawthorne was inclined to interpret figuratively events, nature, and art. Little Pearl runs from her mother and cannot be coaxed to return; that is typical of a moral gulf separating them. The sunless wood in which Hester stands alone images a moral solitude. Light streaming through the painted windows of a Gothic church is a foretaste of the 'glories of the better world.' As Hawthorne views a half-finished bust, and sees the human face struggling to get out of the marble, he remarks: 'As this bust in the block of marble, so does our individual fate exist in the limestone of time.' It has been said that Poe was a myth maker; Hawthorne likewise built up his own myths, and then he allegorized them like Bacon, turning them into apologues. Even the allegorical interpretation sometimes given to *The Marble Faun* is not to be ridiculed, for the allegory is there. Whatever may have been the origin of language, it has now become, in its common use, a direct representation of things, ideas, and feelings. Hawthorne did not always so treat it, but rather conceived of it as a system of hieroglyphics; a secret he does not call a secret, 'it is a wild venomous thing' imprisoned in the heart. This is the way of Spenser.

The story of Hawthorne is only half told when we say he refined Gothic art and fashioned it to high ethical purposes. As in the case of Poe, one of his great charms is his workmanship in structure and style. In the technique of the short tale, Poe was at least his equal; in the longer tale, where Poe left many loose ends, Hawthorne succeeded twice—in *The Scarlet Letter* (1850) and *The House of the Seven Gables* (1851). Poe modelled his style on Defoe and De Quincey, now suggesting the one and now the other. Hawthorne by laborious practice acquired a more individual style; the good taste of Addison and Irving are visible in it, and the brooding and dreamy fancy of Tieck, disguised however in the fusion.

—Wilbur L. Cross, *The Development of the English Novel*, 1899, pp. 163–66

Bradford Torrey
"Writers That Are Quotable" (1899)

Hawthorne's work you may read from end to end without the temptation to transfer so much as a line to the commonplace book. The road has taken you through many interesting scenes, and past many a beautiful landscape; you may have felt much and learned much; you might be glad to turn back straightway and travel the course over again; but you will have picked up no coin or jewel to put away in a cabinet. This characteristic of Hawthorne is the more noteworthy because of the moral quality of his work. A mere story-teller may naturally keep his narrative on the go, as we say,—that is one of the chief secrets of his art; but Hawthorne was not a mere story-teller. He was a moralist,—Emerson himself hardly more so; yet he has never a moral sentence. The fact is, he did not make sentences; he made books. The story, not the sentence, nor even the paragraph or the chapter, was the unit. The general truth—the moral—informed the work. Not only was it not affixed as a label; it was not given anywhere a direct and separable verbal expression. If the story does not convey it to you, you will never get it. Hawthorne, in short, was what, for lack of a better word, we may call a literary artist.

> —Bradford Torrey, "Writers That Are Quotable,"
> *Atlantic*, March 1899, p. 407

T.S. Eliot "The Hawthorne Aspect" (1918)

Thomas Stearns Eliot was the American poet who revolutionized verse in 1922 with the publication of *The Waste Land*. Like Hawthorne and Henry James, he was an American who spent some years in Europe. Like James, he became naturalized as a British citizen and, like James, he was seen by his fellow Americans as a terrible snob and a fawning Anglophile. This essay will principally be of interest to students examining the relationship between Hawthorne and Henry James. Eliot's argument is that Hawthorne is the forerunner of James. The essay is important also for voicing the views of a leading modernist on Hawthorne.

It is unsurprising that Eliot meditates first on the American quality of Hawthorne and James. He specifies that there is a "New England genius" present in Emerson, Thoreau, Hawthorne, and Lowell, also evident in James. Eliot sees New England letters as dominated by the figure of the "man of leisure." The idea of indolence recurs in his criticism of Hawthorne

(Eliot himself worked for a bank and then for a publisher). Hawthorne was lazy, Eliot argues, without substantiating this claim. His tone is faintly facetious as he dismisses Boston as "quite uncivilized but refined beyond the point of civilization" (Eliot had studied at Harvard University).

When Eliot ends his discussion of Henry James and turns to the nominal subject of his essay, it is to note that the American soil produced Hawthorne and—"just as inevitably"—it stunted him. Hawthorne exceeds James in one way only: his acute sense of history. Eliot, unlike other critics contained in this volume, finds Hawthorne erudite and exacting. He considers this "sense of the past" peculiarly American. Students examining Hawthorne's use of history and his "American" qualities might find this of use. Students interested in Hawthorne's influence on James should also turn to this particular entry.

Eliot finds both Hawthorne and James writing novels of "the deeper psychology," removed from their contemporaries in England and on the European continent (Dickens, Thackeray, George Eliot, Stendhal, and Flaubert). They "perceive by antennae" rather than by sight. Students mounting a psychological study of Hawthorne's works should read T.S. Eliot's analysis.

Hawthorne wrote of the past, Eliot explains, because his present was "so narrowly barren." This is a state Eliot regrets. Hawthorne's characters, he continues, are *aware* of each other," a phenomenon that occurs nowhere else in the English-language novel prior to Henry James. Eliot restates Hawthorne's lack of influences ("his limited culture" and his mind "closed to new impressions") but, unlike other critics, he sees this as a drawback rather than a virtue.

After a lengthy dissertation on James's small debt to Hawthorne, Eliot explains that Hawthorne's best work is *The House of the Seven Gables*.

—————

My object is not to discuss critically even one phase or period of [Henry] James, but merely to provide a note, *Beitrage*, toward any attempt to determine his antecedents, affinities, and 'place'. Presumed that James's relation to Balzac, to Turgenev, to any one else on the continent is known and measured—I refer to Mr Hueffer's book and to Mr Pound's article—and presumed that his relation to the Victorian novel is negligible, it is not concluded that James was simply a clever young man who came to Europe and improved himself, but that the soil of his origin contributed a flavour discriminible after transplantation in his latest fruit. We may even draw the instructive conclusion that this flavour was precisely improved and given its chance, not worked off, by transplantation. If there is this strong native taste, there will probably be some relation to Hawthorne; and if there is any relation to Hawthorne, it will probably help us to analyse the flavour of which I speak.

When we say that James is 'American', we must mean that this 'flavour' of his, and also more exactly definable qualities, are more or less diffused throughout the vast continent rather than anywhere else; but we cannot mean that this flavour and these qualities have found literary expression throughout the nation, or that they permeate the work of Mr Frank Norris or Mr Booth Tarkington. The point is that James is positively a continuator of the New England genius; that there is a New England genius, which has discovered itself only in a very small number of people in the middle of the nineteenth century—and which is *not* significantly present in the writings of Miss Sara Orne Jewett, Miss Eliza White, or the Bard of Appledore whose name I forget. I mean whatever we associate with certain purlieus of Boston, with Concord, Salem, and Cambridge, Mass.: notably Emerson, Thoreau, Hawthorne and Lowell. None of these men, with the exception of Hawthorne, is individually very important; they all can, and perhaps ought to be made to look very foolish; but there is a 'something' there, a dignity, about Emerson for example, which persists after we have perceived the taint of commonness about some English contemporary, as for instance the more intelligent, better educated, more alert Matthew Arnold. Omitting such men as Bryant and Whittier as absolutely plebeian, we can still perceive this halo of dignity around the men I have named, and also Longfellow, Margaret Fuller and her crew, Bancroft and Motley, the faces of (later) Norton and Child pleasantly shaded by the Harvard elms. One distinguishing mark of this distinguished world was very certainly leisure; and importantly not in all cases a leisure given by money, but insisted upon. There seems no easy reason why Emerson or Thoreau or Hawthorne should have been men of leisure; it seems odd that the New England conscience should have allowed them leisure; yet they would have it, sooner or later. That is really one of the finest things about them, and sets a bold frontier between them and a world which will at any price avoid leisure, a world in which Theodore Roosevelt is a patron of the arts. An interesting document, of this latter world is the *Letters* of a nimbly dull poet of a younger generation, of Henry James's generation, Richard Watson Gilder, Civil Service Reform, Tenement House Commission, Municipal Politics.

Of course leisure in a metropolis, with a civilized society (the society of Boston was and is quite uncivilized but refined beyond the point of civilisation) with exchange of ideas and critical standards would have been better, but these men could not provide the metropolis, and were right in taking the leisure under possible conditions.

Precisely this leisure, this dignity, this literary aristocracy, this unique character of a society in which the men of letters were also of the beat people, clings to Henry James. It is some consciousness of this kinship which makes him so tender and gentle in his appreciations of Emerson, Norton and the beloved Ambassador. With Hawthorne, as much the most important of these people in any question of literary art, his relation is more personal; but no more in the case of Hawthorne than with any of the other figures of the background is there any consideration of influence. James owes little, very little, to anyone; there are certain writers whom he consciously studied, of whom Hawthorne was not one; but in any case his relation to Hawthorne is on another plane from his relation to Balzac, for example. The influence of Balzac, not on the whole a good influence, is perfectly evident in some of the earlier novels; the influence of Turgenev is vaguer, but more useful. That James was, at a certain period, more moved by Balzac, that he followed him with more concentrated admiration, is clear from the tone of his criticism of that writer compared with the tone of his criticism of either Turgenev or Hawthorne. In *French Poets and Novelists*, though an early work, James's attitude toward Balzac is exactly that of having been very much attracted from his orbit, perhaps very wholesomely stimulated at an age when almost any foreign stimulus may be good, and having afterwards reacted from Balzac, though not to the point of injustice. He handles Balzac shrewdly and fairly. From the essay on Turgenev there is on the other hand very little to be got but a touching sense of appreciation; from the essay on Flaubert even less. The charming study of Hawthorne is quite different from any of these. The first conspicuous quality in it is tenderness, the tenderness of a man who had escaped too early from an environment to be warped or thwarted by it, who had escaped so effectually that he could afford the gift of affection. At the same time he places his finger, now mid then, very gently, on some of Hawthorne's more serious defects as well as his limitations.

> The best things come, as a general thing, from the talents that are members of a group; every man works better when he has companions working in the same line, and yielding uric stimulus of suggestion, comparison, emulation.

Though when he says that 'there was manifestly a strain of generous indolence in his (Hawthorne's) composition' he is understating the fault of laziness for which Hawthorne can chiefly be blamed. But gentleness is needed in criticising Hawthorne, a necessary thing to remember about whom is precisely the difficult fact that the soil which produced him with his essential flavour is the soil which produced, just as inevitably, the environment which stunted him.

In one thing alone Hawthorne is more solid than James: he had a very acute historical sense. His erudition in the small field of American colonial history was extensive, and he made most fortunate use of it. Both men had that sense of the past which is peculiarly American, but in Hawthorne this sense exercised itself in a grip on the past itself; in James it is a sense of the sense. This, however, need not be dwelt upon here. The really vital thing, in finding any personal kinship between Hawthorne and James, is what James touches lightly when he says that 'the fine thing in Hawthorne is that he cared for the deeper psychology, and that, in his way, he tried to become familiar with it.' There are other points of resemblance, not directly included under this, but this one is of the first importance. It is, in fact, almost enough to ally the two novelists, in comparison with whom almost all others maybe accused of either superficiality or aridity. I am not saying that the 'deeper psychology' is essential, or that it can always be had without loss of other qualities, or that a novel need be any the less a work of art without it. It is a definition; and it separates the two novelists at once from the English contemporaries of either. Neither Dickens nor Thackeray, certainly, had the smallest notion of the 'deeper psychology'; George Eliot had a kind of heavy intellect for it (Tito) but all her genuine feeling went into the visual realism of *Amos Barton*. On the continent it is known; but the method of Stendhal or of Flaubert is quite other. A situation is for Stendhal something deliberately constructed, often an illustration. There is a bleakness about it, vitalised by force rather than feeling, and its presentation is definitely visual. Hawthorne and James have a kind of sense, a receptive medium, which is not of sight. Not that they fail to make you *see*, so far as necessary, but sight is not the essential sense. They perceive by antennae; and the 'deeper psychology' is here. The deeper psychology indeed led Hawthorne to some of his absurdest and most characteristic excesses; it was for ever tailing off into the fanciful, even the allegorical, which is a lazy substitute for profundity. The fancifulness is the 'strain of generous indolence', the attempt to get the artistic effect by meretricious means. On this side a critic might seize hold of *The Turn of the Screw*, a tale about which I have many doubts; but the actual working out of this is different from Hawthorne's, and we are not interested in approximation of the two men on the side of their weakness. The point is that Hawthorne was acutely sensitive to the situation; that he did grasp character through the relation of two or more persons to each other, and this is what no one else, except James, has done. Furthermore, he does establish, as James establishes, a solid atmosphere, and he does, in his quaint way, get New England, as James gets a larger part of America, and as none of their respective contemporaries get anything above a village or two, or a jungle. Compare, with anything that any English contemporary could do, the situation which Hawthorne sets up in the relation of Dimmesdale and Chillingworth. Judge Pyncheon and Clifford, Hepzibah and Phoebe, are similarly achieved by their relation to each other, Clifford, for one, being simply the intersection of a relation to three other characters. The only dimension in which Hawthorne could expand was the past, his present being so narrowly barren. It is a great pity, with his remarkable gift of observation, that the present did not offer him more to observe. But he is the one English-writing predecessor of James whose characters are *aware* of each other, the one whose novels were in any deep sense a criticism of even a slight civilization; and here is something more definite and closer than any derivation we can trace from Richardson or Marivaux.

The fact that the sympathy with Hawthorne is most felt in the last of James's novels, *The Sense of the Past*, makes me the more certain of its genuineness. In the meantime, James has been through a much more elaborate development than poor Hawthorne ever knew. Hawthorne, with his very limited culture, was not exposed to any bewildering variety of influences. James, in his astonishing career of self-improvement, touches Hawthorne most evidently at the beginning and end of his course; at the beginning simply as a young New Englander of letters; at the end, with almost a gesture of approach. *Roderick Hudson* is the novel of a clever and expanding young New Englander; immature, but just coming out to a self-consciousness where Hawthorne never arrived at all. Compared with *Daisy Miller* or *The Europeans* or *The American*, its critical spirit is very crude. But *The Marble Faun* (Transformation), the only European novel of Hawthorne, is of Cimmerian opacity; the mind of its author was closed to new impressions though with all its Walter Scott-Mysteries of Udolpho upholstery the old man does establish a kind of solid moral atmosphere which the young James does not get. James in *Roderick Hudson* does very little better with Rome than Hawthorne, and as he confesses in the later preface, rather fails with Northampton.

He does in the later edition tone down the absurdities of Roderick's sculpture a little. the pathetic Thirst and the gigantic Adam; Mr Striker remains a failure, the judgement of a young man consciously humourising, too suggestive of Martin Chuzzlewit. The generic resemblance to Hawthorne is in the occasional heavy facetiousness of the style, the tedious whimsicality how different from the exactitude of *The American Scene*, the verbalism. He too much identifies himself with Rowland, does not see through the solemnity he has created in that character, commits the cardinal sin of failing to 'detect' one of his own characters. The failure to create a situation is evident: with Christina and Mary, each nicely adjusted, but never quite set in relation to each other. The interest of the book for our present purpose is what he does *not* do in the Hawthorne way, in the instinctive attempt to get at something larger, which will bring him to the same success with much besides.

The interest in the 'deeper psychology', the observation, and the sense for situation, developed from book to book, culminate in *The Sense of the Past* (by no means saying that this is his best) uniting with other qualities both personal and racial. James's greatness is apparent both in his capacity for development as an artist and his capacity for keeping his mind alive to the changes in the world during twenty-five years: It is remarkable (for the mastery of a span of American history) that the man who did the Wentworth family in the '80s could do the Bradhams in the '00s. In *The Sense of the Past* the Midmores belong to the same generation as the Bradhams; Ralph belongs to the same race as the Wentworths, indeed as the Pyncheons. Compare the book with *The House of the Seven Gables* (Hawthorne's best novel after all); the situation, the 'shrinkage and extinction of a family' is rather more complex, on the surface, than James's with (so far as the book was done) fewer character-relations. But James's real situation here, to which Ralph's mounting the step is the key, as Hepzibah's opening of her shop, is a situation of different states of mind. James's situation is the shrinkage and extinction of an idea. The Pyncheon tragedy is simple; the 'curse' upon the family a matter of the simplest fairy mechanics. James has taken Hawthorne's ghost-sense and given it substance. At the same time making the tragedy much more etherial: the tragedy of that 'Sense', the hypertrophy, in Ralph, of a partial civilization; the vulgar vitality of the Midmores in their financial decay contrasted with the decay of Ralph in his financial prosperity, when they precisely should have been the civilisation he had come to seek. All this watched over by the absent, but conscious Aurora. I do not want to insist upon the Hawthorneness of the confrontation of the portrait, the importance of the opening of a door. We need surely not insist that this book is the most important, most substantial sort of thing that James did; perhaps there is more solid wear even in that other unfinished *Ivory Tower*. But I consider that it was an excursion which we could well permit him, after a lifetime in which he had taken talents similar to Hawthorne's and made them yield far greater returns than poor Hawthorne could harvest from his granite soil; a permissible exercise, in which we may by a legitimately cognate fancy seem to detect Hawthorne coming to a mediumistic existence again, to remind a younger and incredulous generation of what he really was, had he had the opportunity, and to attest his satisfaction that that opportunity had been given to James.

—T.S. Eliot, "The Hawthorne Aspect,"
Little Review, 4, August 1918, pp. 47–53

HENRY LOUIS MENCKEN "MARK TWAIN" (1919)

Mencken was the "sage of Baltimore"—a journalist, critic, essayist, and encyclopædic authority on the American language, famed for his brilliant but often withering criticism. His evaluation of Hawthorne comes from an essay on Mark Twain (who Mencken valued above all other American writers). Mencken's loathing of Puritans may contribute to his opinion.

Mencken was one of the earliest writers to connect Hawthorne with psychoanalysis, pronouncing that Hawthorne's "enterprise, in his chief work, might almost be called an attempt to psychoanalyze the dead." His view of Hawthorne opposes many of those printed here. He finds Hawthorne not to be the great native hope, the first true portrayer of America in high literature (that would be Mark Twain), but to be—like Henry James—uncomfortable in his own country, only at ease when abroad. Mencken slams Hawthorne's remoteness as un-American. Hawthorne—with Whitman, Emerson, and Poe—was too isolated from the American people, and this limited his native quality. Mencken's view will prove significant to any student writing on Hawthorne's "Americanism" and also anyone writing a psychoanalytical study of Hawthorne's work.

Hawthorne concerned himself with psychological problems that were not only inordinately obscure and labored, but even archaic; his enterprise, in his chief work, might almost be called an attempt to psychoanalyze the dead. It would be ridiculous to say that there was anything in his books that was characteristic of his time and his country. The gusto of a man thoroughly at home in his surroundings was simply not in him, and it is surely not surprising to hear that while he was physically present in America he lived like a hermit, and that his only happiness was found abroad.

—Henry Louis Mencken, "Mark Twain,"
Smart Set 60, No. 2 (October 1919), pp. 139–143

WORKS

TWICE-TOLD TALES

HENRY WADSWORTH LONGFELLOW
"HAWTHORNE'S *TWICE-TOLD TALES*" (1837)

Henry Wadsworth Longfellow was the American poet best known for his long poem *The Song of Hiawatha*. He was also Hawthorne's classmate at Bowdoin College in Brunswick, Maine. They remained close friends. There is more poetry than criticism in this first review; however, Longfellow significantly defines Hawthorne's fiction as "written by a poet," although in prose form. Longfellow draws attention to the clarity of Hawthorne's writing and differentiates his work from the prevailing school of gothic fiction then in vogue. While those works "need a translation for many of the crowd," Hawthorne's stories are delivered in "a language that is generally understood." Hawthorne is viewed, in the time of Jacksonian democracy, as a democratic writer. Students connecting Hawthorne to an American gothic tradition should read Longfellow's review; readers trying to locate Hawthorne within a democratic tradition should do likewise.

When a new star rises in the heavens, people gaze after it for a season with the naked eye, and with such telescopes as they may find. In the stream of thought, which flows so peacefully deep and clear, through the pages of this book, we see the bright reflection of a spiritual star, after which men will be fain to gaze "with the naked eye and with the spy-glasses of criticism." This star is but newly risen; and ere long the observations of numerous star-gazers, perched up on armchairs and editors' tables, will inform the world of its magnitude and its place in the heaven of poetry, whether it be in the paw of the Great Bear, or on the forehead of Pegasus, or on the strings of the Lyre, or in the wing of the Eagle. Our own observations are as follows. To this little work we would say, "Live ever, sweet, sweet book." It comes from the hand of a man of genius. Everything about it has the freshness of morning and of May. These flowers and green leaves of poetry have not the dust of the highway upon them. They have been gathered fresh from the secret places of a peaceful and gentle heart. There flow deep waters, silent, calm, and cool; and the green trees look into them, and "God's blue heaven." The book, though in prose, is written nevertheless by a poet. He looks upon all things in the spirit of love, and with lively sympathies; for to him external form is but the representation of internal being, all things having a life, an end and aim. . . .

Another characteristic of this writer is the exceeding beauty of his style. It is as clear as running waters are. Indeed he uses words as mere stepping-stones, upon which, with a free and youthful bound, his spirit crosses and recrosses the bright and rushing stream of thought. Some writers of the present day have introduced a kind of Gothic architecture into their style. All is fantastic, vast, and wondrous in the outward form, and within is mysterious twilight, and the swelling sound of an organ, and a voice chanting hymns in Latin, which need a translation for many of the crowd. To this we do not object. Let the priest chant in what language he will, so long as he understands his own mass-book. But if he wishes the world to listen and be edified, he will do well to choose a language that is generally understood.

—Henry Wadsworth Longfellow, "Hawthorne's *Twice-Told Tales*,"
North American Review, July 1837, pp. 59, 63

Henry Wadsworth Longfellow (1842)

This second review anticipates many of the themes that would endure in Hawthorne criticism for the next century. Longfellow views Hawthorne as standing independent of other literatures: "He gives us no poor copies of poor originals in English magazines and souvenirs." He also notes Hawthorne's novel use of native materials ("His writings retain the racy flavor of the soil"). Longfellow identifies Hawthorne's capacity for seamlessly merging "the picturesque, the romantic, and even the supernatural, in the every-day, common-place life, that is constantly going on around us." As Richard Holt Hutton would later note, Longfellow praises Hawthorne's ability to "detect the essentially poetic in that which is superficially prosaic."

Longfellow highlights how Hawthorne "blends together, with a skillful hand, the two worlds of the seen and the unseen." Hawthorne's subjects verge on the supernatural, but stay within the realm of the possible, as all the while he "passes as near as possible to the dividing line." In this respect, Hawthorne resembles no other writer. Students examining the fantastic element in Hawthorne's fiction would do well to consult Longfellow.

Longfellow notes how New England, which had not previously been the subject for the novelist/romance writer, is transformed by Hawthorne. Longfellow mentions Hawthorne's affinity for writing about female characters, noting especially the "womanly knowledge of a child's mind and character" in "Little Annie's Ramble."

Again Longfellow observes that, unlike his gothic contemporaries (and unlike Poe), Hawthorne never stoops to "vulgar horrors or physical clap-traps." Longfellow discerns humor in Hawthorne's tales, albeit a quiet sort that "never begets a laugh." Rather—in stories such as "A Rill from the Town Pump" or "Chippings with a Chisel"—his humor is gentle and deals with "the mind." Readers studying Hawthorne's use of humor will find much of relevance in this passage.

Finally Longfellow turns to Hawthorne's use of language. He reiterates his earlier view that Hawthorne's language is clear, "correct and careful." As subsequent critics would notice, Hawthorne is exacting without being laborious. Anticipating later critics again, Longfellow notes Hawthorne's lack of any model.

The lovers of delicate humor, natural feeling, observation 'like a blind man's touch,' unerring taste, and magic grace of style, will greet with pleasure this new, improved, and enlarged edition of Hawthorne's 'Twice-told Tales.' The first volume appeared several years since, and received notice and fit commendation in a former Number of our Journal. The second volume is made up of tales and sketches, similar in character to those of the first volume, and not inferior in merit. We are disposed, on the strength of these volumes, to accord to Mr. Hawthorne a high rank among the writers of this country, and to predict, that his contributions to its imaginative literature will enjoy a permanent and increasing reputation. Though he has not produced any elaborate and long-sustained work of fiction, yet his writings are most strikingly characterized by that creative originality, which is the essential life-blood of genius. He does not see by the help of other men's minds, and has evidently been more of an observer and thinker, than of a student. He gives us no poor copies of poor originals in English magazines and souvenirs. He has caught nothing of the intensity of the French, or the extravagance of the German, school of writers of fiction. Whether he writes a story or a sketch, or describes a character or a scene, he employs his own materials, and gives us transcripts of images painted on his own mind. Another characteristic merit of his writings is, that he seeks and finds his subjects at home, among his own people, in the characters, the events, and the traditions of his own country. His writings retain the racy flavor of the soil. They have the healthy vigor and free grace of indigenous plants.

Perhaps there is no one thing for which he is more remarkable than his power of finding the elements of the picturesque, the romantic, and even the supernatural, in the every-day, common-place life, that is constantly going on around us. He detects the essentially poetical in that which is superficially prosaic. In the alembic of his genius, the subtile essence of poetry is extracted from prose. The history, the traditions, the people, and the scenes of New England, have not generally been supposed favorable to the romance-writer or the poet; but, in his hands, they are fruitful and suggestive, and dispose themselves into graceful attitudes and dramatic combinations. In his little sketch called 'David Swan,' the subject is nothing more or less than an hour's sleep, by the way-side, of a youth, while waiting for the coach that is to carry him to Boston; yet how much of thoughtful and reflective beauty is thrown round it, what strange and airy destinies brush by the youth's unconscious face, how much matter for deep meditation of life and death, the past and future, time and eternity, is called forth by the few incidents in this simple drama. As illustrations of the same power, we would refer to 'The Minister's Black Veil,' 'The Seven Vagabonds,' and 'Edward Fane's Rosebud,' not to speak of many others, in which this peculiarity is more or less perceptible.

One of Mr. Hawthorne's most characteristic traits is the successful manner in which he deals with the supernatural. He blends together, with a skilful hand, the two worlds of the seen and the unseen. He never fairly goes out of the limits of probability, never calls up an actual ghost, or dispenses with the laws of nature; but he passes as near as possible to the dividing line, and his skill and ingenuity are sometimes tasked to explain, by natural laws, that which produced upon the reader all the effect of the supernatural. In this, too, his originality is conspicuously displayed. We know of no writings which resemble his in this respect.

His genius, too, is characterized by a large proportion of feminine elements, depth and tenderness of feeling, exceeding purity of mind, and a certain airy grace and arch vivacity in narrating incidents and delineating characters. The strength and beauty of a mother's love are poured over that exquisite story, which we are tempted to pronounce, as, on the whole, the finest thing he ever wrote,—'The Gentle Boy.' What minute delicacy of touch, and womanly knowledge of a child's mind and character, are perceptible in 'Little Annie's Ramble.' How much of quiet pathos is contained in 'The Shaker Bridal,' and of tranquil beauty in 'The Three-fold Destiny.' His female characters are sketched with a pencil equally fine and delicate; steeped in the finest hues of the imagination, yet not

    too bright and good
    For human nature's daily food.

Every woman owes him a debt of gratitude for those lovely visions of womanly faith, tenderness, and truth, which glide so gracefully through his pages.

All that Mr. Hawthorne has written is impressed with a strong family likeness. His range is not very extensive, nor has he any great versatility of mind. He is not extravagant or excessive in any thing. His tragedy is tempered with a certain smoothness; it solemnizes and impresses us, but it does not freeze the blood, still less offend the most fastidious taste. He stoops to no vulgar horrors or physical clap-traps. The mind, in its highest and deepest moods of feeling, is the only subject with which he deals. There is, however, a great deal of calm power, as well as artist-like skill, in his writings of this kind, such as 'Howe's Masquerade,' 'The White Old Maid,' 'Lady Eleanor's Mantle.' In his humor, too, there is the same quiet tone. It is never riotous, or exuberant; it never begets a laugh, and seldom a smile, but it is most unquestioned humor, as any one may see, by reading 'A Rill from the Town Pump,' or 'Chippings with a Chisel.' It is a thoughtful humor, of kindred with sighs as well as tears. Indeed, over all that he has written, there hangs, like an atmosphere, a certain soft and calm melancholy, which has nothing diseased or mawkish in it, but is of that kind which seems to flow naturally from delicacy of organization and a meditative spirit. There is no touch of despair in his pathos, and his humor subsides into that minor key, into which his thoughts seem naturally cast.

As a writer of the language merely, Mr. Hawthorne is entitled to great praise, in our judgment. His style strikes us as one of marked and uncommon excellence. It is fresh and vigorous, not formed by studying any particular model, and has none of the stiffness which comes from imitation; but it is eminently correct and careful. His language is very pure, his words are uniformly well chosen, and his periods are moulded with great grace and skill. It is also a very perspicuous style, through which his thoughts shine like natural objects seen through the purest plate-glass. He has no affectations or prettinesses of phrases, and none of those abrupt transitions, or of that studied inversion and uncouth abruptness, by which attention is often attempted to be secured to what is feeble or commonplace. It is characterized by that same unerring good taste, which presides over all the movements of his mind.

We feel that we have hardly done justice to Mr. Hawthorne's claims in this brief notice, and that they deserve an extended analysis and criticism; but we have not done this, partly on account of our former attempt to do justice to his merits, and partly because his writings have now become so well known, and are so justly appreciated, by all discerning minds, that they do not need our commendation. He is not an author to create a sensation, or have a tumultuous popularity. His works are not stimulating or impassioned, and they minister nothing to a feverish love of excitement. Their tranquil beauty and softened tints, which do not win the notice of the restless many, only endear them the more to the thoughtful few. We commend them for their truth and healthiness of feeling, and their moral dignity, no less than for their literary merit. The pulse of genius beats vigorously through them, and the glow of life is in them. It is the voice of a man who has seen and thought for himself, which addresses us; and the treasures which he offers to us are the harvests of much observation and deep reflection on man, and life, and the human heart.

—Henry Wadsworth Longfellow,
North American Review, April 1842, pp. 496–97

Margaret Fuller (1842)

Margaret Fuller was a writer, thinker, historian, and "chronicler of intellectual advents and apparitions" who was closely attached to Emerson's transcendentalist circle. She was also involved with the Brook Farm social experiment at the same time as Hawthorne. This review was written nine months after Hawthorne left Brook Farm.

Biographers have described a rivalry that existed between Hawthorne and Fuller. When Hawthorne turned his brief exposure to communal living into *The Blithedale Romance*, soon after Fuller's tragic death by drowning, it was generally understood that the character Zenobia was based, however loosely, on her. Despite Hawthorne's blithe insistence that none of the characters in the book was a caricature of the living (or the dead), this view has—probably rightly—prevailed. When Hawthorne's notebooks were published, his caustic comments about Fuller—unusually bitter and cruel—shocked literary society. Hawthorne's son, Julian, compounded the shock and hurt with further jibes and slanders in his biography *Nathaniel Hawthorne and His Wife*.

These rivalries and resentments seem far from this review, in which Fuller praises Hawthorne, although occasional niggles can be discerned coursing beneath her positive assessment. She lauds Hawthorne's "great reserve of thought and strength never yet all brought forward." Hawthorne withholds matter, is sparing and exacting—"how little yet is told." This trait should be noted by students of Hawthorne's style.

Fuller interestingly declares that Hawthorne is "a favorite writer for children, with whom he feels at home, as all manliness does." Readers interested in Hawthorne's intended audience should take note; he wrote several books expressly for children. Can *Twice-Told Tales* be considered one of them?

Hawthorne's greatest success, however, lies in his presentation of "familiar life." Fuller finds his "mere imaginative pieces" phantasmal and flimsy. She suggests that Hawthorne is undermotivated ("this would be otherwise, probably, were the genius fully roused to its work"), a view later echoed by T.S. Eliot. Hawthorne needs to write from life, Fuller reasons; she seems to suggest he needs to enter life, to find "deeper experiences," that he might "paint with blood-warm colors." Given Fuller's personal acquaintance with Hawthorne, particularly at Brook Farm (where, after all, the intention was for writers and artists to exist "within life," among the workers), this personal judgment is significant. Ironically, when Hawthorne did write from life it was to depict Brook Farm, and possibly Fuller.

Fuller's text joins the portraits of Hawthorne as cerebral and reclusive. Readers interested in Hawthorne's transformation of his own life into fiction will find here an articulate advocate.

⸺⧫⧫⧫⸺ ⸺⧫⧫⧫⸺ ⸺⧫⧫⧫⸺

Ever since 'The Gentle Boy' first announced among us the presence of his friend and observer, the author of the *Twice-told Tales* has been growing more and more dear to his readers, who now have the pleasure of seeing all the leaves they had been gathering up here and there collected in these two volumes.

It is not merely the soft grace, the playfulness, and genial human sense for the traits of individual character, that have pleased, but the perception of what is rarest in this superficial, bustling community, a great reserve of thought and strength never yet at all brought forward. Landor says, 'He is not over-rich in knowledge who cannot afford to let the greater part lie fallow, and to bring forward his produce according to the season and the demand.' We can seldom recur to such a passage as this with pleasure, as we turn over the leaves of a new book. But here we may. Like gleams of light on a noble tree which stands untouched and self-sufficing in its fulness of foliage on a distant hill-slope,—like slight ripples wrinkling the smooth surface, but never stirring the quiet depths of a wood-embosomed lake, these tales distantly indicate the bent of the author's mind, and the very frankness with which they impart to us slight outward details and habits shows how little yet is told. He is a favorite writer for children, with whom he feels at home, as true manliness always does, and the *Twice-told Tales* scarce call him out more than the little books for his acquaintance of fairy stature.

In the light of familiar letters, written with ready hand, by a friend, from the inns where he stops in a journey through the varied world-scenes, the tales are most pleasing: but they seem to promise more, should their author ever hear a voice that truly calls upon his solitude to ope his study door.

In his second volume, 'The Village Uncle,' 'Lily's Guest,' 'Chippings with a Chisel,' were new to us, and pleasing for the same reasons as former favorites from the same hand. We again admired the sweet grace of the little piece, 'Footprints on the Sea-shore.'

'Chippings with a Chisel,' from its mild, common-sense philosophy, and genial love of the familiar plays of life, would have waked a brotherly smile on the lips of the friend of Dr Dry-as-dust.

It is in the studies of familiar life that there is most success. In the mere imaginative pieces, the invention is not clearly woven, far from being all compact, and seems a phantom or shadow, rather than a real growth. The men and women, too, flicker large and unsubstantial, like 'shadows from the evening firelight,' seen 'upon the parlor wall.' But this would be otherwise, probably, were the genius fully roused to its work, and initiated into its own life, so as to paint with blood-warm colors. This frigidity and thinness of design usually bespeaks a want of the deeper experiences, for which no talent at observation, no sympathies, however ready and delicate, can compensate. We wait new missives from the same hand.

—Margaret Fuller, *The Dial*, III, July 1842, pp. 130–31

EDGAR ALLAN POE "TWICE-TOLD TALES" (1842)

As writers working broadly in the same field (dealing with the eerie and the uncanny and pioneering the tale as a literary form) critical comparisons between Hawthorne and Edgar Allan Poe were frequent. They still are. It is of immense interest to scholars of both writers, then, that Poe published these reviews of Hawthorne. Poe was such a prolific and outspoken critic of his contemporaries that he leaves us a treasure trove of criticism. While he could be stinging in his dismissals of his peers, Poe's praise of Hawthorne is effusive. This is despite Poe's natural and enduring antipathy for New England and its "impudent *cliques*," which he had suspected of promoting—and corrupting—Hawthorne.

Students comparing the two writers should undoubtedly consult these reviews. Poe's identification with Hawthorne is clear, as the review veers into a personal manifesto by Poe on the tale form, albeit one inspired by Hawthorne. Both reviews appeared within a month of each other, and the latter is essentially an expansion of the former. After quibbling about the aptness of the collection's title, Poe notes how Hawthorne's tales are often not tales—a recurring claim—rather, they are "pure essays." In this category he includes "Sights from a Steeple," "Little Annie's Ramble," "A Rill from the Town Pump," "Snow-Flakes" and "Foot-Prints on the Sea-Shore." These Poe dismisses as "discrepancies" from the best of Hawthorne's work.

Nevertheless, Poe credits the novelty of Hawthorne's "subdued" tone in the so-called essays, and notices a similarity to Washington Irving's writing, "with more of originality, and less of finish." He also invokes the essayists of the English magazine *The Spectator*. Students covering Hawthorne's influences should consider this. Poe finds an "absence of novel combination" in Irving and *The Spectator* which is present in Hawthorne, who evidences a "truly imaginative intellect, restrained . . . by fastidiousness of taste, by constitutional melancholy and by indolence."

Poe argues that the tale form "affords unquestionably the fairest field for the exercise of the loftiest talent" in the "wide domains of mere prose." The novel form is objectionable, since a novel requires more than one sitting to read it, the reader thereby losing the "immense force derived from *totality*." "Worldly interests" break the spell of the fiction. This is not the case for the prose tale, as employed by Hawthorne, which takes between thirty minutes and two hours to read. "During the hour of perusal the soul of the reader is at the writer's control."

Authorial control is essential to Hawthorne (and, implicitly, Poe); not one word is misused or excessive, and each fits; a concept comparable to Flaubert's *mot juste*. Writing of "The Hollow of the Three Hills," Poe notes that "Not only is all done that should be done but . . . there is nothing done which should not be. Every word tells and there is not a word which does *not* tell." Similar claims redound throughout criticism of Hawthorne, and should be of note to any readers studying Hawthorne's literary style.

Truth is "the aim of the tale." The "style is purity itself." There are no great American tales, Poe avers, except Irving's *Tales of a Traveller* and now those reviewed here. He claims that the United States lags behind Great Britain in this regard. However, in his estimation, Hawthorne shines—"As Americans, we feel proud of this book." Hawthorne's singular strength is "invention, creation, imagination, originality." Poe especially praises "Wakefield," "The Wedding Knell," "The Minister's Black Veil" and "Dr. Heidegger's Experiment."

Mr. Hawthorne's volumes appear to us misnamed in two respects. In the first place they should not have been called *Twice-Told Tales*—for this is a title which will not bear *repetition*. If in the first collected edition they were twice-told, of course now they are thrice-told.—May we live to hear them told a hundred times! In the second place, these compositions are by no means *all* "Tales." The most of them are essays properly so called. It would have been wise in their author to have modified his title, so as to have had reference to all included. This point could have been easily arranged.

But under whatever titular blunders we receive this book, it is most cordially welcome. We have seen no prose composition by any American which can compare with *some* of these articles in the higher merits, or indeed in the lower; while there is not a single piece which would do dishonor to the best of the British essayists.

"The Rill from the Town Pump" which, through the *ad captandum* nature of its title, has attracted more of public notice than any one other of Mr. Hawthorne's compositions, is perhaps, the *least* meritorious. Among his best, we may briefly mention "The Hollow of the Three Hills;" "The Minister's Black Veil;" "Wakefield;" "Mr. Higginbotham's Catastrophe;" "Fancy's Show-Box;" "Dr. Heidegger's Experiment;" "David Swan;" "The Wedding Knell;" and "The White Old Maid." It is remarkable that all these, with one exception, are from the first volume.

The style of Mr. Hawthorne is purity itself. His *tone* is singularly effective— wild, plaintive, thoughtful, and in full accordance with his themes. We have only to object that there is insufficient diversity in these themes themselves, or rather in their character. His *originality* both of incident and of reflection |is very remarkable; and this trait alone would ensure him at least *our* warmest regard and commendation. We speak here chiefly of the tales; the essays are not so markedly novel. Upon the whole we look upon him as one of the few men of indisputable genius to whom our country has as yet given birth.

—Edgar Allan Poe, "Twice-Told Tales,"
Graham's Magazine, April 1842, p. 254

EDGAR ALLAN POE "TWICE-TOLD TALES" (1842)

We said a few hurried words about Mr. Hawthorne in our last number, with the design of speaking more fully in the present. We are still, however, pressed for room, and must necessarily discuss his volumes more briefly and more at random than their high merits deserve.

The book professes to be a collection of *tales* yet is, in two respects, misnamed. These pieces are now in their third republication, and, of course, are thrice-told. Moreover, they are by no means all tales, either in the ordinary or in the legitimate understanding of the term. Many of them are pure essays; for example, "Sights from a Steeple," "Sunday at Home," "Little Annie's Ramble," "A Rill from the Town Pump," "The Toll-Gatherer's Day," "The Haunted Mind," "The Sister Years," "Snow-Flakes," "Night Sketches," and "Foot-Prints on the Sea-Shore." We mention these matters chiefly on account of their discrepancy with that marked precision and finish by which the body of the work is distinguished.

Of the essays just named, we must be content to speak in brief. They are each and all beautiful, without being characterised by the polish and adaptation so visible in the tales proper. A painter would at once note their leading or predominant feature, and style it *repose*. There is no attempt at effect. All is quiet, thoughtful, subdued. Yet this repose may exist simultaneously with high originality of thought; and Mr. Hawthorne has demonstrated the fact. At every turn we meet with novel combinations; yet these combinations never surpass the limits of the quiet. We are soothed as we read; and withal is a calm astonishment that ideas so apparently obvious have never occurred or been presented to us before. Herein our author differs materially from Lamb or Hunt or Hazlitt—who, with vivid originality of manner and expression. have less of the true novelty of thought than is generally supposed, and whose originality, at best, has an uneasy and meretricious quaintness, replete with startling effects unfounded in nature, and inducing trains of reflection which lead to no satisfactory result. The Essays of Hawthorne have much of the character of Irving, with more of originality, and less of finish; while, compared with the Spectator, they have a vast superiority at all points. The Spectator, Mr. Irving, and Mr. Hawthorne have in common that tranquil and subdued manner which we have chosen to denominate *repose*; but, in the case of the two former, this repose is attained rather by the absence of novel combination, or of originality, than otherwise, and consists chiefly in the calm, quiet, unostentatious expression of commonplace thoughts, in an unambitious, unadulterated Saxon. In them, by strong effort, we are made to conceive the absence of all. In the essays before us the absence of effort is too obvious to be mistaken, and a strong undercurrent of *suggestion* runs continuously beneath the upper stream of the tranquil thesis. In short, these effusions of Mr. Hawthorne are the product of a truly imaginative intellect, restrained, and in some measure repressed, by fastidiousness of taste, by constitutional melancholy and by indolence.

But it is of his tales that we desire principally to speak. The tale proper, in our opinion, affords unquestionably the fairest field for the exercise of the loftiest talent, which can be afforded by the wide domains of mere prose. Were we bidden to say how the highest genius could be most advantageously employed for the best display of its own powers, we should answer, without hesitation—in the composition of a rhymed poem, not to exceed in length what might be perused in an hour. Within this limit alone can the highest order of true poetry exist. We need only here say, upon this topic, that, in almost all classes of composition, the unity of effect or impression is a point of the greatest importance. It is clear, moreover, that this unity cannot be thoroughly preserved in productions whose perusal cannot be completed at one sitting. We may continue the reading of a prose composition, from the very nature of prose itself, much longer than we can persevere, to any good purpose, in the perusal of a poem. This latter, if truly fulfilling the demands of the poetic sentiment, induces an exaltation of the soul which cannot be long sustained. All high excitements are necessarily transient. Thus a long poem is a paradox. And, without unity of impression, the deepest effects cannot be brought about. Epics were the offspring of an imperfect sense of Art, and their reign is no more. A poem *too* brief may produce a vivid, but never an intense or enduring impression. Without a certain continuity of effort—without a certain duration or repetition of purpose—the soul is never deeply moved. There must be the dropping of the water upon the rock. De Béranger has wrought brilliant things—pungent and spirit-stirring—but, like all immassive bodies, they lack *momentum,* and thus fail to satisfy the Poetic Sentiment. They sparkle and excite, but, from want of continuity, fail deeply to impress. Extreme brevity will degenerate into epigrammatism; but the sin of extreme length is even more unpardonable. *In medio tutissimus ibis.*

Were we called upon, however, to designate that class of composition which, next to such a poem as we have suggested, should best fulfil the demands of high genius—should offer it the most advantageous field of exertion—we should unhesitatingly speak of the prose tale, as Mr. Hawthorne has here exemplified it. We allude to the short prose narrative, requiring from a half-hour to one or two hours in its perusal. The ordinary novel is objectionable, from its length, for reasons already stated in substance. As it cannot be read at one sitting, it deprives itself, of course, of the immense force derivable from *totality.* Worldly interests intervening during the pauses of perusal, modify, annul, or counteract, in a greater or less degree, the impressions of the book. But simple cessation in reading, would, of itself, be sufficient to destroy the true unity. In the brief tale, however, the author is enabled to carry out the fullness of his intention, be it what it may. During the hour of perusal the soul of the reader is at the writer's control. There are no external or extrinsic influences—resulting from weariness or interruption.

A skilful literary artist has constructed a tale. If wise, he has not fashioned his thoughts to accommodate his incidents; but having conceived, with deliberate care, a certain unique or single effect to be wrought out, he then invents such incidents—he then combines such events as may best aid him in establishing this preconceived effect. If his very initial sentence tend not to the outbringing of this effect, then he has failed in his first step. In the whole composition there should be no word written, of which the tendency, direct or indirect, is not to the one pre-established design. And by such means, with such care and skill, a picture is at length painted which leaves in the mind of him who contemplates it with a kindred art, a sense of the fullest satisfaction. The idea of the tale has been presented unblemished, because undisturbed; and this is an end unattainable by the novel. Undue brevity is just as exceptionable here as in the poem; but undue length is yet more to be avoided.

We have said that the tale has a point of superiority even over the poem. In fact, while the *rhythm* of this latter is an essential aid in the development of the poet's highest idea—the idea of the Beautiful—the artificialities of this rhythm are an inseparable bar to the development of all points of thought or expression which have their basis in *Truth*. But Truth is often, and in very great degree, the aim of the tale. Some of the finest tales are tales of ratiocination. Thus the field of this species of composition, if not in so elevated a region on the mountain of Mind, is a table-land of far vaster extent than the domain of the mere poem. Its products are never so rich, but infinitely more numerous, and more appreciable by the mass of mankind. The writer of the prose tale, in short, may bring to his theme a vast variety of modes or inflections of thought and expression—(the ratiocinative, for example, the sarcastic, or the humorous) which are not only antagonistical to the nature of the poem, but absolutely forbidden by one of its most peculiar and indispensable adjuncts; we allude, of course, to rhythm. It may be added here, *par parenthèse*, that the author who aims at the purely beautiful in a prose tale is laboring at great disadvantage. For Beauty can be better treated in the poem. Not so with terror, or passion, or horror, or a multitude of such other points. And here it will be seen how full of prejudice are the usual animadversions against those *tales of effect,* many fine examples of which were found in the earlier numbers of Blackwood. The impressions produced were wrought in a legitimate sphere of action, and constituted a legitimate although sometimes an exaggerated interest. They were relished by every man of genius: although there were found many men of genius who condemned them without just ground. The true critic will but demand that the design intended be accomplished, to the fullest extent, by the means most advantageously applicable.

We have very few American tales of real merit—we may say, indeed, none, with the exception of "The Tales of a Traveller" of Washington Irving, and these "Twice-Told Tales" of Mr. Hawthorne. Some of the pieces of Mr. John Neal abound in vigor and originality; but in general, his compositions of this class are excessively diffuse, extravagant, and indicative of an imperfect sentiment of Art. Articles at random are, now and then, met with in our periodicals which might be advantageously compared with the best effusions of the British Magazines; but, upon the whole, we are far behind our progenitors in this department of literature

Of Mr. Hawthorne's Tales we would say, emphatically, that they belong to the highest region of Art—an Art subservient to genius of a very lofty order. We had supposed, with good reason for so supposing, that he had been thrust into his present position by one of the impudent *cliques* which beset our literature, and whose pretensions it is our full purpose to expose at the earliest opportunity; but we have been most agreeably mistaken. We know of few compositions which the critic can more honestly commend than these "Twice-Told Tales." As Americans, we feel proud of the book.

Mr. Hawthorne's distinctive trait is invention, creation, imagination, originality—a trait which, in the literature of fiction, is positively worth all the rest. But the nature of originality, so far as regards its manifestation in letters, is but imperfectly understood. The inventive or original mind as frequently displays itself in novelty of *tone* as in novelty of matter. Mr. Hawthorne is original at *all* points.

It would be a matter of some difficulty to designate the best of these tales; we repeat that, without exception, they are beautiful. "Wakefield" is remarkable for the skill with which an old idea—a well-known incident—is worked up or discussed. A man of whims conceives the purpose of quitting his wife and residing *incognito*, for twenty years, in her immediate neighborhood. Something of this kind actually happened in London. The force of Mr. Hawthorne's tale lies in the analysis of the motives which must or might have impelled the husband to such folly, in the first instance, with the possible causes of his perseverance. Upon this thesis a sketch of singular power has been constructed.

"The Wedding Knell" is full of the boldest imagination—an imagination fully controlled by taste. The most captious critic could find no flaw in this production.

"The Minister's Black Veil" is a masterly composition of which the sole defect is that to the rabble its exquisite skill will be *caviare*. The *obvious* meaning of this article will be found to smother its insinuated one. The *moral* put into the mouth of the dying minister will be supposed to convey the *true* import of the narrative; and that a crime of dark dye (having reference to the "young lady"), has been committed, is a point which only minds congenial with that of the author will perceive.

"Mr. Higginbotham's Catastrophe" is vividly original and managed most dexterously.

"Dr. Heidegger's Experiment" is exceedingly well imagined and executed with surpassing ability. The artist breathes in every line of it.

"The White Old Maid" is objectionable, even more than the "Minister's Black Veil," on the score of its mysticism. Even with the thoughtful and analytic, there will be much trouble in penetrating its entire import.

"The Hollow of the Three Hills" we would quote in full, had we space;— not as evincing higher talent than any of the other pieces, but as affording an excellent example of the author's peculiar ability. The subject is commonplace. A witch subjects the Distant and the Past to the view of a mourner. It has been the fashion to describe, in such cases, a mirror in which the images of the absent appear; or a cloud of smoke is made to arise, and thence the figures are gradually unfolded. Mr. Hawthorne has wonderfully heightened his effect by making the ear, in place of the eye, the medium by which the fantasy is conveyed. The head of the mourner is enveloped in the cloak of the witch, and within its magic folds there arise sounds which have an all-sufficient intelligence. Throughout this article also, the artist is conspicuous—not more in positive than in negative merits. Not only is all done that should be done, but (what perhaps is an end with more difficulty attained) there is nothing done which should not be. Every word *tells* and there is not a word which does *not* tell.

In "Howe's Masquerade" we observe something which resembles plagiarism—but which *may be* a very flattering coincidence of thought. We quote the passage in question.

"*With a dark flush of wrath* upon his brow they saw the general *draw his sword* and *advance to meet* the figure *in the cloak* before the latter had stepped one pace upon the floor.

"*'Villain, unmuffle yourself,*' cried he. 'you pass no farther!'

"The figure, without blenching a hair's breadth from the sword which was pointed at his breast, made a solemn pause, and *lowered the cape* of the cloak from his face, yet sufficiently for the spectators to catch a glimpse of it. But Sir

William Howe had evidently seen enough. The sternness of his countenance gave place to a look of wild amazement, if not horror, while he recoiled several steps from the figure, *and let fall his sword* upon the floor."—See vol. 2, page 20.

The idea here is, that the figure in the cloak is the phantom or reduplication of Sir William Howe; but in an article called "William Wilson," one of the "Tales of the Grotesque and Arabesque," we have not only the same idea, but the same idea similarly presented in several respects. We quote two paragraphs, which our readers may compare with what has been already given. We have italicized, above, the immediate particulars of resemblance.

"The brief moment in which I averted my eyes had been sufficient to produce, apparently, a material change in the arrangement at the upper or farther end of the room. A large mirror, it appeared to me, now stood where none had been perceptible before: and as I stepped up to it in extremity of terror, mine own image, but with features all pale and dabbled in blood, *advanced* with a feeble and tottering gait to meet me.

"Thus it appeared I say, but was not. It was Wilson, who then stood before me in the agonies of dissolution. Not a line in all the marked and singular lineaments of that face which was not even identically mine own. *His mask and cloak lay where he had thrown them, upon the floor.*"—Vol. 2 p. 57.

Here it will be observed that, not only are the two general conceptions identical, but there are various *points* of similarity. In each case the figure seen is the wraith or duplication of the beholder. In each case the scene is a masquerade. In each case the figure is cloaked. In each, there is a quarrel—that is to say, angry words pass between the parties. In each the beholder is enraged. In each the cloak and sword fall upon the floor. The "villain, unmuffle yourself," of Mr. H. is precisely paralleled by a passage at page 56 of "William Wilson."

In the way of objection we have scarcely a word to say of these tales. There is, perhaps, a somewhat too general or prevalent *tone*—a tone of melancholy and mysticism. The subjects are insufficiently varied. There is not so much of *versatility* evinced as we might well be warranted in expecting from the high powers of Mr. Hawthorne. But beyond these trivial exceptions we have really none to make. The style is purity itself. Force abounds. High imagination gleams from every page. Mr. Hawthorne is a man of the truest genius. We only regret that the limits of our Magazine will not permit us to pay him that full tribute of commendation, which, under other circumstances, we should be so eager to pay.

—Edgar Allan Poe, "Twice-Told Tales,"
Graham's Magazine, May 1842, pp. 298–300

NATHANIEL HAWTHORNE (1853)

From the press of Munroe & Co., Boston, in the year 1837 appeared *Twice-Told Tales*. Though not widely successful in their day and generation, they had the effect of making me known in my own immediate vicinity; insomuch that, however reluctantly, I was compelled to come out of my owl's nest and lionize in a small way. Thus I was gradually drawn somewhat into the world, and became pretty much like other people. My long seclusion had not made me melancholy or misanthropic, nor wholly unfitted me for the bustle of life; and perhaps it was the kind of discipline which my idiosyncrasy demanded, and chance and my own instincts, operating together, had caused me to do what was fittest.

> —Nathaniel Hawthorne, Letter to Richard Henry Stoddard
> (1853), cited in Julian Hawthorne, *Nathaniel Hawthorne*
> *and His Wife*, 1884, Vol. 1, p. 98

ALEXANDER SMITH
"A SHELF IN MY BOOKCASE" (1863)

Alexander Smith was a Scottish poet of the Victorian era. He was a member of the so-called and much maligned Spasmodic School. He also wrote novels and essays.

In this essay, Smith values Hawthorne's *Twice-Told Tales* over the later novels. He compares the two forms, and finds that he prefers the tales because "the novels were written for the world, while the tales seem written for the author." The tales provide a more intimate view of the author (Poe, too, valued the tale form over the novel for similar reasons).

Hawthorne has "none of the characteristics of a Yankee," but resembles rather the Puritan (a view echoed by Sir Leslie Stephen). "There is nothing modern about him." Smith praises above all the "monologues," and values most highly Hawthorne's use of humor. Students comparing Hawthorne's earlier and later work, his tales with his novels, may find Smith's sentiments useful.

First, then, on this special shelf stands Nathaniel Hawthorne's *Twice-Told Tales*. It is difficult to explain why I like these short sketches and essays, written in the author's early youth, better than his later, more finished, and better-known novels and romances. The world sets greater store by *The Scarlet Letter* and *Transformation* than by this little book—and, in such matters of liking against the judgment of the world, there is no appeal. I think the reason of my liking consists in this—that the novels were written for the world, while the tales seem written for the author; in these he is actor and audience in one. Consequently, one gets nearer him, just as one gets nearer an artist in his first sketch than in his finished picture. And after all, one takes the greatest pleasure in those books in which a peculiar personality is most clearly revealed. A thought may be very commendable *as* a thought, but I value it chiefly as a window through which I can obtain insight on the thinker; and Mr Hawthorne's personality is peculiar, and specially peculiar in a new country like America. He is quiet, fanciful, quaint, and his humour is shaded by a certain meditativeness of spirit. Although a Yankee, he partakes of none of the characteristics of a Yankee. His thinking and his style have an antique air. His roots strike down through the visible mould of the present, and draw sustenance from the generations under ground. The ghosts that haunt the chamber of his mind are the ghosts of dead men and women. He has a strong smack of the Puritan; he wears around him, in the New-England town, something of the darkness and mystery of the aboriginal forest. He is a shy, silent, sensitive, much-ruminating man, with no special overflow of animal spirits. He loves solitude and the things which age has made reverent. There is nothing modern about him. Emerson's writing has a cold cheerless glitter, like the new furniture in a warehouse, which will come of use by and by; Hawthorne's, the rich, subdued colour of furniture in a Tudor mansion-house—which has winked to long-extinguished fires, which has been toned by the usage of departed generations. In many of the *Twice-Told Tales* this peculiar personality is charmingly exhibited. He writes of the street or the sea-shore, his eye takes in every object, however trifling, and on these he hangs comments melancholy and humorous. He does not require to go far for a subject; he will stare on the puddles in the street of a New-England village, and immediately it becomes a Mediterranean Sea with empires lying on its muddy shores. If the sermon be written out fully in your heart, almost any text will be suitable—if you have to find your sermon *in* your text, you may search the Testament, New and Old, and be as poor at the close of Revelation as when you started at the first book of Genesis. Several of the papers which I like best are monologues, fanciful, humorous, or melancholy; and of these, my chief favourites are—"Sunday at Home," "Night Sketches," "Foot-prints on the Sea-shore," and the "Seven Vagabonds." This last seems to me almost the most exquisite thing which has flowed from its author's pen—a perfect little drama, the place a showman's waggon, the time the falling of a summer shower, full of subtle suggestions, which, if followed, will lead the reader away out of the story altogether; and illuminated by a grave, wistful kind of humour, which plays in turns upon the author's companions, and upon the author himself. Of all Mr Hawthorne's gifts, this gift of humour—which would light up the skull and cross-bones of a village churchyard, which would be silent at a dinner-table—is to me the most delightful.

Then this writer has a strangely weird power. He loves ruins like the ivy, he skims the twilight like the bat, he makes himself a familiar of the phantoms of the heart and brain. He believes in ghosts; perhaps he has seen one burst on him from the impalpable air. He is fascinated by the jarred brain and the ruined heart. Other men collect china, books, pictures, jewels, this writer collects singular human experiences, ancient wrongs and agonies, murders done on unfrequented roads, crimes that seem to have no motive, and all the dreary mysteries of the world of will. To his chamber of horrors Madame Tussaud's is nothing. With proud, prosperous, healthy men, Mr Hawthorne has little sympathy; he prefers a cracked piano to a new one, he likes cobwebs in the corner of his rooms. All this peculiar taste comes out strongly in the little book in whose praise I am writing. I read "The Minister's Black Veil," and find it the first sketch of the *Scarlet Letter*. In "Wakefield"—the story of the man who left his wife, remaining away twenty years, but who yet looked upon her every day to appease his burning curiosity as to her manner of enduring his absence—I find the keenest analysis of an almost incomprehensible act. And then Mr Hawthorne has a skill in constructing allegories which no one of his contemporaries, either English or American, possesses. These allegorical papers may be read with pleasure, for their ingenuity, their grace, their poetical feeling; but just as, gazing on the surface of a stream, admiring the ripples and eddies, and the widening rings made by the butterfly falling into it, you begin to be conscious that there is something at the bottom, and gradually a dead face wavers upwards from the oozy weeds, becoming every moment more clearly defined, so through Mr Hawthorne's graceful sentences, if read attentively, begins to flash the hidden meaning, a meaning, perhaps, the writer did not care to express formally and in set terms, and which he merely suggests and leaves the reader to make out for himself. If you have the book I am writing about, turn up "David Swan," "The Great Carbuncle," "The Fancy Show-box," and after you have read these, you will understand what I mean.

—Alexander Smith, "A Shelf in My Bookcase,"
Dreamthorp, 1863, pp. 190–94

MOSSES FROM AN OLD MANSE

Nathaniel Hawthorne
(1846)

This fascinating letter will be vital to any study comparing Hawthorne's work to Poe's. The extent to which Hawthorne agrees with Poe is spelled out succinctly here, as is the extent of their disagreement.

Poe's subsequent review follows. Written in November but published more than a year later, it should be read in light of Hawthorne's letter. The first part quotes Poe's views from July 1846, immediately after receiving the book and the letter. Poe's opinions have altered somewhat. He is more willing to find fault with Hawthorne. His identification with Hawthorne five years earlier seems to have ended. One biographer has described this review as "marred by an overall incoherence that bespeaks much conflict and even a difficulty in thinking clearly." The reason for Poe's disenchantment and his befuddlement may well be Hawthorne's identification (however ironic) with Emerson and New England in the book's preface and title. Poe detested Emerson and his Concord circle.

Like Melville and Fuller, Poe discourses on Hawthorne's notable lack of popularity. Poe seeks to justify this, however, while the other critics lament it. Poe points to Hawthorne's over-reliance on allegory—a device he derides at some length—and on the limits of Hawthorne's originality and peculiarity. Poe particularly insists on Hawthorne's stylistic borrowings from the German writer of tales Ludwig Tieck (a claim seconded later by Lowell in his "A Fable for Critics"). This is perhaps another case of Poe's unwitting doubling of himself with Hawthorne, since critics found Poe's own early tales to be derivative of Tieck.

My dear Sir,

I presume the publishers will have sent you a copy of 'Mosses from an Old Manse'—the latest (and, probably, the last) collection of my tales and sketches. I have read your occasional notices of my productions with great interest—not so much because your judgment was, upon the whole, favourable, as because it seemed to be given in earnest. I care for nothing but the truth; and shall always much more readily accept a harsh truth, in regard to my writings, than a sugared falsehood.

I confess, however, that I admire you rather as a writer of Tales, than as a critic upon them. I might often—and often do—dissent from your opinions, in the latter capacity, but could never fail to recognize your force and originality, in the former.

> —Nathaniel Hawthorne, Letter to Edgar Allan Poe, June 17, 1846,
> in Joel Myerson (ed.), *Selected Letters of Nathaniel Hawthorne,*
> Columbus, OH: Ohio State University, 2002, p. 123

MARGARET FULLER (1846)

In this review, Fuller addresses the disparity between Hawthorne's reputation and his popularity (a theme continued by Melville in his entry from 1850). Fuller meditates on American expansion—the development of the frontier as well as the development of print media—and laments the glut of middling or poor fiction appearing on the market. The sheer proliferation of titles and the excessive amount of promotion and uncritical endorsement many of them received means that Hawthorne's work is lost in the welter of available books. Students interested in Hawthorne's place in the marketplace will find much valuable insight here.

Fuller finds Hawthorne's "range of subjects" has increased since *Twice-Told Tales*, but regrets that his apparitions remain intangible. Hawthorne does not explain; he "intimates and suggests," but does not "lay bear the mysteries of our being." Fuller describes "Young Goodman Brown" in terms that seem, to the contemporary reader, to anticipate twentieth-century existentialism. Hawthorne describes a scene where "the gods of the hearth . . . crumble and nothing, nothing is left." Any student considering the philosophical aspect of Hawthorne's work may also find Fuller's insights pertinent.

We have been seated here the last ten minutes, pen in hand, thinking what we can possibly say about this book that will not be either superfluous or impertinent.

Superfluous, because the attractions of Hawthorne's writings cannot fail of one and the same effect on all persons who possess the common sympathies of men. To all who are still happy in some groundwork of unperverted Nature, the delicate, simple, human tenderness, unsought, unbought and therefore precious morality, the tranquil elegance and playfulness, the humour which never breaks the impression of sweetness and dignity, do an inevitable message which requires no comment of the critic to make its meaning clear. Impertinent, because the influence of this mind, like that of some loveliest aspects of Nature, is to induce silence from a feeling of repose. We do not think of any thing particularly worth saying about this that has been so fitly and pleasantly said.

Yet it seems *un*fit that we, in our office of chronicler of intellectual advents and apparitions, should omit to render open and audible honour to one whom we have long delighted to honour. It may be, too, that this slight notice of ours may awaken the attention of those distant or busy who might not otherwise search for the volume, which comes betimes in the leafy month of June.

So we will give a slight account of it, even if we cannot say much of value. Though Hawthorne has now a standard reputation, both for the qualities we have mentioned and the beauty of the style in which they are embodied, yet we believe he has not been very widely read. This is only because his works have not been published in the way to ensure extensive circulation in this new, hurrying world of ours. The immense extent of country over which the reading (still very small in proportion to the mere working) community is scattered, the rushing and pushing of our life at this electrical stage of development, leave no work a chance to be speedily and largely known that is not trumpeted and placarded. And, odious as are the features of a forced and artificial circulation, it must be considered that it does no harm in the end. Bad books will not be read if they are bought instead of good, while the good have an abiding life in the log-cabin settlements and Red River steamboat landings, to which they would in no other way penetrate. Under the auspices of Wiley and Putnam, Hawthorne will have a chance to collect all his own public about him, and that be felt as a presence which before was only a rumor.

The volume before us shares the charms of Hawthorne's earlier tales: the only difference being that his range of subjects is a little wider. There is the same gentle and sincere companionship with Nature, the same delicate but fearless scrutiny of the secrets of the heart, the same serene independence of petty and artificial restrictions, whether on opinions or conduct, the same familiar, yet pensive sense of the spiritual or demoniacal influences that haunt the palpable life and common walks of men, not by many apprehended except in results. We have here to regret that Hawthorne, at this stage of his mind's life, lays no more decisive hand upon the apparition—brings it no nearer than in former days. We had hoped that we should see, no more as in a glass darkly, but face to face. Still, still brood over his page the genius of revery and the nonchalance of Nature, rather than the ardent earnestness of the human soul which feels itself born not only to see and disclose, but to understand and interpret such things. Hawthorne intimates and suggests, but he does not lay bare the mysteries of our being.

The introduction to the *Mosses*, in which the old manse, its inhabitants and visitants are portrayed, is written with even more than his usual charm of placid grace and many strokes of his admirable good sense. Those who are not, like ourselves, familiar with the scene and its denizens, will still perceive how true that picture must be; those of us who are thus familiar will best know how to prize the record of objects and influences unique in our country and time.

'The Birth Mark' and 'Rapaccini's [sic] Daughter,' embody truths of profound importance in shapes of aerial elegance. In these, as here and there in all these pieces, shines the loveliest ideal of love, and the beauty of feminine purity (by which we mean no mere acts or abstinences, but perfect single truth felt and done in gentleness) which is its root.

'The Celestial Railroad,' for its wit, wisdom, and the graceful adroitness with which the natural and material objects are interwoven with the allegories, has already won its meed of admiration. 'Fire-worship' is a most charming essay for its domestic sweetness and thoughtful life. 'Goodman Brown' is one of those disclosures we have spoken of, of the secrets of the breast. Who has not known such a trial that is capable indeed of sincere aspiration toward that only good, that infinite essence, which men call God. Who has not known the hour when even that best beloved image cherished as the one precious symbol left, in the range of human nature, believed to be still pure gold when all the rest have turned to clay, shows, in severe ordeal, the symptoms of alloy. Oh, hour of anguish, when the old familiar faces grow dark and dim in the lurid light—when the gods of the hearth, honoured in childhood, adored in youth, crumble, and nothing, nothing is left which the daily earthly feelings can embrace—can cherish with unbroken faith! Yet some survive that trial more happily than young Goodman Brown. They are those who have not sought it—have never of their own accord walked forth with the Tempter into the dim shades of Doubt. Mrs Bull-Frog is an excellent humourous [sic] picture of what is called to be 'content at last with substantial realities!!' The 'Artist of the Beautiful' presents in a form that is, indeed, beautiful, the opposite view as to what are the substantial realities of life. Let each man choose between them according to his kind. Had Hawthorne written 'Roger Malvin's Burial' alone, we should be pervaded with the sense of the poetry and religion of his soul.

As a critic, the style of Hawthorne, faithful to his mind, shows repose, a great reserve of strength, a slow secure movement. Though a very refined, he is also a very clear writer, showing, as we said before, a placid grace, and an indolent command of language.

And now, beside the full, calm yet romantic stream of his mind, we will rest. It has refreshment for the weary, islets of fascination no less than dark recesses and shadows for the imaginative, pure reflections for the pure of heart and eye, and like the Concord he so well describes, many exquisite lilies for him who knows how to get at them.

—Margaret Fuller, *New York Daily Tribune*,
June 22, 1846, p. 1, reported in *Papers on
Literature and Art*, London, 1846, pp. 143–46

ANONYMOUS (1846)

Under this somewhat quaint title Mr Hawthorne has given us an exquisite collection of essays, allegories, and stories, replete with fancy, humor and sentiment. Many of them have been published before in the magazines, but are well worthy of their present permanent form. The description of the old Manse, Buds and Bird Voices, The Hall of Fantasy, The Celestial Railroad, The Procession of Life, P's Correspondence, and Earth's Holocaust, are among the most striking in the collection and, in the finer qualities of mind and style, rank among the best productions of American literature. There is a felicity and evanescent grace to Mr Hawthorne's humor, to which no other American can lay claim. We fear that it is almost too fine for popularity. It provokes no laughter, yet makes the 'sense of satisfaction ache' with its felicity of touch, and nicety of discrimination. He is even a finer and deeper humorist, we think, than Addison or Goldsmith, or Irving, though not so obvious and striking in his mirth. As he is a poet and man of genius in his humor, he is as felicitous in his representation of the serious as of the comic side of things; or rather, he so interlaces the serious with the comic that their division lines are scarcely observable. These *Mosses*, and the *Twice-told Tales*, are certain of a life far beyond the present generation of readers.

—Anonymous, *Graham's Magazine*, XXIX, August 1846, pp. 107–08

EDGAR ALLAN POE (1847)

In the preface to my sketches of New York Literati [June 1846], while speaking of the broad distinction between the seeming public and real private opinion respecting our authors, I thus alluded to Nathaniel Hawthorne:—

"For example, Mr. Hawthorne, the author of 'Twice-Told Tales,' is scarcely recognized by the press or by the public, and when noticed at all, is noticed merely to be damned by faint praise. Now, my own opinion of him is, that although his walk is limited and he is fairly to be charged with mannerism, treating all subjects in a similar tone of dreamy innuendo, yet in this walk he evinces extraordinary genius, having no rival either in America or elsewhere; and this opinion I have never heard gainsaid by any one literary person in the country. That this opinion, however, is a spoken and not a written one, is referable to the facts, first, that Mr. Hawthorne *is* a poor man, and, secondly, that he is *not* an ubiquitous quack."

The reputation of the author of "Twice-Told Tales" has been confined, indeed, until very lately, to literary society; and I have not been wrong, perhaps, in citing him as the example, *par excellence*, in this country, of the privately-admired and publicly-unappreciated man of genius. Within the last year or two, it is true, an occasional critic has been urged, by honest indignation, into very warm approval. Mr. Webber, for instance, (than whom no one has a keener relish for that kind of writing which Mr. Hawthorne has best illustrated,) gave us, in a late number of "The American Review," a cordial and certainly a full tribute to his talents; and since the issue of the "Mosses from an Old Manse," criticisms of similar tone have been by no means infrequent in our more authoritative journals. I can call to mind few reviews of Hawthorne published *before* the "Mosses." One I remember in "Arcturus" (edited by Matthews and Duyckinck) for May, 1841; another in the "American Monthly" (edited by Hoffman and Herbert) for March, 1838; a third in the ninety-sixth number of the "North American Review." These criticisms, however, seemed to have little effect on the popular taste—at least, if we are to form any idea of the popular taste by reference to its expression in the newspapers, or by the sale of the author's book. It was never the fashion (until lately) to speak of him in any summary of our best authors. The daily critics would say, on such occasions, "Is there not Irving and Cooper, and Bryant and Paulding, and—Smith?" or, "Have we not Halleck and Dana, and Longfellow and—Thompson?" or, "Can we not point triumphantly to our own Sprague, Willis, Channing, Bancroft, Prescott and—Jenkins?" but these unanswerable queries were never wound up by the name of Hawthorne.

Beyond doubt, this inappreciation of him on the part of the public arose chiefly from the two causes to which I have referred—from the facts that he is neither a man of wealth nor a quack;—but these are insufficient to account for the whole effect. No small portion of it is attributable to the very marked idiosyncrasy of Mr. Hawthorne himself. In one sense, and in great measure, to be peculiar is to be original, and than the true originality there is no higher literary virtue. This true or commendable originality, however, implies not the uniform, but the continuous peculiarity—a peculiarity springing from ever-active vigor of fancy—better still if from ever-present force of imagination, giving its own hue, its own character to everything it touches, and, especially *self impelled to touch everything.*

It is often said, inconsiderately, that very original writers always fail in popularity—that such and such persons are too original to be comprehended by the mass. "Too peculiar," should be the phrase, "too idiosyncratic." It is, in fact, the excitable, undisciplined and child-like popular mind which most keenly feels the original. The criticism of the conservatives, of the hackneys, of the cultivated old clergymen of the "North American Review," is precisely the criticism which condemns and alone condemns it. "It becometh not a divine," saith Lord Coke, "to be of a fiery and salamandrine spirit." Their conscience allowing them to move nothing themselves, these dignitaries have a holy horror of being moved. "Give us *quietude*," they say. Opening their mouths with proper caution, they sigh forth the word "*Repose*." And this is, indeed, the one thing they should be permitted to enjoy, if only upon the Christian principle of give and take.

The fact is, that if Mr. Hawthorne were really original, he could not fail of making himself felt by the public. But the fact is, he is *not* original in any sense. Those who speak of him as original, mean nothing more than that he differs in his manner or tone, and in his choice of subjects, from any author of their acquaintance—their acquaintance not extending to the German Tieck, whose manner, in *some* of his works, is absolutely identical with that *habitual* to Hawthorne. But it is clear that the element of the literary originality is novelty. The element of its appreciation by the reader is the reader's sense of the new. Whatever gives him a new and insomuch a pleasurable emotion, he considers original, and whoever frequently gives him such emotion, he considers an original writer. In a word, it is by the sum total of these emotions that he decides upon the writer's claim to originality. I may observe here, however, that there is clearly a point at which even novelty itself would cease to produce the legitimate originality, if we judge this originality, as we should, by the effect designed: this point is that at which *novelty becomes nothing novel*; and here the artist, *to preserve his originality*, will subside into the common-place. . . .

These points properly understood, it will be seen that the critic (unacquainted with Tieck) who reads a single tale or essay by Hawthorne, may be justified in thinking him original; but the tone, or manner, or choice of subject, which induces in this critic the sense of the new, will—if not in a second tale, at least in a third and all subsequent ones—not only fail of inducing it, but bring about an exactly antagonistic impression. In concluding a volume and more especially in concluding all the volumes of the author, the critic will abandon his first design of calling him "original," and content himself with styling him "peculiar." . . .

The "peculiarity" or sameness, or monotone of Hawthorne, would, in its mere character of "peculiarity," and without reference to what is the peculiarity, suffice to deprive him of all chance of popular appreciation. But at his failure to be appreciated, we can, of course, no longer wonder, when we find him monotonous at decidedly the worst of all possible points—at that point which, having the least concern with Nature, is the farthest removed from the popular intellect, from the popular sentiment and from the popular taste. I allude to the strain of allegory which completely overwhelms the greater number of his subjects, and which in some measure interferes with the direct conduct of absolutely all.

In defence of allegory, (however, or for whatever object, employed,) there is scarcely one respectable word to be said. Its best appeals are made to the fancy that is to say, to our sense of adaptation, not of matters proper, but of matters improper for the purpose, of the real with the unreal, having never more of intelligible connection than has something with nothing, never half so much of effective affinity as has the substance for the shadow. The deepest emotion aroused within us by the happiest allegory, as allegory, is a very, very imperfectly satisfied sense of the writer's ingenuity in overcoming a difficulty we should have preferred his not having attempted to overcome. The fallacy of the idea that allegory, in any of its moods, can be made to enforce a truth— that metaphor, for example, may illustrate as well as embellish an argument— could be promptly demonstrated: the converse of the supposed fact might be shown, indeed, with very little trouble—but these are topics foreign to my present purpose. One thing is clear, that if allegory ever establishes a fact, it is by dint of overturning a fiction. Where the suggested meaning runs through the obvious one in a very profound under-current, so as never to interfere with the upper one without our own volition, so as never to show itself unless called to the surface, there only, for the proper uses of fictitious narrative, is it available at all. Under the best circumstances, it must always interfere with that unity of effect which, to the artist, is worth all the allegory in the world. Its vital injury, however, it rendered to the most vitally important point in fiction—that of earnestness or verisimilitude. That "The Pilgrim's Progress" is a ludicrously over-rated book, owing its seeming popularity to one or two of those accidents in critical literature which by the critical are sufficiently well understood, is a matter upon which no two thinking people disagree; but the pleasure derivable from it, in any sense, will be found in the direct ratio of the reader's capacity to smother its true purpose, in the direct ratio of his ability to keep the allegory out of sight, or of his inability to comprehend it. Of allegory properly handled, judiciously subdued, seen only as a shadow or by suggestive glimpses, and making its nearest approach to truth in a not obtrusive and therefore not unpleasant appositeness, the "Undine" of De La Motte Fouqué is the best, and undoubtedly a very remarkable specimen.

The obvious causes, however, which have prevented Mr. Hawthorne's popularity, do not suffice to condemn him in the eyes of the few who belong properly to books, and to whom books, perhaps, do not quite so properly belong. These few estimate an author, not as do the public, altogether by what he does, but in great measure—indeed, even in the greatest measure—by what he evinces a capability of doing. In this view, Hawthorne stands among literary people in America in much the same light as Coleridge in England. The few, also, through a certain warping of the taste, which long pondering upon books as books never fails to induce, are not in condition to view the errors of a scholar as errors altogether. At any time these gentlemen are prone to think the public not right rather than an educated author wrong. But the simple truth is, that the writer who aims at impressing the people, is always wrong when he fails in forcing that people to receive the impression. How far Mr. Hawthorne has addressed the people at all, is, of course, not a question for me to decide. His books afford strong internal evidence of having been written to himself and his particular friends alone.

—Edgar Allan Poe, *Godey's Lady's Book*, November 1847,
reprinted in Poe, *Essays and Reviews*
(Ed. G.R. Thompson), pp. 577–83

Herman Melville
"Hawthorne and His Mosses. By a Virginian Spending July in Vermont" (1850)

Melville's whimsical but penetrating essay has been called "one of the strangest pieces of literary criticism by an American in the nineteenth-century." It is as much fiction as it is criticism. Ostensibly penned "by a Virginian Spending July in Vermont," Melville was actually a New Yorker residing, at the time of the essay's composition, in Pittsfield,

Massachusetts. He was also given Hawthorne's book by his aged Aunt Mary, not, as he claims, by a dryadic cousin Cherry. More significantly, he had already met Hawthorne—although only very recently—when he wrote the piece. The air of ecstatic conjecture is only a pose.

Like Poe's review of *Twice-Told Tales*, Melville's essay is more about the author than about Hawthorne. Poe's seemed like a personal manifesto; Hawthorne's is a campaign tract. "True, I have been braying myself," he concedes. Yet "as I now write, I am Posterity speaking by proxy." Importantly, Melville is allying himself with Hawthorne in print. "I cannot but be charmed by the coincidence; especially, when it shows such a parity of ideas, at least, in this one point, between a man like Hawthorne and a man like me."

When he does write directly about Hawthorne, his subject mirrors Fuller's; Melville discusses popularity and the exploding fictional marketplace, lamenting that "so many books [are] called 'excellent'." Hawthorne is a victim of this glut of praise for what are essentially mediocre creations. He is "perhaps too deserving of popularity to be popular." (Contrast this with Melville's later letter to Hawthorne celebrating the ubiquity of *The Blithedale Romance*). Melville ponders the reason for this lack of popularity. Maintaining his inquiry into the state of authorship, Melville examines the public's misperceptions of Hawthorne. He is seen as "a pleasant writer, with a pleasant style," but essentially "harmless." Melville's insights will be of particular use to students exploring public perceptions and receptions of Hawthorne and his work.

Melville suspects that Hawthorne fosters this persona: "he rather prefers to be generally esteemed a so-so sort of author." Correcting this error is Melville's subject and object: Hawthorne's is "a great, deep intellect, which drops down into the universe like a plummet." Melville's own version of Hawthorne is, of course, biased. It is almost mythical ("this Mossy Man" "this sweet Man of Mosses") and often it seems more like a representation of Melville himself.

Melville muses about Hawthorne's "intricate, profound heart" and expounds at some length on his capacity for darkness ("that blackness in Hawthorne"), deducing that Hawthorne must have suffered at "some time or other and in some shape or other," since only then can one depict suffering in others. When Julian Hawthorne visited Melville, much later and when the novelist languished in obscurity, Melville cryptically claimed that he always sensed that Hawthorne had some dark secret that he had never revealed. Such a conjecture clashes with Margaret Fuller's plaint that Hawthorne was altogether too bookish and outside the true thrust of life. Students exploring Hawthorne's pragmatism and use of his own life should consider Melville's views.

Melville becomes most insistent when he discusses nationalism and American independence from English and European literatures. He explicitly challenges Sidney Smith's famous question "in the four quarters of the globe, who reads an American book?" Shakespeare becomes for Melville a symbol of how America is cowed and strangled by English literature. Melville challenges anxieties about originality, fame, and influence and calls for the yoke to be thrown off. This he does by challenging the precedents, and vaunting the alternative: Hawthorne. (Emerson is pointedly rejected.) "I do not say that Nathaniel of Salem, is a greater than William of Avon, or as great. But the difference between the two men is by no means immeasurable."

"This Hawthorne is here almost alone in his generation," Melville opines, asserting that *Mosses from an Old Manse* will be considered Hawthorne's masterpiece. This essay will especially gratify students tracing the extent of Hawthorne's debt to English precedents. It will serve students interested in Hawthorne's place in the literary marketplace, and of course students focusing particularly on Hawthorne's relationship with Melville.

—ⁿⁿⁿ— —ⁿⁿⁿ— —ⁿⁿⁿ—

A papered chamber in a fine old farm-house—a mile from any other dwelling, and dipped to the eaves in foliage—surrounded by mountains, old woods, and Indian ponds,—this, surely is the place to write of Hawthorne. Some charm is in this northern air, for love and duty seem both impelling to the task. A man of a deep and noble nature has seized me in this seclusion. His wild, witch voice rings through me; or, in softer cadences, I seem to hear it in the songs of the hill-side birds, that sing in the larch trees at my window.

Would that all excellent books were foundlings, without father or mother, that so it might be, we could glorify them, without including their ostensible authors. Nor would any true man take exception to this;—least of all, he who writes,—"When the Artist rises high enough to achieve the Beautiful, the symbol by which he makes it perceptible to mortal senses becomes of little value in his eyes, while his spirit possesses itself in the enjoyment of the reality."

But more than this, I know not what would be the right name to put on the title-page of an excellent book, but this I feel, that the names of all fine authors are fictitious ones, far more than that of Junius,—simply standing, as they do, for the mystical, ever-eluding Spirit of all Beauty, which ubiquitously possesses men of genius. Purely imaginative as this fancy may appear, it nevertheless seems to receive some warranty from the fact, that on a personal interview no great author has ever come up to the idea of his reader. But that dust of which our bodies are composed, how can it fitly express the nobler intelligences among us? With reverence be it spoken, that not even in the case of one deemed more than man, not even in our Saviour, did his visible frame betoken anything of the augustness of the nature within. Else, how could those Jewish eyewitnesses fail to see heaven in his glance.

It is curious, how a man may travel along a country road, and yet miss the grandest, or sweetest of prospects, by reason of an intervening hedge, so like all other hedges, as in no way to hint of the wide landscape beyond. So has it been with me concerning the enchanting landscape in the soul of this Hawthorne, this most excellent Man of Mosses. His "Old Manse" has been written now four years, but I never read it till a day or two since. I had seen it in the book-stores—heard of it often—even had it recommended to me by a tasteful friend, as a rare, quiet book, perhaps too deserving of popularity to be popular. But there are so many books called "excellent," and so much unpopular merit, that amid the thick stir of other things, the hint of my tasteful friend was disregarded; and for four years the Mosses on the Old Manse never refreshed me with their perennial green. It may be, however, that all this while, the book, like wine, was only improving in flavor and body. At any rate, it so chanced that this long procrastination eventuated in a happy result. At breakfast the other day, a mountain girl, a cousin of mine, who for the last two weeks has every morning helped me to strawberries and raspberries,—which like the roses and pearls in the fairy-tale, seemed to fall into the saucer from those strawberry-beds her cheeks,—this delightful creature, this charming Cherry says to me—"I see you spend your mornings in the hay-mow; and yesterday I found there 'Dwight's Travels in New England'. Now I have something far better than that,—something more congenial to our summer on these hills. Take these raspberries, and then I will give you some moss."—"Moss!" said I—"Yes, and you must take it to the barn with you, and good-bye to 'Dwight.'"

With that she left me, and soon returned with a volume, verdantly bound, and garnished with a curious frontispiece in green,—nothing less, than a fragment of real moss cunningly pressed to a fly-leaf.—"Why this," said I, spilling my raspberries, "this is the 'Mosses from an Old Manse.'" "Yes," said cousin Cherry, "yes, it is that flowery Hawthorne."—"Hawthorne and Mosses," said I, "no more: it is morning: it is July in the country: and I am off for the barn."

Stretched on that new mown clover, the hill-side breeze blowing over me through the wide barn door, and soothed by the hum of the bees in the meadows around, how magically stole over me this Mossy Man! And how amply, how bountifully, did he redeem that delicious promise to his guests in the Old Manse, of whom it is written—"Others could give them pleasure, or amusement, or instruction—these could be picked up anywhere—but it was for me to give them rest. Rest, in a life of trouble! What better could be done for weary and world-worn spirits? what better could be done for anybody, who came within our magic circle, than to throw the spell of a magic spirit over them?"—So all that day, half-buried in the new clover, I watched this Hawthorne's "Assyrian dawn, and Paphian sunset and moonrise, from the summit of our Eastern Hill."

The soft ravishments of the man spun me round in a web of dreams, and when the book was closed, when the spell was over, this wizard "dismissed me with but misty reminiscences, as if I had been dreaming of him."

What a mild moonlight of contemplative humor bathes that Old Manse!— the rich and rare distilment of a spicy and slowly-oozing heart. No rollicking rudeness, no gross fun fed on fat dinners, and bred in the lees of wine,—but a humor so spiritually gentle, so high, so deep, and yet so richly relishable, that it were hardly inappropriate in an angel. It is the very religion of mirth; for nothing so human but it may be advanced to that. The orchard of the Old Manse seems the visible type of the fine mind that has described it. Those twisted, and contorted old trees, "that stretch out their crooked branches, and take such hold of the imagination, that we remember them as humorists and odd-fellows." And then, as surrounded by these grotesque forms, and hushed in the noon-day repose of this Hawthorne's spell, how aptly might the still fall of his ruddy thoughts into your soul be symbolized by "the thump of a great apple, in the stillest afternoon, falling without a breath of wind, from the mere necessity of perfect ripeness"! For no less ripe than ruddy are the apples of the thoughts and fancies in this sweet Man of Mosses.

"Buds and Bird-Voices"—What a delicious thing is that!—"Will the world ever be so decayed, that Spring may not renew its greenness?"—And the "Fire-Worship." Was ever the hearth so glorified into an altar before? The mere title of that piece is better than any common work in fifty folio volumes. How exquisite is this:—"Nor did it lessen the charm of his soft, familiar courtesy and helpfulness, that the mighty spirit, were opportunity offered him, would run riot through the peaceful house, wrap its inmates in his terrible embrace, and leave nothing of them save their whitened bones. This possibility of mad destruction only made his domestic kindness the more beautiful and touching. It was so sweet of him, being endowed with such power, to dwell, day after day, and one long, lonesome night after another, on the dusky hearth, only now and then betraying his wild nature, by thrusting his red tongue out of the chimney-top! True, he had done much mischief in the world, and was pretty certain to do more, but his warm heart atoned for all. He was kindly to the race of man."

But he has still other apples, not quite so ruddy, though full as ripe:— apples, that have been left to wither on the tree, after the pleasant autumn gathering is past. The sketch of "The Old Apple Dealer" is conceived in the subtlest spirit of sadness; he whose "subdued and nerveless boyhood prefigured his abortive prime, which, likewise, contained within itself the prophecy and image of his lean and torpid age." Such touches as are in this piece can not proceed from any common heart. They argue such a depth of tenderness, such a boundless sympathy with all forms of being, such an omnipresent love, that we must needs say, that this Hawthorne is here almost alone in his generation,—at least, in the artistic manifestation of these things. Still more. Such touches as these,—and many, very many similar ones, all through his chapters—furnish clews, whereby we enter a little way into the intricate, profound heart where they originated. And we see, that suffering, some time or other and in some shape or other,—this only can enable any man to depict it in others. All over him, Hawthorne's melancholy rests like an Indian summer, which, though bathing a whole country in one softness, still reveals the distinctive hue of every towering hill, and each far-winding vale.

But it is the least part of genius that attracts admiration. Where Hawthorne is known, he seems to be deemed a pleasant writer, with a pleasant style,—a sequestered, harmless man, from whom any deep and weighty thing would hardly be anticipated:—a man who means no meanings. But there is no man, in whom humor and love, like mountain peaks, soar to such a rapt height, as to receive the irradiations of the upper skies;—there is no man in whom humor and love are developed in that high form called genius; no such man can exist without also possessing, as the indispensable complement of these, a great, deep intellect, which drops down into the universe like a plummet. Or, love and humor are only the eyes, through which such an intellect views this world. The great beauty in such a mind is but the product of its strength. What, to all readers, can be more charming than the piece entitled "Monsieur du Miroir"; and to a reader at all capable of fully fathoming it, what at the same time, can possess more mystical depth of meaning?—Yes, there he sits, and looks at me,—this "shape of mystery," this "identical Monsieur du Miroir."—"Methinks I should tremble now, were his wizard power of gliding through all impediments in search of me, to place him suddenly before my eyes."

How profound, nay appalling, is the moral evolved by the "Earth's Holocaust"; where—beginning with the hollow follies and affectations of the world,—all vanities and empty theories and forms, are, one after another, and by an admirably graduated, growing comprehensiveness, thrown into the allegorical fire, till, at length, nothing is left but the all-engendering heart of man; which remaining still unconsumed, the great conflagration is naught.

Of a piece with this, is the "Intelligence Office," a wondrous symbolizing of the secret workings in men's souls. There are other sketches, still more charged with ponderous import.

"The Christmas Banquet" and "The Bosom Serpent" would be fine subjects for a curious and elaborate analysis, touching the conjectural parts of the mind that produced them. For spite of all the Indian-summer sunlight on the hither side of Hawthorne's soul, the other side—like the dark half of the physical sphere—is shrouded in a blackness, ten times black. But this darkness but gives more effect to the ever-moving dawn, that forever advances through it, and circumnavigates his world. Whether Hawthorne has simply availed himself of this mystical blackness as a means to the wondrous effects he makes it to produce in his lights and shades; or whether there really lurks in him, perhaps unknown to himself, a touch of Puritanic gloom,—this, I cannot altogether tell. Certain it is, however, that this great power of blackness in him derives its force from its appeals to that Calvinistic sense of Innate Depravity and Original Sin, from whose visitations, in some shape or other, no deeply thinking mind is always and wholly free. For, in certain moods, no man can weigh this world, without throwing in something, somehow like Original Sin, to strike the uneven balance. At all events, perhaps no writer has ever wielded this terrific thought with greater terror than this same harmless Hawthorne. Still more: this black conceit pervades him, through and through. You may be witched by his sunlight,—transported by the bright gildings in the skies he builds over you;—but there is the blackness of darkness beyond; and even his bright gildings but fringe, and play upon the edges of thunder-clouds.—In one word, the world is mistaken in this Nathaniel Hawthorne. He himself must often have smiled at its absurd misconceptions of him. He is immeasurably deeper than the plummet of the mere critic. For it is not the brain that can test such a man; it is only the heart. You cannot come to know greatness by inspecting it; there is no glimpse to be caught of it, except by intuition; you need not ring it, you but touch it, and you find it is gold.

Now it is that blackness in Hawthorne, of which I have spoken, that so fixes and fascinates me. It may be, nevertheless, that it is too largely developed in him. Perhaps he does not give us a ray of his light for every shade of his dark. But however this may be, this blackness it is that furnishes the infinite obscure of his background,—that background, against which Shakespeare plays his grandest conceits, the things that have made for Shakespeare his loftiest, but most circumscribed renown, as the profoundest of thinkers. For by philosophers Shakespeare is not adored as the great man of tragedy and comedy.—"Off with his head! so much for Buckingham!" this sort of rant, interlined by another hand, brings down the house,—those mistaken souls, who dream of Shakespeare as a mere man of Richard-the-Third humps, and Macbeth daggers. But it is those deep far-away things in him; those occasional flashings-forth of the intuitive Truth in him; those short, quick probings at the very axis of reality:—these are the things that make Shakespeare, Shakespeare. Through the mouths of the dark characters of Hamlet, Timon, Lear, and Iago, he craftily says, or sometimes insinuates the things, which we feel to be so terrifically true, that it were all but madness for any good man, in his own proper character, to utter, or even hint of them. Tormented into desperation, Lear the frantic King tears off the mask, and speaks the sane madness of vital truth. But, as I before said, it is the least part of genius that attracts admiration. And so, much of the blind, unbridled admiration that has been heaped upon Shakespeare, has been lavished upon the least part of him. And few of his endless commentators and critics seem to have remembered, or even perceived, that the immediate products of a great mind are not so great, as that undeveloped, (and sometimes undevelopable) yet dimly-discernible greatness, to which these immediate products are but the infallible indices. In Shakespeare's tomb lies infinitely more than Shakespeare ever wrote. And if I magnify Shakespeare, it is not so much for what he did do, as for what he did not do, or refrained from doing. For in this world of lies, Truth is forced to fly like a scared white doe in the woodlands; and only by cunning glimpses will she reveal herself, as in Shakespeare and other masters of the great Art of Telling the Truth,—even though it be covertly, and by snatches.

But if this view of the all-popular Shakespeare be seldom taken by his readers, and if very few who extol him, have ever read him deeply, or, perhaps, only have seen him on the tricky stage, (which alone made, and is still making him his mere mob renown)—if few men have time, or patience, or palate, for the spiritual truth as it is in that great genius;—it is, then, no matter of surprise that in a contemporaneous age, Nathaniel Hawthorne is a man, as yet, almost utterly mistaken among men. Here and there, in some quiet armchair in the noisy town, or some deep nook among the noiseless mountains, he may be appreciated for something of what he is. But unlike Shakespeare, who was forced to the contrary course by circumstances, Hawthorne (either from simple disinclination, or else from inaptitude) refrains from all the popularizing noise and show of broad farce, and blood-besmeared tragedy; content with the still, rich utterances of a great intellect in repose, and which sends few thoughts into circulation, except they be arterialized at his large warm lungs, and expanded in his honest heart.

Nor need you fix upon that blackness in him, if it suit you not. Nor, indeed, will all readers discern it, for it is, mostly, insinuated to those who may best understand it, and account for it; it is not obtruded upon every one alike.

Some may start to read of Shakespeare and Hawthorne on the same page. They may say, that if an illustration were needed, a lesser light might have sufficed to elucidate this Hawthorne, this small man of yesterday. But I am not, willingly, one of those, who as touching Shakespeare at least, exemplify the maxim of Rochefoucauld, that "we exalt the reputation of some, in order to depress that of others";—who, to teach all noble-souled aspirants that there is no hope for them, pronounce Shakespeare absolutely unapproachable. But Shakespeare has been approached. There are minds that have gone as far as Shakespeare into the universe. And hardly a mortal man, who, at some time or other, has not felt as great thoughts in him as any you will find in Hamlet. We must not inferentially malign mankind for the sake of any one man, whoever he may be. This is too cheap a purchase of contentment for conscious mediocrity to make. Besides, this absolute and unconditional adoration of Shakespeare has grown to be a part of our Anglo Saxon superstitions. The Thirty-Nine Articles are now Forty. Intolerance has come to exist in this matter. You must believe in Shakespeare's unapproachability, or quit the country. But what sort of belief is this for an American, an man who is bound to carry republican progressiveness into Literature, as well as into Life? Believe me, my friends, that men not very much inferior to Shakespeare, are this day being born on the banks of the Ohio. And the day will come, when you shall say who reads a book by an Englishman that is a modern? The great mistake seems to be, that even with those Americans who look forward to the coming of a great literary genius among us, they somehow fancy he will come in the costume of Queen Elizabeth's day,—be a writer of dramas founded upon old English history, or the tales of Boccaccio. Whereas, great geniuses are parts of the times; they themselves are the time; and possess an correspondent coloring. It is of a piece with the Jews, who while their Shiloh was meekly walking in their streets, were still praying for his magnificent coming; looking for him in a chariot, who was already among them on an ass. Nor must we forget, that, in his own life-time, Shakespeare was not Shakespeare, but only Master William Shakespeare of the shrewd, thriving business firm of Condell, Shakespeare & Co., proprietors of the Globe Theater in London; and by a courtly author, of the name of Chettle, was hooted at, as an "upstart crow" beautified "with other birds' feathers." For, mark it well, imitation is often the first charge brought against real originality. Why this is so, there is not space to set forth here. You must have plenty of sea-room to tell the Truth in; especially, when it seems to have an aspect of newness, as America did in 1492, though it was then just as old, and perhaps older than Asia, only those sagacious philosophers, the common sailors, had never seen it before; swearing it was all water and moonshine there.

Now, I do not say that Nathaniel of Salem is a greater than William of Avon, or as great. But the difference between the two men is by no means immeasurable. Not a very great deal more, and Nathaniel were verily William.

This too, I mean, that if Shakespeare has not been equalled, give the world time, and he is sure to be surpassed, in one hemisphere or the other. Nor will it at all do to say, that the world is getting grey and grizzled now, and has lost that fresh charm which she wore of old, and by virtue of which the great poets of past times made themselves what we esteem them to be. Not so. The world is as young today, as when it was created, and this Vermont morning dew is as wet to my feet, as Eden's dew to Adam's. Nor has Nature been all over ransacked by our progenitors, so that no new charms and mysteries remain for this latter generation to find. Far from it. The trillionth part has not yet been said, and all that has been said, but multiplies the avenues to what remains to be said. It is not so much paucity, as superabundance of material that seems to incapacitate modern authors.

Let America then prize and cherish her writers, yea, let her glorify them. They are not so many in number, as to exhaust her good-will. And while she has good kith and kin of her own, to take to her bosom, let her not lavish her embraces upon the household of an alien. For believe it or not England, after all, is, in many things, an alien to us. China has more bowels of real love for us than she. But even were there no strong literary individualities among us, as there are some dozen at least, nevertheless, let America first praise mediocrity even, in her own children, before she praises (for everywhere, merit demands acknowledgment from every one) the best excellence in the children of any other land. Let her own authors, I say, have the priority of appreciation. I was very much pleased with a hot-headed Carolina cousin of mine, who once said,—"If there were no other American to stand by, in Literature,—why, then, I would stand by Pop Emmons and his 'Fredoniad,' and till a better epic came along, swear it was not very far behind the 'Iliad.'" Take away the words, and in spirit he was sound.

Not that American genius needs patronage in order to expand. For that explosive sort of stuff will expand though screwed up in a vice, and burst it, though it were triple steel. It is for the nation's sake, and not for her authors' sake, that I would have America be heedful of the increasing greatness among her writers. For how great the shame, if other nations should be before her, in crowning her heroes of the pen. But this is almost the case now. American authors have received more just and discriminating praise (however loftily and ridiculously given, in certain cases) even from some Englishmen, than from their own countrymen. There are hardly five critics in America, and several of them are asleep. As for patronage, it is the American author who now patronizes the country, and not his country him. And if at times some among them appeal to the people for more recognition, it is not always with selfish motives, but patriotic ones.

It is true, that but few of them as yet have evinced that decided originality which merits great praise. But that graceful writer, who perhaps of all Americans has received the most plaudits from his own country for his productions,—that very popular and amiable writer, however good, and self-reliant in many things, perhaps owes his chief reputation to the self-acknowledged imitation of a foreign model, and to the studied avoidance of all topics but smooth ones. But it is better to fail in originality, than to succeed in imitation. He who has never failed somewhere, that man can not be great. Failure is the true test of greatness. And if it be said, that continual success is a proof that a man wisely knows his powers,—it is only to be added, that, in that case, he knows them to be small. Let us believe it, then, once for all, that there is no hope for us in these smooth pleasing writers that know their powers. Without malice, but to speak the plain fact, they but furnish an appendix to Goldsmith, and other English authors. And we want no American Goldsmiths, nay, we want no American Miltons. It were the vilest thing you could say of a true American author, that he were an American Tompkins. Call him an American, and have done, for you can not say a nobler thing of him.—But it is not meant that all American writers should studiously cleave to nationality in their writings; only this, no American writer should write like an Englishman, or a Frenchman; let him write like a man, for then he will be sure to write like an American. Let us away with this leaven of literary flunkyism towards England. If either we must play the flunky in this thing, let England do it, not us. While we are rapidly preparing for that political supremacy among the nations, which prophetically awaits us at the close of the present century; in a literary point of view, we are deplorably unprepared for it; and we seem studious to remain so. Hitherto, reasons might have existed why this should be; but no good reason exists now. And all that is requisite to amendment in this matter, is simply this: that, while freely acknowledging all excellence, everywhere, we should refrain from unduly lauding foreign writers, and, at the same time, duly recognize the meritorious writers that are our own,—those writers, who breathe that unshackled, democratic spirit of Christianity in all things, which now takes the practical lead in the world, though at the same time led by ourselves—us Americans. Let us boldly contemn all imitation, though it comes to us graceful and fragrant as the morning; and foster all originality, though, at first, it be crabbed and ugly as our own pine knots. And if any of our authors fail, or seem to fail, then, in the words of my enthusiastic Carolina cousin, let us clap him on the shoulder, and back him against all Europe for his second round. The truth is, that in our point of view, this matter of a national literature has come to such a pass with us, that in some sense we must turn bullies, else the day is lost, or superiority so far beyond us, that we can hardly say it will ever be ours.

And now, my countrymen, as an excellent author, of your own flesh and blood,—an unimitating, and perhaps, in his way, an inimitable man—whom better can I commend to you, in the first place, than Nathaniel Hawthorne. He is one of the new, and far better generation of your writer. The smell of your beeches and hemlocks is upon him; your own broad prairies are in his soul; and if you travel away inland into his deep and noble nature, you will hear the far roar of his Niagara. Give not over to future generations the glad duty of acknowledging him for what he is. Take that joy to yourself, in your own generation; and so shall he feel those grateful impulses in him, that may possibly prompt him to the full flower of some still greater achievement in your eyes. And by confessing him, you thereby confess others, you brace the whole brotherhood. For genius, all over the world, stands hand in hand, and one shock of recognition runs the whole circle round.

In treating of Hawthorne, or rather of Hawthorne in his writings (for I never saw the man; and in the chances of a quiet plantation life, remote from his haunts, perhaps never shall) in treating of his works, I say, I have thus far omitted all mention of his "Twice Told Tales," and "Scarlet Letter." Both are excellent, but full of such manifold, strange and diffusive beauties, that time would all but fail me, to point the half of them out. But there are things in those two books, which, had they been written in England a century ago, Nathaniel Hawthorne had utterly displaced many of the bright names we now revere on authority. But I am content to leave Hawthorne to himself, and to the infallible finding of posterity; and however great may be the praise I have bestowed upon him, I feel, that in so doing, I have more served and honored myself, than him. For at bottom, great excellence is praise enough to itself; but the feeling of a sincere and appreciative love and admiration towards it, this is relieved by utterance; and warm, honest praise ever leaves a pleasant flavor in the mouth; and it is an honorable thing to confess to what is honorable in others.

But I cannot leave my subject yet. No man can read a fine author, and relish him to his very bones, while he reads, without subsequently fancying to himself some ideal image of the man and his mind. And if you rightly look for it, you will almost always find that the author himself has somewhere furnished you with his own picture. For poets (whether in prose or verse), being painters of Nature, are like their brethren of the pencil, the true portrait-painters, who, in the multitude of likenesses to be sketched, do not invariably omit their own; and in all high instances, they paint them without any vanity, though, at times, with a lurking something, that would take several pages to properly define.

I submit it, then, to those best acquainted with the man personally, whether the following is not Nathaniel Hawthorne,—to himself, whether something involved in it does not express the temper of this mind,—that lasting temper of all true, candid men—a seeker, not a finder yet:—

A man now entered, in neglected attire, with the aspect of a thinker, but somewhat too rough-hewn and brawny for a scholar. His face was full of sturdy vigor, with some finer and keener attribute beneath; though harsh at first, it was tempered with the glow of a large, warm heart, which had force enough to heat his powerful intellect through and through. He advanced to the Intelligencer, and looked at him with a glance of such stern sincerity, that perhaps few secrets were beyond its scope.

"'I seek for Truth,' said he."

Twenty-four hours have elapsed since writing the foregoing. I have just returned from the hay mow, charged more and more with love and admiration of Hawthorne. For I have just been gleaning through the "Mosses," picking up many things here and there that had previously escaped me. And I found that but to glean after this man, is better than to be in at the harvest of others. To be frank (though, perhaps, rather foolish), notwithstanding what I wrote yesterday of these Mosses, I had not then culled them all; but had, nevertheless, been sufficiently sensible of the subtle essence, in them, as to write as I did. To what infinite height of loving wonder and admiration I may yet be borne, when by repeatedly banquetting on these Mosses, I shall have thoroughly incorporated their whole stuff into my being,—that, I can not tell. But already I feel that this Hawthorne has dropped germinous seeds into my soul. He expands and deepens down, the more I contemplate him; and further, and further, shoots his strong New-England roots into the hot soil of my Southern soul.

By careful reference to the "Table of Contents," I now find, that I have gone through all the sketches; but that when I yesterday wrote, I had not at all read two particular pieces, to which I now desire to call special attention,—"A Select Party," and "Young Goodman Brown." Here, be it said to all those whom this poor fugitive scrawl of mine may tempt to the perusal of the "Mosses," that they must on no account suffer themselves to be trifled with, disappointed, or deceived by the triviality of many of the titles to these Sketches. For in more than one instance, the title utterly belies the piece. It is as if rustic demijohns containing the very best and costliest of Falernian and Tokay, were labeled "Cider," "Perry," and "Elder-berry Wine." The truth seems to be, that like many other geniuses, this Man of Mosses takes great delight in hoodwinking the world,—at least, with respect to himself. Personally, I doubt not, that he rather prefers to be generally esteemed but a so-so sort of author; being willing to reserve the thorough and acute appreciation of what he is, to that party most qualified to judge—that is, to himself. Besides, at the bottom of their natures, men like Hawthorne, in many things, deem the plaudits of the public such strong presumptive evidence of mediocrity in the object of them, that it would in some degree render them doubtful of their own powers, did they hear much and vociferous braying concerning them in the public pastures. True, I have been braying myself (if you please to be witty enough, to have it so) but then I claim to be the first that has so brayed in this particular matter; and therefore, while pleading guilty to the charge, still claim all the merit due to originality.

But with whatever motive, playful or profound, Nathaniel Hawthorne has chosen to entitle his pieces in the manner he has, it is certain, that some of them are directly calculated to deceive—egregiously deceive—the superficial skimmer of pages. To be downright and candid once more, let me cheerfully say, that two of these titles did dolefully dupe no less an eagle-eyed reader than myself, and that, too, after I had been impressed with a sense of the great depth and breadth of this American man. "Who in the name of thunder," (as the country-people say in this neighborhood), "who in the name of thunder, would anticipate any marvel in a piece entitled "Young Goodman Brown"? You would of course suppose that it

was a simple little tale, intended as a supplement to "Goody Two Shoes."
Whereas, it is deep as Dante; nor can you finish it, without addressing the
author in his own words—"It is yours to penetrate, in every bosom, the
deep mystery of sin." And with Young Goodman, too, in allegorical pursuit
of his Puritan wife, you cry out in your anguish,—

"Faith!" shouted Goodman Brown, in a voice of agony and desperation;
and the echoes of the forest mocked him, crying Faith! Faith!" as if bewildered
wretches were seeking her all through the wilderness.

Now this same piece, entitled "Young Goodman Brown," is one of the two
that I had not all read yesterday; and I allude to it now, because it is, in itself,
such a strong positive illustration of that blackness in Hawthorne, which I
had assumed from the mere occasional shadows of it, as revealed in several of
the other sketches. But had I previously perused "Young Goodman Brown,"
I should have been at no pains to draw the conclusion, which I came to, at
a time, when I was ignorant that the book contained one such direct and
unqualified manifestation of it.

The other piece of the two referred to, is entitled "A Select Party," which
in my first simplicity upon originally taking hold of the book, I fancied must
treat of some pumpkin-pie party in Old Salem, or some Chowder Party on
Cape Cod. Whereas, by all the gods of Peedee! it is the sweetest and sublimest
thing that has been written since Spenser wrote. Nay, there is nothing in
Spenser that surpasses it, perhaps, nothing that equals it. And the test is this:
read any canto in "The Faery Queen," and then read "A Select Party," and
decide which pleases you the most,—that is, if you are qualified to judge. Do
not be frightened at this; for when Spenser was alive, he was thought of very
much as Hawthorne is now—was generally accounted just such a "gentle"
harmless man. It may be, that to common eyes, the sublimity of Hawthorne
seems lost in his sweetness,—as perhaps in this same "Select Party" his; for
whom, he has builded so august a dome of sunset clouds, and served them on
richer plate, than Belshazzar's when he banquetted his lords in Babylon.

But my chief business now, is to point out a particular page in this piece,
having reference to an honored guest, who under the name of "The Master
Genius" but in the guise "of a young man of poor attire, with no insignia
of rank or acknowledged eminence," is introduced to the Man of Fancy,
who is the giver of the feast. Now the page having reference to this "Master
Genius", so happily expresses much of what I yesterday wrote, touching the
coming of the literary Shiloh of America, that I cannot but be charmed by the
coincidence; especially, when it shows such a parity of ideas, at least, in this
one point, between a man like Hawthorne and a man like me.

And here, let me throw out another conceit of mine touching this American Shiloh, or "Master Genius," as Hawthorne calls him. May it not be, that this commanding mind has not been, is not, and never will be, individually developed in any one man? And would it, indeed, appear so unreasonable to suppose, that this great fullness and overflowing may be, or may be destined to be, shared by a plurality of men of genius? Surely, to take the very greatest example on record, Shakespeare cannot be regarded as in himself the concretion of all the genius of his time; nor as so immeasurably beyond Marlowe, Webster, Ford, Beaumont, Johnson, that those great men can be said to share none of his power? For one, I conceive that there were dramatists in Elizabeth's day, between whom and Shakespeare the distance was by no means great. Let anyone, hitherto little acquainted with those neglected old authors, for the first time read them thoroughly, or even read Charles Lamb's Specimens of them, and he will be amazed at the wondrous ability of those Anaks of men, and shocked at this renewed example of the fact, that Fortune has more to do with fame than merit,—though, without merit, lasting fame there can be none.

Nevertheless, it would argue too illy of my country were this maxim to hold good concerning Nathaniel Hawthorne, a man, who already, in some minds, has shed "such a light, as never illuminates the earth, save when a great heart burns as the household fire of a grand intellect."

The words are his,—in the "Select Party"; and they are a magnificent setting to a coincident sentiment of my own, but ramblingly expressed yesterday, in reference to himself. Gainsay it who will, as I now write, I am Posterity speaking by proxy—and after times will make it more than good, when I declare—that the American, who up to the present day, has evinced, in Literature, the largest brain with the largest heart, that man is Nathaniel Hawthorne. Moreover, that whatever Nathaniel Hawthorne may hereafter write, "The Mosses from an Old Manse" will be ultimately accounted his masterpiece. For there is a sure, though a secret sign in some works which proves the culmination of the power (only the developable ones, however) that produced them. But I am by no means desirous of the glory of a prophet. I pray Heaven that Hawthorne may *yet* prove me an impostor in this prediction. Especially, as I somehow cling to the strange fancy, that, in all men, hiddenly reside certain wondrous, occult properties—as in some plants and minerals—which by some happy but very rare accident (as bronze was discovered by the melting of the iron and brass in the burning of Corinth) may chance to be called forth here on earth, not entirely waiting for their better discovery in the more congenial, blessed atmosphere of heaven.

Once more—for it is hard to be finite upon an infinite subject, and all subjects are infinite. By some people, this entire scrawl of mine may be esteemed altogether unnecessary, inasmuch, "as years ago" (they may say) "we found out the rich and rare stuff in this Hawthorne, whom you now parade forth, as if only *yourself* were the discoverer of this Portuguese diamond in our Literature."—But even granting all this; and adding to it, the assumption that the books of Hawthorne have sold by the five-thousand,—what does that signify?—They should be sold by the hundred-thousand, and read by the million; and admired by every one who is capable of Admiration.

> —Herman Melville, "Hawthorne and His Mosses.
> By a Virginian Spending July in Vermont,"
> *The Literary World*, VII, 185 and 186,
> August 17 and 24, 1850, pp. 125–7, 145–7

THE SCARLET LETTER

As is apparent from the following reviews, Hawthorne's novel *The Scarlet Letter* was a *cause célèbre*. Whereas his previous work suffered from popular indifference, this novel gained him the attention he had formerly lacked, no small part of it negative. Actually a conservative in many regards, with the publication of *The Scarlet Letter*, Hawthorne became viewed as a radical and a subversive by conservative reviewers.

The Scarlet Letter is a divisive, divided book. It has been termed "subversive-benign" by one critic. It could arouse the Christian conservative moralists to vituperation, but it could also seduce and convert critics from the same faction. Hawthorne himself, on reading it back to his wife, found himself "tossed up and down . . . in a very nervous state," flustered by the novel. Hawthorne's intentions were not obvious. Was he a seditious radical, spreading sympathy for the devil, or was he a Puritan moralist reasserting biblical convention?

Arthur Coxe found the novel a threat to female chastity. He saw it as corrupting, its intention to "Ethiopize the snowiest conscience." Such loaded, racialized language played to the psychosexual anxieties and stereotypes of conservative readers in antebellum America. E.P. Whipple—almost as pious and reverend a gentleman as Coxe—found the book reminiscent of the sensuous novels of France, but differing vitally in its ethical resolution. Dimmesdale and Hester are dispatched in a manner consistent with holy writ.

The novel was published at a time when genteel conservatism was at the fore. One critic has termed the decade the Feminine Fifties. What might be unusual to contemporary eyes is the anxiety about the effect novels could have in society. Readers should be aware that *The Scarlet Letter* was published amidst a torrent of sensationalist novels (Hawthorne himself condemned the "mob of d——— scribbling women"), not only from home soil but also from Europe.

Many reviewers note the divided nature of the novel itself in another respect. The novel's preface, "The Custom-House," a semi-autobiographical frame narrative written in a jocular and ironic tone, is quite removed from the story proper.

Salient for students seeking precedents for the novel, both James Herbert Morse and Francis Hovey Stoddard compare *The Scarlet Letter* specifically to the Greek tragedies of Aeschylus. George E. Woodberry also remarks on the theatrical basis of the novel.

E.A. DUYCKINCK
"THE SCARLET LETTER: A ROMANCE" (1850)

Evert Duyckinck was the editor of the New York publication *Literary World* and of numerous books and periodicals. With his brother George, he was the editor of an early encyclopedia of American writers. The Duyckincks were also important figures in literary society, acquainted with many writers including Hawthorne, Melville, Poe, Cooper, and Irving.

Duyckinck rigorously claims that *The Scarlet Letter* is not a novel but a "psychological romance . . . a study of character in which the human heart is anatomized." Like Hawthorne in the preface to *The House of the Seven Gables*, Duyckinck places great import in this differentiation. Students analyzing Hawthorne's preference for the romance as a literary form should note Duyckinck's observations.

Duyckinck calls the actual scarlet letter "the hero of the volume." Students attempting to unpack the meaning of the letter might inquire here.

———

Mr. Hawthorne introduces his new story to the public, the longest of all that he has yet published, and most worthy in this way to be called a romance, with one of those pleasant personal descriptions which are the most charming of his compositions, and of which we had so happy an example in the preface to his last collection, the *Mosses from an Old Manse*. In these narratives everything seems to fall happily into its place. The style is simple and flowing, the observation accurate and acute; persons and things are represented in their minutest shades, and difficult traits of character presented with an instinct which art might be proud to imitate. They are, in fine, little cabinet pictures exquisitely painted. The readers of the *Twice-told Tales* will know the pictures to which we allude. They have not, we are sure, forgotten 'Little Annie's Ramble,' or the 'Sights from a Steeple.' This is the Hawthorne of the present day in the sunshine. There is another Hawthorne less companionable, of sterner Puritan aspect, with the shadow of the past over him, a reviver of witchcrafts and of those dark agencies of evil which lurk in the human soul, and which even now represent the old gloomy historic era in the microcosm and eternity of the individual; and this Hawthorne is called to mind by such tales as the 'Minister's Black Veil' or the 'Old Maid in the Winding Sheet,' and reappears in *The Scarlet Letter, a Romance*. Romantic in sooth! Such romance as you may read in the intensest sermons of old Puritan divines, or in the mouldy pages of that Marrow of Divinity, the ascetic Jeremy Taylor.

The Scarlet Letter is a psychological romance. The hardiest Mrs. Malaprop would never venture to call it a novel. It is a tale of remorse, a study of character in which the human heart is anatomized, carefully, elaborately, and with striking poetic and dramatic power. Its incidents are simply these. A woman in the early days of Boston becomes the subject of the discipline of the court of those times, and is condemned to stand in the pillory and wear henceforth, in token of her shame, the scarlet letter A attached to her bosom. She carries her child with her to the pillory. Its other parent is unknown. At this opening scene her husband from whom she had been separated in Europe, preceding him by ship across the Atlantic, reappears from the forest, whither he had been thrown by shipwreck on his arrival. He was a man of a cold intellectual temperament, and devotes his life thereafter to search for his wife's guilty partner and a fiendish revenge. The young clergyman of the town, a man of a devout sensibility and warmth of heart, is the victim, as this Mephistophilean old physician fixes himself by his side to watch over him and protect his health, an object of great solicitude to his parishioners, and, in reality, to detect his suspected secret and gloat over his tortures. This slow, cool, devilish purpose, like the concoction of some sublimated hell broth, is perfected gradually and inevitably. The wayward, elfish child, a concentration of guilt and passion, binds the interests of the parties together, but throws little sunshine over the scene. These are all the characters, with some casual introductions of the grim personages and manners of the period, unless we add the scarlet letter, which, in Hawthorne's hands, skilled to these allegorical, typical semblances, becomes vitalized as the rest. It is the hero of the volume.

The denouement is the death of the clergyman on a day of public festivity, after a public confession in the arms of the pilloried, branded woman. But few as are these main incidents thus briefly told, the action of the story, or its passion, is 'long, obscure, and infinite.' It is a drama in which thoughts are acts. The material has been thoroughly fused in the writer's mind, and springs forth an entire, perfect creation. We know of no American tales except some of the early ones of Mr Dana, which approach it in conscientious completeness. Nothing is slurred over, superfluous, or defective. The story is grouped in scenes simply arranged, but with artistic power, yet without any of those painful impressions which the use of the words, as it is the fashion to use them, 'grouping' and 'artistic' excite, suggesting artifice and effort at the expense of nature and ease.

Mr Hawthorne has, in fine, shown extraordinary power in this volume, great feeling and discrimination, a subtle knowledge of character in its secret springs and outer manifestations. He blends, too, a delicate fancy with this metaphysical insight. We would instance the chapter towards the close, entitled 'The Minister in a Maze,' where the effects of a diabolic temptation are curiously depicted, or 'The Minister's Vigil,' the night scene in the pillory. The atmosphere of the piece also is perfect. It has the mystic element, the weird forest influences of the old Puritan discipline and era. Yet there is no affrightment which belongs purely to history, which has not its echo even in the unlike and perversely commonplace custom-house of Salem. Then for the moral. Though severe, it is wholesome, and is a sounder bit of Puritan divinity than we have been of late accustomed to hear from the degenerate successors of Cotton Mather. We hardly know another writer who has lived so much among the new school who would have handled this delicate subject without an infusion of George Sand. The spirit of his old Puritan ancestors, to whom he refers in the preface, lives in Nathaniel Hawthorne.

We will not mar the integrity of *The Scarlet Letter* by quoting detached passages. Its simple and perfect unity forbids this. Hardly will the introductory sketch bear this treatment without exposing the writer to some false impressions; but as evidence of the possession of a style faithfully and humorously reflective of the scenes of the passing hour, which we earnestly wish he may pursue in future volumes, we may give one or two separable sketches.

There is a fine, natural portrait of General Miller, the collector; equal in its way to the Old Inspector, the self-sufficing gourmand lately presented in our journal; and there are other officials as well done. A page, however, of as general application, and of as sound profit as any in this office-seeking age, is that which details, in its mental bearing,

THE PARALYSIS OF OFFICE.

An effect—which I believe to be observable, more or less, in every individual who has occupied the position—is, that while he leans on the mighty arm of the Republic, his own proper strength departs from him . . . Whoever touches it should look well to himself, or he may find the bargain to go hard against him, involving, if not his soul, yet many of its better attributes; its sturdy force, its courage and constancy, its truth, its self-reliance, and all that gives the emphasis to manly character.

The personal situation of Nathaniel Hawthorne—in whom the city by his removal lost an indifferent official, and the world regained a good author—is amusingly presented in this memoir of

A DECAPITATED SURVEYOR.

A remarkable event of the third year of my Surveyorship—to adopt the tone of 'P.P.'—was the election of General Taylor to the Presidency . . . The real human being, all this time, with his head safely on his shoulders, had brought himself to the comfortable conclusion that everything was for the best; and making an investment in ink, paper, and steel-pens, had opened his long-disused writing-desk, and was again a literary man.

And a literary man long may he remain, an honor and a support to the craft, of genuine worth and fidelity, to whom no word is idle, no sentiment insincere. Our literature has given to the world no truer product of the American soil, though of a peculiar culture, than Nathaniel Hawthorne.

—E.A. Duyckinck, "The Scarlet Letter: A Romance,"
The Literary World, VI, No. 165, March 30, 1850, pp. 323–25

GEORGE RIPLEY (1850)

George Ripley was the founder of the Brook Farm community. A Unitarian minister turned liberal theologian and social reformer, he was also a reviewer and essayist. At Brook Farm he edited *The Harbinger*, the community newspaper. If he resented Hawthorne for his departure and subsequent lawsuit against Brook Farm, it is not apparent in this review.

Ripley praises *The Scarlet Letter* and compares Hawthorne favorably to Poe. While both excel in inspiring "terrible excitement" in the reader,

Hawthorne is "always *motived* with a wonderful insight and skill," his intimation of the supernatural always "relieved, softened, made tolerable, and almost attractive, by a strong admixture of the human." Poe, meanwhile, seemed arbitrary in his use of the "horrible and infernal": Poe's reader is only infuriated by the "superfluous introduction to the company of the devils and his angels." Writing soon after Poe's ignoble alcohol-related death, Ripley alludes to this by comparing Hawthorne's literary effect to a "serene sense of refreshment," while Poe's tales recall "a drugged cup of intoxication."

This review will doubtless benefit any reader comparing Hawthorne and Poe.

The weird and ghostly legends of the Puritanic history present a singularly congenial field for the exercise of Mr. Hawthorne's peculiar genius. From this fruitful source, he has derived the materials for his most remarkable creations. He never appears so much in his element as when threading out some dim, shadowy tradition of the twilight age of New England, peering into the faded records of our dark-visaged forefathers for the lingering traces of the preternatural, and weaving into his gorgeous web of enchantment the slender filaments which he has drawn from the distaff of some muttering witch on Gallows-Hill. He derives the same terrible excitement from these legendary horrors, as was drawn by Edgar Poe from the depths of his own dark and perilous imagination, and brings before us pictures of death-like, but strangely fascinating agony, which are described with the same minuteness of finish—the same slow and fatal accumulation of details—the same exquisite coolness of coloring, while everything creeps forward with irresistible certainty to a soul-harrowing climax—which made the last-named writer such a consummate master of the horrible and infernal in fictitious composition. Hawthorne's tragedies, however, are always *motived* with a wonderful insight and skill, to which the intellect of Poe was a stranger. In the most terrific scenes with which he delights to scare the imagination, Hawthorne does not wander into the region of the improbable; you scarcely know that you are in the presence of the supernatural, until your breathing becomes too thick for this world; it is the supernatural relieved, softened, made tolerable, and almost attractive, by a strong admixture of the human; you are tempted onward by the mild, unearthly light, which seems to shine upon you like a healthful star; you are blinded by no lurid glare; you acquiesce in the necessity of the wizard journey; instead of being provoked to anger by a superfluous introduction to the company of the devil and his angels.

The elements of terror, which Mr. Hawthorne employs with such masterly effect, both in the original conceptions of his characters and the scenes of mystery and dread in which they are made to act, are blended with such sweet gushes of natural feeling, such solemn and tender relations of the deepest secrets of the heart, that the painful impression is greatly mitigated, and the final influence of his most startling creation is a serene sense of refreshment, without the stupor and bewilderment occasioned by a drugged cup of intoxication.

—George Ripley, *New York Tribune Supplement*, IX,
April 1, 1850, p. 2

E.P. WHIPPLE (1850)

Edwin Percy Whipple was a critic and a popular lecturer. His was an earnest endeavor to bring literature to the masses, and he had a moral purpose, which is apparent in this review.

In this positive (if squeamish) review of *The Scarlet Letter*, Whipple esteems Hawthorne over the "libertine" school of French novelists (he names Eugene Sue, George Sand, and Alexandre Dumas). While Hawthorne's novel is "too painfully analytical" of the "psychological details of a strange crime," the "painful emotions" and "dark passions," Hawthorne differs from the French school by investing his story with "moral purpose." Hawthorne's use of stark subject matter is aimed at a genteel moral end. His story and his characters find their resolution not according to the author's fancy or kinder sympathies, but as "the spiritual laws" dictate. *The Scarlet Letter* "has undermined the whole philosophy on which the French novels rest."

This review is significant to any student writing about Hawthorne's relation to his European contemporaries, and also for any readers interested in how *The Scarlet Letter* was perceived—and valued—by the American conservative press and its readership.

In this beautiful and touching romance Hawthorne has produced something really worthy of the fine and deep genius which lies within him. The *Twice Told Tales*, and *Mosses from an Old Manse*, are composed simply of sketches and stories, and although such sketches and stories as few living men could write, they are rather indications of the possibilities of his mind than realizations of its native power, penetration, and creativeness. In *The Scarlet Letter* we have a complete work, evincing a true artist's certainty of touch and expression in the exhibition of characters and events, and a keen-sighted and far-sighted vision into the essence and purpose of spiritual laws. There is a profound philosophy underlying the story which will escape many of the readers whose attention is engrossed by the narrative.

The book is prefaced by some fifty pages of autobiographical matter, relating to the author, his native city of Salem, and the Custom House, from which he was ousted by the Whigs. These pages, instinct with the vital spirit of humor, show how rich and exhaustless a fountain of mirth Hawthorne has at his command. The whole representation has the dreamy yet distinct remoteness of the purely comic ideal. The view of Salem streets; the picture of the old Custom House at the head of Derby's wharf, with its torpid officers on a summer's afternoon, their chairs all tipped against the wall, chatting about old stories, 'while the frozen witticisms of past generations were thawed out, and came bubbling with laughter from their lips'—the delineation of the old Inspector, whose 'reminiscences of good cheer, however ancient the date of the actual banquet, seemed to bring the savor of pig or turkey under one's very nostrils,' and on whose palate there were flavors 'which had lingered there not less than sixty or seventy years, and were still apparently as fresh as that of the mutton-chop which he had just devoured for his breakfast,' and the grand view of the stout Collector, in his aged heroism, with the honors of Chippewa and Fort Erie on his brow, are all encircled with that visionary atmosphere which proves the humorist to be a poet, and indicates that his pictures are drawn from the images which observation has left on his imagination. The whole introduction, indeed, is worthy of a place among the essays of Addison and Charles Lamb.

With regard to *The Scarlet Letter*, the readers of Hawthorne might have expected an exquisitely written story, expansive in sentiment, and suggestive in characterization, but they will hardly be prepared for a novel of so much tragic interest and tragic power, so deep in thought and so condensed in style, as is here presented to them. It evinces equal genius in the region of great passions and elusive emotions, and bears on every page the evidence of a mind thoroughly alive, watching patiently the movements of morbid hearts when stirred by strange experiences, and piercing, by its imaginative power, directly through all the externals to the core of things. The fault of the book, if fault it have, is the almost morbid intensity with which the characters are realized, and the consequent lack of sufficient geniality in the delineation. A portion of the pain of the author's own heart is communicated to the reader, and although there is great pleasure received while reading the volume, the general impression left by it is not satisfying to the artistic sense. Beauty bends to power throughout the work, and therefore the power displayed is not always beautiful. There is a strange fascination to a man of contemplative genius in the psychological details of a strange crime like that which forms the plot of *The Scarlet Letter*, and he is therefore apt to become, like Hawthorne, too painfully anatomical in his exhibition of them.

If there be, however, a comparative lack of relief to the painful emotions which the novel excites, owing to the intensity with which the author concentrates attention on the working of dark passions, it must be confessed that the moral purpose of the book is made more definite by this very deficiency. The most abandoned libertine could not read the volume without being thrilled into something like virtuous resolution, and the roué would find that the deep-seeing eye of the novelist had mastered the whole philosophy of that guilt of which practical roués are but childish disciples. To another class of readers, those who have theories of seduction and adultery modeled after the French school of novelists, and whom libertinism is of the brain, the volume may afford matter for very instructive and edifying contemplation; for, in truth, Hawthorne, in *The Scarlet Letter*, has utterly undermined the whole philosophy on which the French novels rest, by seeing farther and deeper into the essence both of conventional and moral laws; and he has given the results of his insight, not in disquisitions and criticisms, but in representations more powerful even than those of Sue, Dumas, or George Sand. He has made his guilty parties end, not as his own fancy of his own benevolent sympathies might dictate, but as the spiritual laws, lying back of all persons, dictated to him. In this respect there is hardly a novel in English literature more purely objective.

As everybody will read *The Scarlet Letter*, it would be impertinent to give a synopsis of the plot. The principal characters, Dimmesdale, Chillingworth, Hester, and little Pearl, all indicate a firm grasp of individualities, although from the peculiar method of the story, they are developed more in the way of logical analysis than by events. The descriptive portions of the novel are in a high degree picturesque and vivid, bringing the scenes directly home to the heart and imagination, and indicating a clear vision of the life as well as forms of nature. Little Pearl is perhaps Hawthorne's finest poetical creation, and is the very perfection of ideal impishness.

In common, we trust, with the rest of mankind, we regretted Hawthorne's dismissal from the Custom House, but if that event compels him to exert his genius in the production of such books as the present, we shall be inclined to class the Honorable Secretary of the Treasury among the great philanthropists. In his next work we hope to have a romance equal to *The*

Scarlet Letter in pathos and power, but more relieved by touches of that beautiful and peculiar humor, so serene and so searching, in which he excels almost all living writers.

—E.P. Whipple, *Graham's Magazine,*
XXXVI, May 1850, pp. 345–46

HENRY F. CHORLEY (1850)

Henry Chorley was an English reviewer of art, music, and literature. Like Whipple's text, his is a conservative, somewhat prissy moral endorsement of *The Scarlet Letter.*

Also like Whipple, Chorley finds the novel "more than ordinarily painful." Victorian genteelism customarily recoiled from such fare. Nevertheless Chorley uses strong religious language to laud Hawthorne's achievement: "no tale dealing with crime so sad and revenge so subtly diabolical [is] so clear of fever and of prurient excitement." Fortunately, Hawthorne has a commendable moral compass. Chorley praises Hawthorne for his emphasis on Hester Prynne's suffering: "The misery of the woman is present in every page," he trills. While Chorley is "by no means satisfied" that such passions and tragedies ("Sin and Sorrow") are fit subjects for fiction, Hawthorne is portrayed as exemplary in his handling of them.

Readers interested in the positive perception of *The Scarlet Letter* among moral and religious conservatives should make especial note of this review.

This is a most powerful but painful story. Mr. Hawthorne must be well known to our readers as a favourite with the *Athenaeum.* We rate him as among the most original and peculiar writers of American fiction. There is in his works a mixture of Puritan reserve and wild imagination, of passion and description, of the allegorical and the real, which some will fail to understand, and which others will positively reject,—but which, to ourselves, is fascinating, and which entitles him to be placed on a level with Brockden Brown and the author of *Rip Van Winkle.* *The Scarlet Letter* will increase his reputation with all who do not shrink from the invention of the tale; but this, as we have said, is more than ordinarily painful. When we have announced that the three characters are a guilty wife, openly punished for her guilt,—her tempter, whom she refuses to unmask, and who during the entire story carries a fair front and an unblemished name among his congregation,—and her husband, who, returning from a long absence at the moment of her sentence, sits himself down betwixt the two in the midst of a small and severe community to work out his slow vengeance on both under the pretext of magnanimous forgiveness,—when we have explained that *The Scarlet Letter* is the badge of Hester Prynne's shame, we ought to add that we recollect no tale dealing with crime so sad and revenge so subtly diabolical, that is at the same time so clear of fever and of prurient excitement. The misery of the woman is as present in every page as the heading which in the title of the romance symbolizes her punishment. Her terrors concerning her strange elvish child present retribution in a form which is new and natural:—her slow and painful purification through repentance is crowned by no perfect happiness, such as awaits the decline of those who have no dark and bitter past to remember. Then, the gradual corrosion of heart of Dimmesdale, the faithless priest, under the insidious care of the husband, (whose relationship to Hester is a secret known only to themselves,) is appalling; and his final confession and expiation are merely a relief, not a reconciliation.—We are by no means satisfied that passions and tragedies like these are the legitimate subjects for fiction: we are satisfied that novels such as *Adam Blair* and plays such as *The Stranger* may be justly charged with attracting more persons than they warn by their excitement. But if Sin and Sorrow in their most fearful forms are to be presented in any work of art, they have rarely been treated with a loftier severity, purity, and sympathy than in Mr. Hawthorne's *Scarlet Letter*. The touch of the fantastic befitting a period of society in which ignorant and excitable human creatures conceived each other and themselves to be under the direct 'rule and governance' of the Wicked One, is most skilfully administered. The supernatural here never becomes grossly palpable:—the thrill is all the deeper for its action being indefinite, and its source vague and distant.

—Henry F. Chorley, *Athenaeum*, 1181, June 15, 1850, p. 634

ORESTES BROWNSON (1850)

Orestes Brownson was a New England minister and liberal freethinker—a "seeker," somewhat after Roger Williams, who became notorious (and something of a laughingstock) for his frequent and violent changes of position regarding politics and religion. He progressed from Calvinism to Presbyterianism to Unitarianism (where he indulged in transcendentalism, being a charter member of the Transcendental Club). These he each renounced in turn—becoming a "renegade" critic of transcendentalism—eventually converting to Catholicism, the faith with which he remained.

Before this, Brownson was a prominent radical reformer, associating with the utopians Robert Dale Owen and Fanny Wright. Brownson's son (Orestes Jr.) spent two years studying at Brook Farm. Brownson was also an editor (principally of his own *Brownson's Quarterly Review*), a journalist, and a prolific writer on theology, history, politics, autobiography, and literary criticism. He even wrote fiction. Brownson's notorious about-face from radical to conservative may have provided the model for Hawthorne's character Holgrave in *The House of the Seven Gables*.

Brownson's avowed purpose in this colorful review (almost a sermon) is to inquire as to whether Hawthorne has employed his God-given faculties according to God's design. As a further index to Brownson's position, he lapses into Latin, and falls readily to preaching ("sin is sin"). He finds that while Hawthorne has not perverted God's gifts, his work is by no means "unobjectionable." Hawthorne tells "a story that should not have been told." His audience is "the great body of our countrymen who have no well defined religious belief, and no fixed principles of virtue."

Like Arthur Cleveland Coxe, Brownson finds Hawthorne writes too well, depicting crimes that are actually "loathsome" and repellent as attractive and human. Brownson resents the "fascinations of genius" and the "charms of a highly polished style" by which Hawthorne ensnares readers and corrupts their "moral health." Even when he makes his guilty parties "suffer intensely," it is apparently not sufficient; Hawthorne fails to "excite the horror of his readers for their crime." Again echoing Coxe, Brownson opines that Hawthorne's characters would indeed be "less desperate" without "that external morality and decorum." Sinners must be depicted as conniving and vulgar.

Brownson's objections are broad and highly conservative. The love between Hester and Dimmesdale is "illicit, and highly criminal." As if he was not already making his position clear enough, Brownson sermonizes: "No man has the right to love another man's wife, and no married woman has the right to love any man but her husband." It is a "modern doctrine," one to be "severely reprobated," that supposes that love is "withdrawn from voluntary control." Love, Brownson believes, evolves from the marriage contract. Any students interested in the social context of Hawthorne's novel—the public attitude to the portrayal of private feelings—should consult Brownson's review. He manifests the severity of feeling held by many in the community at the time.

Brownson also raises objections to theological niceties: Hawthorne knows nothing about Christian asceticism. His literary creations strive only to maintain the "integrity of their character," which Brownson roundly translates as pridefulness. (Frances Hovey Stoddard's celebration of Hawthorne's championing of the individual in the novel provides a useful contrast, showing developing attitudes.) Brownson finds Hawthorne himself overly prideful. Brownson then claims that Hawthorne fails to comprehend the act of Christian pardon. Hester finds pardon, but this brings her no "inner peace." This categorically cannot be, according to Catholic scripture ("All this is false"). Pardon and inner peace are synonymous. Finally, Brownson contends that Hawthorne fails to understand the act of Christian confession. The review descends into a Catholic critique of Protestantism. Any students conducting a religious-ethical examination of *The Scarlet Letter* will find a wealth of relevant material here.

——————— ——————— ———————

Mr. Hawthorne is a writer endowed with a large share of genius, and in the species of literature he cultivates has no rival in this country, unless it be Washington Irving. His *Twice-told Tales*, his *Mosses from an Old Manse*, and other contributions to the periodical press, have made him familiarly known, and endeared him to a large circle of readers. The work before us is the largest and most elaborate of the romances he has as yet published, and no one can read half a dozen pages of it without feeling that none but a man of true genius and a highly cultivated mind could have written it. It is a work of rare, we may say of fearful power, and to the great body of our countrymen who have no well defined religious belief, and no fixed principles of virtue, it will be deeply interesting and highly pleasing.

We have neither the space nor the inclination to attempt an analysis of Mr. Hawthorne's genius, after the manner of the fashionable criticism of the day. Mere literature for its own sake we do not prize, and we are more disposed to analyze an author's work than the author himself. Men are not for us mere psychological phenomena, to be studied, classed, and labelled. They are moral and accountable beings, and we look only to the moral and religious effect of their works. Genius perverted, or employed in perverting others, has no charms for us, and we turn away from it with sorrow and disgust. We are not among those who join in the worship of passion, or even of intellect. God gave us our faculties to be employed in his service and in that of our fellow-creatures for his sake, and our only legitimate office as critics is to inquire, when a book is sent us for review, if its author in producing it has so employed them.

Mr. Hawthorne, according to the popular standard of morals in this age and this community, can hardly be said to pervert God's gifts, or to exert an immoral influence. Yet his work is far from being unobjectionable. The story is told with great naturalness, ease, grace, and delicacy, but it is a story that should not have been told. It is a story of crime, of an adulteress and her accomplice, a meek and gifted and highly popular Puritan minister in our early colonial days,—a purely imaginary story, though not altogether improbable. Crimes like the one imagined were not unknown even in the golden days of Puritanism, and are perhaps more common among the descendants of the Puritans than it is at all pleasant to believe; but they are not fit subjects for popular literature, and moral health is not promoted by leading the imagination to dwell on them. There is an unsound state of public morals when the novelist is permitted, without a scorching rebuke, to select such crimes, and invest them with all the fascinations of genius, and all the charms of a highly polished style. In a moral community such crimes are spoken of as rarely as possible, and when spoken of at all, it is always in terms which render them loathsome, and repel the imagination.

Nor is the conduct of the story better than the story itself. The author makes the guilty parties suffer, and suffer intensely, but he nowhere manages so as to make their sufferings excite the horror of his readers for their crime. The adulteress suffers not from remorse, but from regret and, from the disgrace to which her crime has exposed her, in her being condemned to wear emblazoned on her dress the Scarlet Letter which proclaims to all the deed she has committed. The minister, her accomplice, suffers also, horribly, and feels all his life after the same terrible letter branded on his heart, but not from the fact of the crime itself, but from the consciousness of not being what he seems to the world, from his having permitted the partner in his guilt to be disgraced, to be punished, without his having the manliness to avow his share in the guilt, and to bear his share of the punishment. Neither ever really repents of the criminal deed; nay, neither ever regards it as really criminal, and both seem to hold it to have been laudable, because they *loved* one another,—as if the love itself were not illicit, and highly criminal. No man has the right to love another man's wife, and no married woman has the right to love any man but her husband. Mr. Hawthorne, in the present case seeks to excuse Hester Prynne, a married woman, for loving the Puritan minister, on the ground that she had no love for her husband, and it is hard that a woman should not have some one to love; but this only aggravated her guilt, because she was not only forbidden to love the minister, but commanded to love her husband, whom she had vowed to love, honor, cherish, and obey. The modern doctrine that represents the affections as fatal, and wholly withdrawn from voluntary control, and then allows us to plead them in justification of neglect of duty and breach of the most positive precepts of both the natural and the revealed law, cannot be too severely reprobated.

Human nature is frail, and it is necessary for every one who standeth to take heed lest he fall. Compassion for the fallen is a duty which we all owe, in consideration of our own failings, and especially in consideration of the infinite mercy our God has manifested to her erring and sinful children. But however binding may be this duty, we are never to forget that sin is sin, and that it is pardonable only through the great mercy of God, on condition of the sincere repentance of the sinner. But in the present case neither of the guilty parties repents of the sin, neither exclaims with the royal prophet, who had himself fallen into the sin of adultery and murder, *Misere mei Deus, secundum magnam misericordiam; et secundum multidudinem miserationum tuarum, dele iniquitatem meam. Amplius lava me ab iniquitate mea; et a peccato munda me. Quoniam iniquitatem meam cognosco, et peccatummeum contra me est semper.* They hug their illicit love; they cherish their sin; and after the lapse of seven years are ready, and actually agree, to depart into a foreign country, where they may indulge it without disguise and without restraint. Even to the last, even when the minister, driven by his agony, goes so far as to throw off the mask of hypocrisy, and openly confess his crime, he shows no sign of repentance, or that he regarded his deed as criminal.

The Christian who reads *The Scarlet Letter* cannot fail to perceive that the author is wholly ignorant of Christian asceticism, and that the highest principle of action he recognizes is pride. In both the criminals, the long and intense agony they are represented as suffering springs not from remorse, from the consciousness of having offended God, but mainly from the feeling, especially on the part of the minister, that they have failed to maintain the integrity of their character. They have lowered themselves in their own estimation, and cannot longer hold up their heads in society as honest people. It is not their conscience that is wounded, but their pride. *He* cannot bear to think that he wears a disguise, that he cannot be the open, frank, stainless character he had from his youth aspired to be, and *she,* that she is driven from society, lives a solitary outcast, and has nothing to console her but her fidelity to her paramour. There is nothing Christian, nothing really moral, here. The very pride itself is a sin; and pride often a greater sin than that which it restrains us from committing. There are thousands of men and women too proud to commit carnal sins, and to the indomitable price of our Puritan ancestors we may attribute no small share of their external morality and decorum. It may almost be said, that, if they had less of that external morality and decorum, their case would be less desperate; and often the violation of them, or failure to maintain them, by which their pride receives a shock, and their self-complacency is shaken, becomes the occasion, under the grace of God, of their conversion to truth and holiness. As long as they maintain their self-complacency, are satisfied with themselves, and feel that they have outraged none of the decencies of life, no argument can reach them, no admonition can startle them, no exhortation can move them. Proud of their supposed virtue, free from all self-reproach, they are as placid as a summer morning, pass through life without a cloud to mar their serenity, and die as gently and as sweetly as the infant falling asleep in its mother's arms. We have met with these people, and after laboring in vain to waken them to a sense of their actual condition, till completely discouraged, we have been tempted to say, Would that you might commit some overt act, that should startle you from your sleep, and make you feel how far pride is from being either a virtue, or the safeguard of virtue,—or convince you of your own insufficiency for yourselves, and your absolute need of Divine grace. Mr. Hawthorne seems never to have learned that pride is not only sin, but the root of all sin, and that humility is not only a virtue, but the root of all virtue. No genuine contrition or repentance ever springs from pride, and the sorrow for sin because it mortifies our pride, or lessens us in our own eyes, is nothing but the effect of pride. All true remorse, all genuine repentance, springs from humility, and is sorrow for having offended God, not sorrow for having offended ourselves.

Mr. Hawthorne also mistakes entirely the effect of Christian pardon upon the interior state of the sinner. He seems entirely ignorant of the religion that can restore peace to the sinner,—true, inward peace, we mean. He would persuade us, that Hester had found pardon, and yet he shows us that she had found no inward peace. Something like this is common among popular Protestant writers, who, in speaking of great sinners among Catholics that have made themselves monks or hermits to expiate their sins by devoting themselves to prayer, and mortification, and the duties of religion, represent them as always devoured by remorse, and suffering in their interior agony almost the pains of the damned. An instance of this is the Hermit of Engeddi in Sir Walter Scott's *Talisman*. These men know nothing either of true remorse, or of the effect of Divine pardon. They draw from their imagination, enlightened, or rather darkened, by their own experience. Their speculations are based on the supposition that the sinner's remorse is the effect of wounded pride, and that during life the wound can never be healed. All this is false. The remorse does not spring from wounded pride, and the greatest sinner who really repents, who really does penance, never fails to find interior peace. The mortifications he practices are not prompted by his interior agony, nor designed to bring peace to his soul; they are a discipline to guard against his relapse, and an expiation that his interior peace already found, and his overflowing love to God for his superabounding mercy, lead him to offer to God, in union with that made by his blessed Lord and Master on the cross.

Again, Mr. Hawthorne mistakes the character of confession. He does well to recognize and insist on its necessity; but he is wrong in supposing that its office is simply to disburden the mind by communicating its secrets to another, to restore the sinner to his self-complacency, and to relieve him from the charge of cowardice and hypocrisy. Confession is a duty we owe to God, and a means, not of restoring us to our self-complacency, but of restoring us to the favor of God, and reestablishing us in his friendship. The work before us is full of mistakes of this sort, in those portions where the author really means to speak like a Christian, and therefore we are obliged to condemn it, where we acquit him of all unchristian intention.

As a picture of the old Puritans, taken from the position of a moderate transcendentalist and liberal of the modern school, the work has its merits; but as little as we sympathize with those stern old Popery-haters, we do not regard the picture as at all just. We should commend where the author condemns, and condemn where he commends. Their treatment of the adulteress was far more Christian than his ridicule of it. But enough of fault-finding, and as we have no praise, except what we have given, to offer, we here close this brief notice.

—Orestes Brownson, *Brownson's Quarterly Review*,
IV, n.s., October, 1850, pp. 528–32

Arthur Cleveland Coxe
"The Writings of Hawthorne" (1851)

Coxe was an American theologian and writer of Christian verse. His lengthy review of Hawthorne's book, excerpted here, is notorious in its righteous indignation and severity. Coxe writes with an openly pro-fessed agenda: "to make the voice of the Church more audible to the American public."

Coxe's foremost grievance with the novel lies with its duplicity. Hawthorne is guilty of subterfuge and subversion. *The Scarlet Letter* "never hints the shocking things that belong to its words." Coxe would rather have the tone match the content. Hawthorne's language, instead, is "perfectly chaste," has "delicate sensuality" and his novel is "delicately immoral."

Beyond mere criticism, Coxe sees social corruption in the novel; it threatens "that mirror of Heaven, a Christian maiden's imagination." Coxe contrasts The Scarlet Letter with Oliver Goldsmith's The Vicar of Wakefield, which he contends is the coarser novel for its language, but less so in its subject matter. Hawthorne is guilty of sympathizing with the devil—he "insinuates that the arch-fiend himself is a very tolerable sort of person."

Students exploring the social responses to and perceptions of The Scarlet Letter will find here one of the most extreme reactions. Coxe paints the supposedly conservative Hawthorne as a radical. Students interested in Hawthorne's own intentions—the extent of his radicalism and his subversion of linguistic and literary conventions—will find valuable insights here.

=(\/\/\)= =(\/\/\)= =(\/\/\)=

We shall entirely mislead our reader if we give him to suppose that *The Scarlet Letter* is coarse in its details, or indecent in its phraseology. This very article of our own, is far less suited to ears polite, than any page of the romance before us; and the reason is, we call things by their right names, while the romance never hints the shocking words that belong to its things, but, like Mephistophiles, insinuates that the arch-fiend himself is a very tolerable sort of person, if nobody would call him Mr. Devil. We have heard of persons who could not bear the reading of some Old Testament Lessons in the service of the Church: such persons would be delighted with our author's story; and damsels who shrink at the reading of the Decalogue, would probably luxuriate in bathing their imagination in the crystal of its delicate sensuality. The langauge of our author, like patent blacking, "would not soil the whitest linen," and yet the composition itself, would suffice, if well laid on, to Ethiopize the snowiest conscience that ever sat like a swan upon that mirror of heaven, a Christian maiden's imagination. We are not sure we speak quite strong enough, when we say, that we would much rather listen to the coarsest scene of Goldsmith's *Vicar*, read aloud by a sister or daughter, than to hear from such lips, the perfectly chaste language of a scene in *The Scarlet Letter*, in which a married wife and her reverend paramour, with their unfortunate offspring, are introduced as the actors, and in which the whole tendency of the conversation is to suggest a sympathy for their sin, and an anxiety that they may be able to accomplish a successful escape beyond the seas, to some country where their shameful commerce may be perpetuated. Now, in Goldsmith's story there are very coarse words, but we do not remember anything that saps the foundations of the moral sense, or that goes to create unavoidable sympathy with unrepenting sorrow, and deliberate, premeditated sin. The

Vicar of Wakefield is sometimes coarsely virtuous, but *The Scarlet Letter* is delicately immoral.

—Arthur Cleveland Coxe, "The Writings of Hawthorne,"
Church Review, January 1851, p. 507

BRYAN WALLER PROCTER
(1853)

I was reading (rather re-reading) the other evening the introductory chapter to the *Scarlet Letter*. It is admirably written. Not having any great sympathy with a custom-house—nor, indeed, with Salem, except that it seems to be Hawthorne's birth-place—all my attention was concentrated on the *style*, which seems to me excellent.

—Bryan Waller Procter, Letter to James T. Fields
(February 1853), cited in James T. Fields,
"'Barry Cornwall' and Some of His Friends," *Harper's New
Monthly Magazine*, December 1875, pp. 59–60

NATHANIEL HAWTHORNE
(1855)

Speaking of Thackeray, I cannot but wonder at his coolness in respect to his own pathos, and compare it with my emotions, when I read the last scene of *The Scarlet Letter* to my wife, just after writing it,—tried to read it rather, for my voice swelled and heaved, as if I were tossed up and down on an ocean as it subsides after a storm. But I was in a very nervous state then, having gone through a great diversity of emotion, while writing it, for many months. I think I have never overcome my own adamant in any other instance.

—Nathaniel Hawthorne, *The English Note-Books*, 1855

BERKELEY AIKIN
(1862)

I believe and am sure that *The Scarlet Letter* will endure as long as the language in which it is written; and should that language become dead, the wonderful work will be translated. Mr. S. C. Hall says I am to tell you that your works will live when marble crumbles into dust. I can well understand that even genius stands breathless in silence, watching events; still, master, you must send us forth some fresh enchantment ere-long, though you have done so much.

—Berkeley Aikin, Letter to Nathaniel Hawthorne
(1862), cited in Julian Hawthorne, *Nathaniel Hawthorne and His Wife*, 1884, Vol. 2, p. 305

HENRY JAMES (1879)

Henry James was an important American novelist, essayist, and literary critic, author of many books including *The Ambassadors*, *The Bostonians*, and *The Golden Bowl*. His long study of Hawthorne was written—strangely perhaps—for the "English Men of Letters" series in 1879. Classified by James as an "essay," it has been erroneously described by Edmund Wilson as the "first extended study ever made of an American writer." As Wilson notes, the study is still invaluable. Commissioned by an English publisher, it prompted controversy in the United States where it was deemed to be unpatriotic and snooty. It remains challenging and insightful, if occasionally wilful, the testament of one great novelist keenly regarding another.

In this critique of *The Scarlet Letter*, James praises the novel highly, albeit in equivocal language. He remains ambivalent, sometimes paradoxically so, throughout the "essay," once even correcting himself midsentence. James calls *The Scarlet Letter* "the finest piece of imaginative writing yet put forth in this country" but also finds it "the most consistently gloomy of English novels of the first order."

Students concerned with Hawthorne's debt to popular and genre fiction will find much of use here. James describes *The Scarlet Letter's* status as a popular best-seller, encouraging the student to consider Hawthorne's relation to the literary marketplace and how he variously conforms to and subverts literary conventions. *The Scarlet Letter* has a "well-worn theme," James writes, in "the familiar combination of the wife, the lover and the husband." However, this is not a typical love story; "no story of love was ever less of a love-story." Hawthorne's imagination "plays . . . incessantly" and "leads . . . a dance."

James finds *The Scarlet Letter* to be "absolutely American" and describes the national "satisfaction" felt after its publication, "America having produced a novel that belonged to literature." Students looking at the nationalist aspect of Hawthorne's writing (and, therefore, the nature of his debt to Europe) should investigate James's text and the potential questions its raises. How "American" is *The Scarlet Letter*? How does Hawthorne differ from his British contemporaries?

James compares *The Scarlet Letter* with *Adam Blair* (1822), an earlier (and largely forgotten) novel by the Scotsman John Gibson Lockhart. James claims that a prominent difference lies in Hawthorne's "passionless tone," in his "cold and ingenious fantasy" which James attributes to the author's "subjective Puritanism." He accuses Hawthorne of a cold, intellectual moralism whereas Lockhart is warm and sentimental, if not "vulgar." Students researching Hawthorne's relation to Puritanism will be gratified here.

This excerpt will also appeal to students investigating Hawthorne's representation of history. James faults Hawthorne as a historian, finding his "historical colouring . . . rather weak than otherwise," and lacking in "elaboration of detail, of the modern realism of research." Hawthorne's characters do not speak in "the English of the period." James had strict expectations for historical accuracy in the novel. His criticism of *The Scarlet Letter*'s "want of reality" and Hawthorne's "abuse of the fanciful element" comes at a time when realism, as espoused in America by James's friend William Dean Howells, was a keenly contested subject. Students exploring the extent of Hawthorne's influence on realism—and to what degree he was its antithesis—should certainly look here.

Students investigating Hawthorne's use of symbols will find much to reflect on as well. James criticizes the novel's symbolism—to many critics one of Hawthorne's signature strengths. Hawthorne's characters are superficial, he writes, mere ciphers for a narrative purpose: "representatives, very picturesquely arranged, of a single frame of mind." The symbolism is overdone and mechanical, James contends, veering between the sublime and the ridiculous, between moral tragedy and "physical comedy." If overused, James says, the scarlet letter, the "A" itself risks "seeming to stand for nothing more serious than itself."

—————   —————   —————

If Hawthorne was in a sombre mood, and if his future was painfully vague, *The Scarlet Letter* contains little enough of gaiety or of hopefulness. It is densely dark, with a single spot of vivid colour in it; and it will probably long remain the most consistently gloomy of English novels of the first order. But I just now called it the author's masterpiece, and I imagine it will continue to be, for other generations than ours, his most substantial title to fame. The subject had probably lain a long time in his mind, as his subjects were apt to do; so that he appears completely to possess it, to know it and feel it. It is simpler and more complete than his other novels; it achieves more perfectly what it attempts, and it has about it that charm, very hard to express, which we find in an artist's work the first time he has touched his highest mark—a sort of straightness and naturalness of execution, an unconsciousness of his public, and freshness of interest in his theme. It was a great success, and he immediately found himself famous. The writer of these lines, who was a child at the time, remembers dimly the sensation the book produced, and the little shudder with which people alluded to it, as if a peculiar horror were mixed with its attractions. He was too young to read it himself; but its title, upon which he fixed his eyes as the book lay upon the table, had a mysterious charm. He had a vague belief, indeed, that the "letter" in question was one of the documents that come by the post, and it was a source of perpetual wonderment to him that it should be of such an unaccustomed hue. Of course it was difficult to explain to a child the significance of poor Hester Prynne's blood-coloured A. But the mystery was at last partly dispelled by his being taken to see a collection of pictures (the annual exhibition of the National Academy), where he encountered a representation of a pale, handsome woman, in a quaint black dress and a white coif, holding between her knees an elfish-looking little girl, fantastically dressed, and crowned with flowers. Embroidered on the woman's breast was a great crimson A, over which the child's fingers, as she glanced strangely out of the picture, were maliciously playing. I was told that this was Hester Prynne and little Pearl, and that when I grew older I might read their interesting history. But the picture remained vividly imprinted on my mind; I had been vaguely frightened and made uneasy by it; and when, years afterwards, I first read the novel, I seemed to myself to have read it before, and to be familiar with its two strange heroines. I mention this incident simply as an indication of the degree to which the success of *The Scarlet Letter* had made the book what is called an actuality. Hawthorne himself was very modest about it; he wrote to his publisher, when there was a question of his undertaking another novel, that what had given the history of Hester Prynne its "vogue" was simply the introductory chapter. In fact, the publication of *The Scarlet Letter* was in the United States a literary event of the first importance. The book was the finest piece of imaginative writing yet put forth in the country. There was a consciousness of this in the welcome that was given it—a satisfaction in the idea of America having produced a novel that belonged to literature, and to the forefront of it. Something might at last be sent to Europe as exquisite in quality as anything that had been received, and the best of it was that the thing was absolutely American; it belonged to the soil, to the air; it came out of the very heart of New England.

It is beautiful, admirable, extraordinary; it has in the highest degree that merit which I have spoken of as the mark of Hawthorne's best things—an indefinable purity and lightness of conception, a quality which in a work of art affects one in the same way as the absence of grossness does in a human being. His fancy, as I just now said, had evidently brooded over the subject for a long time; the situation to be represented had disclosed itself to him in all its phases. When I say in all its phases, the sentence demands modification; for it is to be remembered that if Hawthorne laid his hand upon the well-worn theme, upon the familiar combination of the wife, the lover, and the husband, it was, after all, but to one period of the history of these three persons that he attached himself. The situation is the situation after the woman's fault has been committed, and the current of expiation and repentance has set in. In spite of the relation between Hester Prynne and Arthur Dimmesdale, no story of love was surely ever less of a "love-story." To Hawthorne's imagination the fact that these two persons had loved each other too well was of an interest comparatively vulgar; what appealed to him was the idea of their moral situation in the long years that were to follow. The story, indeed, is in a secondary degree that of Hester Prynne; she becomes, really, after the first scene, an accessory figure; it is not upon her the *denoument* depends. It is upon her guilty lover that the author projects most frequently the cold, thin rays of his fitfully-moving lantern, which makes here and there a little luminous circle, on the edge of which hovers the livid and sinister figure of the injured and retributive husband. The story goes on, for the most part, between the lover and the husband—the tormented young Puritan minister, who carries the secret of his own lapse from pastoral purity locked up beneath an exterior that commends itself to the reverence of his flock, while he sees the softer partner of his guilt standing in the full glare of exposure and humbling herself to the misery of atonement—between this more wretched and pitiable culprit, to whom dishonour would come as a comfort and the pillory as a relief, and the older, keener, wiser man, who, to obtain satisfaction for the wrong he has suffered, devises the infernally ingenious plan of conjoining himself with his wronger, living with him, living upon him; and while he pretends to minister to his hidden ailment and to sympathise with his pain, revels in his unsuspected knowledge of these things, and stimulates them by malignant arts. The attitude of Roger Chillingworth, and the means he takes to compensate himself—these are the highly original elements in the situation that Hawthorne so ingeniously treats. None of his works are so impregnated with that after-sense of the old Puritan consciousness of life to which allusion has so often been made. If, as M. Montegut says, the qualities of his ancestors *filtered* down through generations into his composition, *The Scarlet Letter* was, as it were, the vessel that gathered up the last of the precious drops. And I say this not because the story happens to be of so-called historical cast, to be told of the early days of Massachusetts, and of people in steeple-crowned hats and sad-coloured garments. The historical colouring is rather weak than otherwise; there is little elaboration of detail, of the modern realism of research; and the author has made no great point of causing his figures to speak the English of their period. Nevertheless, the book is full of the moral presence of the race that invented Hester's penance—diluted and complicated with other things, but still perfectly recognisable. Puritanism, in a word, is there, not only objectively, as Hawthorne tried to place it there, but subjectively as well. Not, I mean, in his judgment of his characters in any harshness of prejudice, or in the obtrusion of a moral lesson; but in the very quality of his own vision, in the tone of the picture, in a certain coldness and exclusiveness of treatment.

The faults of the book are, to my sense, a want of reality and an abuse of the fanciful element—of a certain superficial symbolism. The people strike me not as characters, but as representatives, very picturesquely arranged, of a single state of mind; and the interest of the story lies, not in them, but in the situation, which is insistently kept before us, with little progression, though with a great deal, as I have said, of a certain stable variation; and to which they, out of their reality, contribute little that helps it to live and move. I was made to feel this want of reality, this over-ingenuity, of *The Scarlet Letter,* by chancing not long since upon a novel which was read fifty years ago much more than to-day, but which is still worth reading—the story of *Adam Blair,* by John Gibson Lockhart. This interesting and powerful little tale has a great deal of analogy with Hawthorne's novel—quite enough, at least, to suggest a comparison between them; and the comparison is a very interesting one to make, for it speedily leads us to larger considerations than simple resemblances and divergences of plot.

Adam Blair, like Arthur Dimmesdale, is a Calvinistic minister who becomes the lover of a married woman, is overwhelmed with remorse at his misdeed, and makes a public confession of it; then expiates it by resigning his pastoral office and becoming a humble tiller of the soil, as his father had been. The two stories are of about the same length, and each is the masterpiece (putting aside, of course, as far as Lockhart is concerned, the *Life of Scott)* of the author. They deal alike with the manners of a rigidly theological society, and even in certain details they correspond. In each of them, between the guilty pair, there is a charming little girl; though I hasten to say that Sarah Blair (who is not the daughter of the heroine, but the legitimate offspring of the hero, a widower) is far from being as brilliant and graceful an apparition as the admirable little Pearl of *The Scarlet Letter.* The main difference between the two tales is the fact that in the American story the husband plays an all-important part, and in the Scottish plays almost none at all. *Adam Blair* is the history of the passion, and *The Scarlet Letter* the history of its sequel; but nevertheless, if one has read the two books at a short interval, it is impossible to avoid confronting them. I confess that a large portion of the interest of *Adam Blair,* to my mind, when once I had perceived that it would repeat in a great measure the situation of *The Scarlet Letter,* lay in noting its difference of tone. It threw into relief the passionless quality of Hawthorne's novel, its element of cold and ingenious fantasy, its elaborate imaginative delicacy. These things do not precisely constitute a weakness in *The Scarlet Letter;* indeed, in a certain way they constitute a great strength; but the absence of a certain something warm and straightforward, a trifle more grossly human and vulgarly natural, which one finds in *Adam Blair,* will always make Hawthorne's tale less touching to a large number of even very intelligent readers, than a love-story told with the robust, synthetic pathos which served Lockhart so well. His novel is not of the first rank (I should call it an excellent second-rate one), but it borrows a charm from the fact that his vigorous, but not strongly imaginative, mind was impregnated with the reality of his subject. He did not always succeed in rendering this reality; the expression is sometimes awkward and poor. But the reader feels that his vision was clear, and his feeling about the matter very strong and rich. Hawthorne's imagination, on the other hand, plays with the theme so incessantly, leads it such a dance through the moon-lighted air of his intellect, that the thing cools off, as it were, hardens and stiffens, and, producing effects much more exquisite, leaves the reader with a sense of having handled a splendid piece of silversmith's work. Lockhart, by means much more vulgar, produces at moments a greater illusion, and satisfies our inevitable desire for something, in the people in whom it is sought to interest us, that shall be of the same pitch and the same continuity with ourselves. Above all, it is interesting to see how the same subject appears to two men of a thoroughly different cast of mind and of a different race. Lockhart was struck with the warmth of the subject that offered itself to him, and Hawthorne with its coldness; the one with its glow, its sentimental interest—the other with its shadow, its moral interest. Lockhart's story is as decent, as severely draped, as *The Scarlet Letter;* but the author has a more vivid sense than appears to have imposed itself upon Hawthorne, of some of the incidents of the situation he describes; his tempted man and tempting woman are more actual and personal; his heroine in especial, though not in the least a delicate or a subtle conception, has a sort of credible, visible, palpable property, a vulgar roundness and relief, which are lacking to the dim and chastened image of Hester Prynne. But I am going too far; I am comparing simplicity with subtlety, the usual with the refined. Each man wrote as his turn of mind impelled him, but each expressed something more than himself. Lockhart was a dense, substantial Briton, with a taste for the concrete, and Hawthorne was a thin New Englander, with a miasmatic conscience.

In *The Scarlet Letter* there is a great deal of symbolism; there is, I think, too much. It is overdone at times, and becomes mechanical; it ceases to be impressive, and grazes triviality. The idea of the mystic A which the young minister finds imprinted upon his breast and eating into his flesh, in sympathy with the embroidered badge that Hester is condemned to wear, appears to me to be a case in point. This suggestion should, I think, have been just made and dropped; to insist upon it and return to it, is to exaggerate the weak side of the subject. Hawthorne returns to it constantly, plays with it, and seems charmed by it; until at last the reader feels tempted to declare that his enjoyment of it is puerile. In the admirable scene, so superbly conceived and beautifully executed, in which Mr. Dimmesdale, in the stillness of the night, in the middle of the sleeping town, feels impelled to go and stand upon the scaffold where his mistress had formerly enacted her dreadful penance, and then, seeing Hester pass along the street, from watching at a sick-bed, with little Pearl at her side, calls them both to come and stand there beside him—in this masterly episode the effect is almost spoiled by the introduction of one of these superficial conceits. What leads up to it is very fine—so fine that I cannot do better than quote it as a specimen of one of the striking pages of the book.

> But before Mr. Dimmesdale had done speaking, a light gleamed far and wide over all the muffled sky. It was doubtless caused by one of those meteors which the nightwatcher may so often observe burning out to waste in the vacant regions of the atmosphere. So powerful was its radiance that it thoroughly illuminated the dense medium of cloud betwixt the sky and earth. The great vault brightened, like the dome of an immense lamp. It showed the familiar scene of the street with the distinctness of mid-day, but also with the awfulness that is always imparted to

familiar objects by an unaccustomed light. The wooden houses, with their jutting stories and quaint gable-peaks; the doorsteps and thresholds, with the early grass springing up about them; the garden-plots, black with freshly-turned earth; the wheel-track, little worn, and, even in the marketplace, margined with green on either side;—all were visible, but with a singularity of aspect that seemed to give another moral interpretation to the things of this world than they had ever borne before. And there stood the minister, with his hand over his heart; and Hester Prynne, with the embroidered letter glimmering on her bosom; and little Pearl, herself a symbol, and the connecting link between these two. They stood in the noon of that strange and solemn splendour, as if it were the light that is to reveal all secrets, and the daybreak that shall unite all that belong to one another.

That is imaginative, impressive, poetic; but when, almost immediately afterwards, the author goes on to say that "the minister looking upward to the zenith, beheld there the appearance of an immense letter—the letter A—marked out in lines of dull red light," we feel that he goes too far, and is in danger of crossing the line that separates the sublime from its intimate neighbour. We are tempted to say that this is not moral tragedy, but physical comedy. In the same way, too much is made of the intimation that Hester's badge had a scorching property, and that if one touched it one would immediately withdraw one's hand. Hawthorne is perpetually looking for images which shall place themselves in picturesque correspondence with the spiritual facts with which he is concerned, and of course the search is of the very essence of poetry. But in such a process discretion is everything, and when the image becomes importunate it is in danger of seeming to stand for nothing more serious than itself. When Hester meets the minister by appointment in the forest, and sits talking with him while little Pearl wanders away and plays by the edge of the brook, the child is represented as at last making her way over to the other side of the woodland stream, and disporting herself there in a manner which makes her mother feel herself, "in some indistinct and tantalising manner, estranged from Pearl; as if the child, in her lonely ramble through the forest, had strayed out of the sphere in which she and her mother dwelt together, and was now vainly seeking to return to it." And Hawthorne devotes a chapter to this idea of the child's having, by putting the brook between Hester and herself, established a kind of spiritual gulf, on the verge of which her little fantastic person innocently mocks at her mother's sense of bereavement. This conception belongs, one would say, quite to the lighter order of a story-teller's devices, and the reader hardly goes with Hawthorne in the large development he gives to it. He hardly goes with him either, I think, in his extreme predilection for a small number of vague ideas which are represented by such terms as "sphere" and "sympathies." Hawthorne makes too liberal a use of these two substantives; it is the solitary defect of his style; and it counts as a defect partly because the words in question are a sort of specialty with certain writers immeasurably inferior to himself.

I had not meant, however, to expatiate upon his defects, which are of the slenderest and most venial kind. *The Scarlet Letter* has the beauty and harmony of all original and complete conceptions, and its weaker spots, whatever they are, are not of its essence; they are mere light flaws and inequalities of surface. One can often return to it; it supports familiarity, and has the inexhaustible charm and mystery of great works of art. It is admirably written. Hawthorne afterwards polished his style to a still higher degree; but in his later productions—it is almost always the case in a writer's later productions—there is a touch of mannerism. In *The Scarlet Letter* there is a high degree of polish, and at the same time a charming freshness; his phrase is less conscious of itself.

—Henry James, *Hawthorne*, 1879, pp. 106–17

JAMES HERBERT MORSE "THE NATIVE ELEMENT IN AMERICAN FICTION" (1883)

In Hawthorne, whose faculty was developed among scholars and with the finest additaments of scholarship, we have our first true artist in literary expression, as well as the most completely equipped genius of romance. His subtle insight into the elements of character was marvelous. He was original and purely American,—Puritan, even, in his cast of thought and in all the internal and external conditions of his creation. But art is of no country. All ages temper the steel of the fine workman; all literatures whet the edge of his tools. In his sense of the controlling influence of powers beyond the individual's grasp, Hawthorne was Grecian. *The Scarlet Letter* and *The Blithedale Romance* are as fierce, unrelenting tragedy—controlling not only the actors but the writer—as anything in Aeschylus. But Hawthorne's Fate came in the more modern form of "heredity." There were no angry gods; the "Sisters Three" had their origin in the ancestral stock a few generations back. His sense of their power, however, was intense, and was deeply based in the constitution of his own mind. He was too sane a man, of course, to yield credence to the Puritan suspicion of demonic influences, yet he was too much of a seer not to have discovered that, whether demons exist in nature or not, there are demons which are the projections of our own minds; and the struggle of his art was so to materialize these projections as to give them, not the reality which Cotton Mather insisted upon, but a spiritualized reality equally potent over the actions of men. Mr. Henry James, Jr., has pointed out—very justly, it would seem—a use made of the "scarlet letter" wherein Hawthorne overreached himself,—where the spiritual projection becomes labored and artificial. As far as Hawthorne attempts to make this image a potent force in Arthur Dimmesdale's mind, his instinct is unerring; but when he tries to make it visible to little Pearl and Roger Chillingworth, he passes from art into artifice. There is, perhaps, no natural person in *The Scarlet Letter,* just as there is no natural Hamlet in life; but we must accept Arthur Dimmesdale as a marvelous embodiment of the Puritan conscience acting upon the finest human clay,—a clay made sensitive to every emotion, quickened by every intellectual force.

The artistic evolution of the plot is as perfect as that of the *Oedipus Tyrannus.* So, too, in *The House of Seven Gables,* Judge Pyncheon is equally an embodiment of the granitic forces of the Puritan temperament, inheriting, not its finer conscience, but its untempered rigidity as acted upon by the forces of life. The man breaks at last, but he never bends. In the same way each character in Hawthorne's small list is a finished study, at once local in its surroundings and general in its psychological elements. It is a study of man in his special environment,—more scientific than the science of to-day, because it does what science fails to do; it tries to settle the spiritual element in its true place as a factor in man's life. Others have surpassed Hawthorne in the management of external conduct, of dialogue, of home life, of local scenery; but none have reached the depth to which he penetrated in the study of the human heart as the creature of its own creation. In every higher qualification of the artist, he easily excels. His style is masterly in ease, grace, clearness,—the winning, absorbing, entrancing quality. His skill in hinting in ideal and spiritual elements is the most perfect in our day. His mastery of light and shade—the power of deepening gloom by sunshine and intensifying sunshine by means of darkness—is of the finest order, at once the gift of original perception and the result of most assiduous practice. Probably few writers ever made so many successes that were failures, or so many failures that were successes; that is, few ever did so much that was to others artistically perfect in order that they might do something artistically perfect to themselves. Mr. James marvels at the existence of the *Note-Books;* yet their publication has thrown a flood of light not only upon the workings of Hawthorne's mind but on the sources of his artistic effects. They supplement with a sunny external quality the gloom of his psychology. They show us in his own nature a capacity for beauty and sweetness, where his own generation saw only a capacity for morbid analysis; that is, they furnish the biography of the sympathetic side of his mind, while the novels represent what was equally real to his emotional nature. No doubt, while his actual life was simple and pure-minded, capable of absorbing beauty and interest, he had, in imagination, lived through the tortures of the damned. He had given to Hester and Dimmesdale no exaltation or despair of which he was not himself capable, and probably none which he had not, by sheer force of imagination, without any adequate external cause, passed through. Others have been capable of such moods—the moods of "angels and ministers of grace" as well as of demons—without being either sinners or angels; but few have obtained the power of expressing them as he did. He spiritualized everything he touched, with a quality which is felt but cannot be analyzed,—which eludes every attempt to fix it. Little Pearl, standing in front of Governor Bellingham's mansion, looking at the "bright wonder of a house, began to caper and dance, and imperatively required that the whole breadth of sunshine should be stripped off its front and given her to play with." It was no harder to strip off that sunshine for little Pearl than it is to detach and handle the spiritual quality of these romances. We had never reached such insight, or such grace of style, before Hawthorne, and we have never reached it since. As a writer, he was long in obscurity and had little influence on other authors. Emerging into something like local note when the first series *of Twice-Told Tales* was published, in 1837, he dawned upon a wider field, in 1842, with the addition of the *Second Series.* The intensity of his gloom was lightened in the *Mosses from an Old Manse* in 1846, and he then reached a larger circle of readers. In 1850, '51, and '52, he became national in fame, and soon reached the height.

—James Herbert Morse, "The Native Element in American Fiction," *Century Magazine,* July 1883, pp. 293–94

FRANCIS HOVEY STODDARD (1900)

Stoddard was an author and an early professor of English language and literature, heading the new department at New York University from 1888. He wrote a leading critical survey of the novel and its development, from which the following excerpt comes.

Stoddard assigns Hawthorne a vital position in a lineage developing the novelistic form, following Jane Austen and then Charlotte Brontë. While *Jane Eyre* depicts a conflict between the individual will and society, *The Scarlet Letter* shows an inner conflict. Hawthorne's work is a "step in advance" in the development of the novel as a form. The "assertion of life" is "the essence of individuality." Students comparing Hawthorne with Charlotte Brontë or Jane Austen should consult Stoddard. Students interested in the theme of individualism in Hawthorne's work may also find this entry of value.

Stoddard continues by analyzing what the novel is, as a genre. This he does by defining what the novel is not, examining which forms it partially partakes of. Like James Herbert Morse, Stoddard sees a semblance ("almost") to the Greek tragedies of Aeschylus. He decides that Hawthorne's book is not a historical novel, nor is it a "mystical romance"—rather, it is an amalgam of historical novel, mystical romance, and Greek tragedy. Students discussing questions of genre relating to *The Scarlet Letter* will find this analysis helpful; students looking into Hawthorne's place in the continuing development of the novel may find Stoddard's insights relevant as well.

It is conflict that we have in *Jane Eyre,* an assertion of individual will, a fine capacity of individual emotion, and all this in conflict with the world opposing. But it is struggle, not conflict, the inner, not the outer, warfare, that we have in Hester Prynne. It is the stir and the struggle of the soul afflicted, punished, but growing into larger development, into riper life, through this stress and struggle and affliction. And if I seemed to indicate that the novel was in process of development when I wrote that the vitality of the assertion of life was the essence of individuality, and that because of this vitality *Jane Eyre* was an indication of an advance in the art of fiction beyond the spirit and the method of Jane Austen's day, then I may further claim now that the completed picture of the soul of Hester Prynne is indicative of a step in advance as great as, if less marked than, the step from Jane Austen to Charlotte Bronte. It is a step in advance because the picture of Hester Prynne portrays a human soul not merely as a strong, demanding individuality, but as under stress of such relation to verdict of law and to the rights of fellow-mortals as to compel its development into a completed personality. The novel of the *Scarlet Letter* is one of the links in the development of the novel from a means of portraying single phases of emotion to a vehicle of highest expressional power. It was written by a psychological student of the problems which harass the human soul. . . .

It is a tragedy—a tragedy sombre, intense, unrelieved. It is almost a fatalistic tragedy; almost as stern as if it had been written by Æschylus. It is not a love story; it is not a story of youth; it is not a story of contemporaneous life; it is not a story of eager hope. Hester Prynne having sinned is doomed for punishment to wear the scarlet letter as the symbol of the seared soul forever on her bosom; made an outcast from social joy forever. And the story is the record of the growth of the thoughtless soul of the girl, Hester Prynne, into the sad, strong soul of a mature woman. As accessories to this record of growth, we have scenery of circumstance and scenery of characters. To get perspective, atmosphere, verisimilitude, Hawthorne goes back to a recognizable era of past history. He paints with steadiness the outward aspects, and makes credible the inner motive, of the Puritan Colony in the Boston of 1658. Yet the book is in no sense an historical novel. To give vividness, concreteness, objectivity, to this story of the inner life, to this record of the growth of the conscience, of the growth of responsibility, of the growth of religion, within the breast of Hester Prynne, Hawthorne uses the symbolism which is the picture language of the infancy of awakening fancy. In the story he carries on the crude symbolism of the Puritan court of justice decreeing a visible A as an objective reminder of the branded heart—carries on this crude symbolism into the most delicate and refined suggestions. The unseen forces, the unseen monitors, the unseen avengers, float before our eyes, are painted on the clouds, are burned upon the flesh, in mystic symbols. These mystic symbols are like the weird sisters in *Macbeth*; they are the objectification of mystery. The revelation of the working of the spirit of regeneration upon the soul of Hester Prynne is embodied for us in the weird child, Pearl. She is a living symbol, at once the incarnation of sin, the personification of the Scarlet Letter, the emblem of hope, and the prophecy of pardon. All this is the poetry of mysticism. Yet the *Scarlet Letter* is no more a mystical romance than it is an historical novel.

But if we have mediaeval mysticism in the symbolism of the work, we have something very like Greek simplicity and Greek directness in the development. The novel is a Greek tragedy. Like the Greek, it is synthetic and creative rather than analytic. Like the Greek tragedy, the novel of the *Scarlet Letter* has a single story, few principal characters, largeness, unity of treatment, directness, sternness, relentlessness. As in the Greek tragedy, also, the story begins after the guilt has been incurred, and the motive of the story is the relation of the soul of man to Nemesis and justice. There is Greek suggestion even in the minor detail; Pearl is as a chorus to voice for us the comment of the unseen powers. There is Greek atmosphere. All the characters seem to be being rather than acting. Yet the novel is no more a Greek tragedy than it is an historical tale; it is no more a Greek tragedy than it is a mediaeval romance. It is, in one, a Greek tragedy, a mediaeval romance, a modern historical tale. It is a master work, limited to no age, belonging to all experiences, to all time.

—Francis Hovey Stoddard,
The Evolution of the English Novel, 1900, pp. 75–80

GEORGE E. WOODBERRY (1902)

George E. Woodberry was an academic, critic, poet, journalist, and biographer—firstly and notably assembling a biography of Poe, whose works he also edited. Woodberry's biography of Hawthorne is recognized as his masterpiece. This excerpt regarding *The Scarlet Letter* provides a counterpoint to the shrill religious excesses of Coxe and Brownson. Woodberry instead offers a scholarly analysis of the text.

Woodberry first addresses the novel's *sui generis* status, or its uniqueness. No novel resembles it. Like Morse and Stoddard, Woodberry notes the novel's closer resemblance to drama ("theatrical in spectacle"). He develops this point further, however, arguing that Hawthorne's characteristic narrative technique is to display a "succession of highly-wrought scenes, tableaux." Unlike the "great novelists," Hawthorne does not "present the scene of life," but shows only its "transitory scaffolding." The background is minimal, "no more than will suffice for the acting of the drama": a town, with its prison, meeting house, pillory, governor's house, "a lonely cottage by the shore, the forest round about all."

Likewise Hawthorne's players number but three (like Stoddard, Woodberry views Pearl as a surrogate Greek chorus). Furthermore, these central characters are isolated, leading largely interior, tormented lives ("the secrecy of men's bosoms"). At least, this is the "simplified" life that Hawthorne shows us. The true drama is played out in the eternal realm: "the life they lived in the soul itself." Woodberry returns to these two words repeatedly. The action takes place in the "soul" and the "eternal"; "it is only incidentally a New England tale." Much of the events are enacted in "a phantasmagoric rather than a realistic world." Students covering Hawthorne's narrative structure will find much material here regarding how the novel is constructed. Students comparing Hawthorne with classical drama should look to this excerpt, as might those readers examining the degree to which Hawthorne used elements of realism.

Woodberry follows this discussion by regarding the relation of the novel to Hawthorne's tales. These tales, too, had only the slightest background. The scarlet letter—the novel's core symbol—evolves out of Hawthorne's earlier tale "Endicott and the Red Cross." Yet with the novel, unlike the tale, Hawthorne manages to "penetrate deep into life."

Woodberry subsequently examines the novel with regard to the larger tradition of "tales." *The Scarlet Letter* (like *Madame Bovary*) upends customary novelistic structure, since it "begins where common tales end." In Hawthorne's story, the actual crime has already been committed, and

Hawthorne "takes no interest" in it. Rather, his is a study of punishment and vengeance, much of it played out in the souls of the offenders. Students examining Hawthorne's subversion of traditional novel forms will find valuable insights in this excerpt.

Woodberry then goes on to examine the nature of the sin. Unlike Orestes Brownson, Woodberry wonders whether the cold and loveless marriage initiated by Chillingworth was not the true sin? For Woodberry, writing fifty years after Brownson and Coxe, the sin of hypocrisy outweighs the original sin of adultery. Again, unlike Brownson, Woodberry celebrates the "moral universality" of the romance. Students interested in the evolving moral responses to the novel should pay particular attention to this part of the entry.

Finally, Woodberry points to the darkness—the before-the-fact existentialism—of the novel. "There is no Christ in this book." Nor does Hawthorne offer room for self-forgiveness or mercy. He has no feelings for his characters; he is a "vivisector," a "moral dissector of their souls." To Hawthorne human nature "is a fallen and ruined thing." "There is no forgiveness in the end . . . to dispel the darkness of evil or promise the dawn of life." This is the void at the book's crux that so terrified Coxe and Brownson. Woodberry, too, questions it. Hawthorne presents but "a half-truth," he argues, "and the darker half; it is the shadow of which the other half is light." Students interested in Hawthorne's pessimism—his anticipation of twentieth-century existentialism—should certainly consult this review.

The Scarlet Letter is a great and unique romance, standing apart by itself in fiction; there is nothing else quite like it. Of all Hawthorne's works it is most identified with his genius in popular regard, and it has the peculiar power that is apt to invest the first work of an author in which his originality finds complete artistic expression. It is seldom that one can observe so plainly the different elements that are primary in a writer's endowment coalesce in the fully developed work of genius; yet in this romance there is nothing either in method or perception which is not to be found in the earlier tales; what distinguishes it is the union of art and intuition as they had grown up in Hawthorne's practice and had developed a power to penetrate more deeply into life. Obviously at the start there is the physical object in which his imagination habitually found its spring, the fantastically embroidered scarlet letter on a woman's bosom which he had seen in the Puritan group described in "Endicott and the Red Cross." It had been in his mind for years, and his thoughts had centred on it and wandered out from it, tracking its mystery. It has in itself that decorative quality, which he sought in the physical object,—the brilliant and rich effect, startling to the eye and yet more to the imagination as it blazes forth with a secret symbolism and almost intelligence of its own. It multiplies itself, as the tale unfolds, with greater intensity and mysterious significance and dread suggestion, as if in mirrors set round about it,—in the slowly disclosed and fearful stigma on the minister's hidden heart over which he ever holds his hand, where it has become flesh of his flesh; in the growing elf-like figure of the child, who, with her eyes always fastened on the open shame of the letter on her mother's bosom or the hidden secret of the hand on her father's breast, has become herself the symbol, half revealed and half concealed, is dressed in it, as every reader remembers, and fantastically embodies it as if the thing had taken life in her; and, as if this were not enough, the scarlet letter, at a climax of the dark story, lightens forth over the whole heavens as a symbol of what cannot be hid even in the intensest blackness of night. The continual presence of the letter seems to have burnt into Hawthorne's own mind, till at the end of the narrative he says he would gladly erase its deep print from the brain where long meditation had fixed it. In no other work is the physical symbol so absorbingly present, so reduplicated, so much alive in itself. It is the brand of sin on life. Its concrete vividness leads the author also by a natural compulsion as well as an artistic instinct to display his story in that succession of high-wrought scenes, tableaux, in fact, which was his characteristic method of narrative, picturesque, pictorial, almost to be described as theatrical in spectacle. The background, also, as in the early tales, is of the slightest, no more than will suffice for the acting of the drama as a stage setting sympathetic with the central scene,—a town, with a prison, a meeting-house, a pillory, a governor's house, other habitations on a street, a lonely cottage by the shore, the forest round about all; and for occasion and accessories, only a woman's sentence, the incidental death of Winthrop unmarked in itself, a buccaneering ship in the harbor, Indians, Spanish sailors, rough matrons, clergy; this will serve, for such was Hawthorne's fine economy, knowing that this story was one in which every materialistic element must be used at its lowest tone. Though the scene lay in this world, it was but transitory scaffolding; the drama was one of the eternal life.

The characteristic markings of Hawthorne's genius are also to be found in other points. He does not present the scene of life, the crowd of the world with its rich and varied fullness of interest, complexity of condition and movement, and its interwoven texture of character, event, and fate, such as the great novelists use; he has only a few individual figures, and these are simplified by being exhibited, not in their complete lives, but only in that single aspect of their experience which was absorbing to themselves and constituted the life they lived in the soul itself. There are three characters, Hester, the minister, and the physician; and a fourth, the child, who fulfills the function of the chorus in the old drama, in part a living comment, in part a spectator and medium of sympathy with the main actors. In all four of these that trait of profound isolation in life, so often used before in the earlier tales, is strongly brought out; about each is struck a circle which separates not only one from another, but from all the world, and in the midst of it, as in a separate orb, each lives an unshared life. It is inherent, too, in such a situation that the mystery that had fascinated Hawthorne in so many forms, the secrecy of men's bosoms, should be a main theme in the treatment. He has also had recourse to that method of violent contrast which has been previously illustrated; on the one hand the publicity of detected wrongdoing, on the other the hidden and unsuspected fact; here the open shame and there the secret sin, whose sameness in a double life is expressed by the identity of the embroidered letter and the flesh-wrought stigma. But it is superfluous to illustrate further the genesis of this romance out of Hawthorne's art and matter in his earlier work, showing how naturally it rose by a concentration of his powers on a single theme that afforded them scope, intensity, and harmony at once. The new thing here is the power of his genius to penetrate, as was said above, deep into life.

The romance begins where common tales end. The crime has been committed; in it, in its motives, circumstances, explanation, its course of passion and human tide of life, Hawthorne takes no interest. All that is past, and, whatever it was, now exists only as sin; it has passed from the region of earthly fact into that of the soul, out of all that was temporal into the world where eternal things only are. Not crime, not passion, not the temptation and the fall, but only sin now staining the soul in consequence is the theme; and the course of the story concerns man's dealing with sin, in his own breast or the breasts of others. It is a study of punishment, of vengeance if one will; this is the secret of its gloom, for the idea of salvation, of healing, is but little present and is not felt; there is no forgiveness in the end, in any sense to dispel the darkness of evil or promise the dawn of new life in any one of these tortured souls. The sin of the lovers is not the centre of the story, but only its initial source; that sin breeds sin is the real

principle of its being; the minister is not punished as a lover, but as the
hypocrite that he becomes, and the physician is punished as the revenger
that he becomes. Hester's punishment is visibly from the law, and illustrates
the law's brutality, the coarse hand of man for justice, the mere physical
blow meant to hurt and crush; it is man's social way of dealing with sin,
and fails because it makes no connection with the soul; the victim rises
above it, is emancipated from its ideas, transforms the symbol of disgrace
into a message of mercy to all who suffer, and annuls the gross sentence
by her own higher soul-power. The minister's punishment, also, is visibly
from the physician, who illustrates man's individual way of dealing with sin
in another; but it is not the minister's suffering under the hand of revenge
working subtly in secret that arrests our attention; it is the physician's
own degeneracy into a devil of hate through enjoyment of the sight and
presence of this punishment, that stamps him into the reader's mind as a
type of the failure of such a revenge. "Vengeance is mine, saith the Lord" is
the text here blazed forth. In the sphere of the soul human law and private
revenge have no place. It is in that sphere that Hester is seen suffering in
the touch of the child, being unable to adjust the broken harmonies of
life; her incapacity to do that is the ever-present problem that keeps her
wound open, not to be stanched, but rather breaking with a more intimate
pain with the unfolding of little Pearl's wide-eyed soul. In that sphere, too,
the minister is seen suffering—not for the original sin, for that is overlaid,
whelmed, forgotten, by the second and heavier transgression of hypocrisy,
cowardice, desertion,—but merely from self-knowledge, the knowledge
that he is a living lie. The characters, so treated, become hardly more than
types, humanly outlined in figure, costume, and event, symbolic pictures
of states of the soul, so simplified, so intense, so elementary as to belong to
a phantasmagoric rather than a realistic world, to that mirror of the soul
which is not found in nature but in spiritual self-consciousness, where the
soul is given back to itself in its nakedness, as in a secret place.

Yet it is in the sense of reality that this romance is most intense. It is a
truthful story, above all; and only its truth could make it tolerable to the
imagination and heart, if indeed it be tolerable to the heart at all. A part of
this reality is due to the fact that there is a story here that lies outside of the
moral scheme in which Hawthorne's conscious thought would confine it;
the human element in it threatens from time to time to break the mould of
thought and escape from bondage, because, simple as the moral scheme
is, human life is too complex to be solved by it even in this small world of the
three guilty ones and the child. This weakness of the moral scheme, this rude

strength of human nature, this sense of a larger solution, are most felt when Hawthorne approaches the love element, and throughout in the character of Hester, in whom alone human nature retains a self-assertive power. The same thing is felt vaguely, but certainly, in the lack of sympathy between Hawthorne and the Puritan environment he depicts. He presents the community itself, its common people, its magistrates and clergy, its customs, temper, and atmosphere, as forbidding, and he has no good word for it; harshness characterizes it, and that trait discredits its ideals, its judgments, and its entire interpretation of life. Hester, outcast from it, is represented as thereby enfranchised from its narrowness, enlightened, escaped into a world of larger truth:—

"The world's law was no law for her mind. It was an age in which the human intellect, newly emancipated, had taken a more active and a wider range than for many centuries before. Men of the sword had overthrown nobles and kings. Men bolder than these had overthrown and rearranged— not actually, but within the sphere of theory, which was their most real abode—the whole system of ancient prejudice, wherewith was linked much of ancient principle. Hester Prynne imbibed this spirit. She assumed a freedom of speculation, then common enough on the other side of the Atlantic, but which our forefathers, had they known it, would have held to be a deadlier crime than that stigmatized by the scarlet letter. In her lonesome cottage, by the sea-shore, thoughts visited her, such as dared to enter no other dwelling in New England; shadowy guests, that would have been as perilous as demons to their entertainer, could they have been seen so much as knocking at her door."

This is the foregleam of the next age, felt in her mind, the coming of a larger day. Hawthorne does not develop this or justify it; he only states it as a fact of life. And in the motive of the story, the love of Hester and Arthur, much is left dim; but what is discerned threatens to be unmanageable within the limits of the scheme. Did Hester love her lover, and he love her, through those seven years in silence? Did either of them ever repent their passion for its own sake? And when Hester's womanhood came back in its bloom and her hair fell shining in the forest sunlight, and she took her lover, hand and head and form, in all his broken suffering to her affectionate care and caress, and planned the bold step that they go out together across the seas and live in each other's lives like lovers in truth and reality,—was this only the resurrection of a moment or the firm vital force of a seven years' silent passion? Had either of them ever repented, though one was a coward and the other a condemned and public criminal before the law, and both had suffered? Was not the true sin, as is suggested, the source of all this error, the act of the physician who had first violated Hester's womanhood in a loveless marriage as he had now in Arthur's breast "violated in cold blood the sanctity of a human heart"? "Thou and I," says Arthur, "never did so." The strange words follow, strange for Hawthorne to have written, but better attesting his truth to human nature than all his morality:—

"Never, never!" whispered she. "What we did had a consecration of its own. We felt it so! We said so to each other! Hast thou forgotten it?"

"Hush, Hester!" said Arthur Dimmesdale, rising from the ground. "No; I have not forgotten!"

That confession is the stroke of genius in the romance that humanizes it with a thrill that is felt through every page of the stubborn, dark, harsh narrative of misery. It was not a sin against love that had been committed; it was a sin against the soul; and the sin against the soul lay in the lack of confession, which becomes the cardinal situation of the romance solved in the minister's dying acknowledgment. But the love problem is never solved, both Hester and Roger Chillingworth, one with her mystery of enduring love, the other with his mystery of insatiable hatred, are left with the issue, the meaning of their lives inexplicable, untold. Yet it is from the presence of these elements in the story that something of its intense reality comes.

It remains true, however, that the essential reality lies in the vivid sense of sin, and its experience in conscience. Hawthorne has not given a historical view of New England life; such a village, with such a tragedy, never existed, in that environing forest of the lone seacoast; but he has symbolized historical New England by an environment that he created round a tragedy that he read in the human heart, and in this tragedy itself he was able also to symbolize New England life in its internal features. One thing stood plainly out in our home Puritanism,—spirituality; the transcendent sense of the reality of the soul's life with God, its conscience, its perils, and its eternal issue. Spirituality remained the inheritance of the New England blood; and Hawthorne, who was no Puritan in doctrine or sympathy even, was Puritan in temperament, and hence to him, too, spirituality in life was its main element. He took that sin of passion which has ever been held typical of sin against the purity of the soul's nature, and transformed it into the symbol of all sin, and in its manifestation revolved the aspects of sin as a presence in the soul after the act,—the broken law disturbing life's external harmonies but working a worse havoc within, mining all with corruption there, while it infects with disease whatever approaches it from without. It is by its moral universality that the romance takes hold of the imagination; the scarlet letter becomes only a pictorial incident, but while conscience, repentance, confession, the modes of punishment, and the modes of absolution remain instant and permanent facts, in the life of the soul, many a human heart will read in this book as in a manual of its own intimate hours.

The romance is thus essentially a parable of the soul's life in sin; in its narrower scope it is the work of the moral intellect allegorizing its view of life; and where creative genius enters into it, in the Shakespearean sense of life in its own right, it tends to be a larger and truer story breaking the bonds of its religious scheme. It has its roots in Puritanism, but it is only incidentally a New England tale; its substance is the most universal experience of human nature in religious life, taking its forms only, its local habitation and name, from the Puritan colony in America, and these in a merely allegorical, not historical manner. Certain traits, however, ally it more closely to New England Puritanism. It is a relentless tale; the characters are singularly free from self-pity, and accept their fate as righteous; they never forgave themselves, they show no sign of having forgiven one another; even God's forgiveness is left under a shadow in futurity. They have sinned against the soul, and something implacable in evil remains. The minister's dying words drop a dark curtain over all.

"Hush, Hester, hush!" said he, with tremulous solemnity. "The law we broke!—the sin here so awfully revealed!—let these alone be in thy thoughts! I fear! I fear! It may be that, when we forgot our God,—when we violated our reverence each for the other's soul,—it was thenceforth vain to hope that we could meet hereafter, in an everlasting and pure reunion." Mercy is but a hope. There is also a singular absence of prayer in the book. Evil is presented as a thing without remedy, that cannot change its nature. The child, even, being the fruit of sin, can bring, Hester and Arthur doubt, no good for others or herself. In the scheme of Puritan thought, however, the atonement of Christ is the perpetual miracle whereby salvation comes, not only hereafter but in the holier life led here by grace. There is no Christ in this book. Absolution, so far as it is hinted at, lies in the direction of public confession, the efficacy of which is directly stated, but lamely nevertheless; it restores truth, but it does not heal the past. Leave the dead past to bury its dead, says Hawthorne, and go on to what may remain; but life once ruined is ruined past recall. So Hester, desirous of serving in her place the larger truth she has come to know, is stayed, says Hawthorne, because she "recognized the impossibility that any mission of divine and mysterious truth should be confided to a woman stained with sin, bowed down with shame, or even burdened with a life-long sorrow." That was never the Christian gospel nor the Puritan faith. Indeed, Hawthorne here and elsewhere anticipates those ethical views which are the burden of George Eliot's moral genius, and contain scientific pessimism. This stoicism, which was in Hawthorne, is a primary element in his moral nature, in him as well as in his work; it is visited with few touches of tenderness and pity; the pity one feels is not in him, it is in the pitiful thing, which he presents objectively, sternly, unrelentingly. It must be confessed that as an artist he appears unsympathetic with his characters; he is a moral dissector of their souls, minute, unflinching, thorough, a vivisector here; and he is cold because he has passed sentence on them, condemned them. There is no sympathy with human nature in the book; it is a fallen and ruined thing suffering just pain in its dying struggle. The romance is steeped in gloom. Is it too much to suggest that in ignoring prayer, the atonement of Christ, and the work of the Spirit in men's hearts, the better part of Puritanism has been left out, and the whole life of the soul distorted? Sin in the soul, the scarlet flower from the dark soil, we see; but, intent on that, has not the eye, and the heart, too, forgotten the large heavens that ensphere all—even this evil flower—and the infinite horizons that reach off to the eternal distance from every soul as from their centre? This romance is the record of a prison-cell, unvisited by any ray of light save that earthly one which gives both prisoners to public ignominy; they are seen, but they do not see. These traits of the book, here only suggested, have kinship with the repelling aspects of Puritanism, both as it was and as Hawthorne inherited it in his blood and breeding; so, in its transcendent spirituality, and in that democracy which is the twin-brother of spirituality in all lands and cultures, by virtue of which Hawthorne here humiliates and strips the minister who is the type of the spiritual aristocrat in the community, there is the essence of New England; but, for all that, the romance is a partial story, an imperfect fragment of the old life, distorting, not so much the Puritan ideal—which were a little matter—but the spiritual life itself. Its truth, intense, fascinating, terrible as it is, is a half-truth, and the darker half; it is the shadow of which the other half is light; it is the wrath of which the other half is love. A book from which light and love are absent may hold us by its truth to what is dark in life; but, in the highest sense, it is a false book. It is a chapter in the literature of moral despair, and is perhaps most tolerated as a condemnation of the creed which, through imperfect comprehension, it travesties.

—George E. Woodberry, *Nathaniel Hawthorne,*
1902, pp. 189–202

D.H. Lawrence "Nathaniel Hawthorne and The Scarlet Letter" (1923)

David Herbert Lawrence was the early-twentieth-century author of novels, short stories, travel books, poetry, and an early critical study of American literature. Lawrence's impressionistic and irreverent style is of its time, the modernist era, when such a flip and bantering tenor could also be found in criticism by writers such as Wyndham Lewis and Ezra Pound.

Lawrence's general method is to assign ungenerous inner motivations to the main, ostensibly sympathetic, characters in the novel. This reading is radical and enlivening, if often implausible. Students examining the motives of Hawthorne's characters will find Lawrence's essay provoking. Lawrence's is the first essay to unflinchingly address the sexual nature of the novel (which he does perhaps to excess). Yet amid Lawrence's psychosexual innuendo students will find material that challenges the surface, Victorian reading of the novel. Any student interested in the sexual politics of the novel will wish to read Lawrence's diatribe. Likewise, any student conducting a Freudian analysis of Hawthorne or his novel will also wish to consult Lawrence's assessment.

Lawrence views Hawthorne ("blue-eyed Nathaniel") as "lovey-dovey" and "goody-goody" on the surface, one who knew "disagreeable things in his inner soul" but "was careful to send them out in disguise." *The Scarlet Letter* has a "diabolic undertone." Hawthorne tells the reader "what's what," although this candor comes "cover[ed] with smarm." Ironically, the sheer attractiveness (or, for Lawrence, the disguise and "smarminess") of Hawthorne's bleak message frightened Coxe and Brownson too.

As an Englishman, Lawrence makes broad, negative observations of the American character: "Americans are destroyers." As a male, he sees women as demonic, "sending out waves of silent destruction of the faltering spirit in men." He makes several sweeping claims, and some of his observations are more salacious than incisive. "The poor hate a salvationist. They smell the devil underneath." Lawrence clearly has his own agenda and his own demons he is unknowingly giving voice to, so the essay speaks more about D.H. Lawrence than it does about Nathaniel Hawthorne. Scattered throughout this seemingly ecstatic and lengthy discourse are some moments of perception or at least useful provocation.

Regarding Hester and Dimmesdale, Lawrence meditates on Adam and Eve and their sin. From this he launches into a protracted reflection on gender relations. Lawrence takes Dimmesdale, Chillingworth, and Hester as representative male and female types. A woman is a devil, but "it is man's fault." Hester destroys Dimmesdale because of his failure of nerve: "Unless a man believes in himself and his gods, *genuinely*; unless he fiercely obeys his own Holy Ghost; his woman will destroy him." The essay lapses into apparent personal bile and misogyny, amplifying private defeats to universal dictums. Lawrence regards Hester (like all women) as entrapping—as variously Abel (to Dimmesdale's Cain), as a witch ("which she was"), as a demon, as Ligeia (from Poe's story), as "the grey nurse" and "the hell-cat." Hester *"hates"* Pearl and vice versa. Hester and Chillingworth are, finally, co-conspirators in "pulling down the spiritual saint" Dimmesdale.

Dimmesdale, meanwhile, is simultaneously saintly and demonic. His last confession is a "coup" of vengeance. He publicly shows Chillingworth up for a cuckold and leaves Hester "dished." His self-torment and ascetic suffering are versions of masturbation. Chillingworth is, like Francis Bacon and also like Roger Bacon, "the old male authority," the "old order of intellect," "a magician on the verge of modern science." Shakespeare's tragedies lament the decline of male authority, Lawrence explains. Queen Elizabeth vanquished male authority, and Queen Victoria ground it underfoot. The castrated male *par excellence*, Chillingworth can only maintain his impotent "intellectual tradition." He has a hatred for Dimmesdale that is "akin to love," Lawrence argues—detecting a homoerotic element to the narrative—and Dimmesdale returns "a hideous kind of love" with his corresponding self-torment. The "crippled masterful male" (Chillingworth) and the "fallen saint" (Dimmesdale) are the "two halves of manhood mutually destroying one another."

⫘ ⫘ ⫘

Nathaniel Hawthorne writes romance.

And what's romance? Usually, a nice little tale where you have everything As You Like It, where rain never wets your jacket and gnats never bite your nose and it's always daisy-time. *As You Like It* and *Forest Lovers*, etc. *Morte D'Arthur.*

Hawthorne obviously isn't this kind of romanticist: though nobody has muddy boots in *The Scarlet Letter*, either.

But there is more to it. *The Scarlet Letter* isn't a pleasant, pretty romance. It is a sort of parable, an earthly story with a hellish meaning.

All the time there is this split in the American art and art-consciousness. On the top it is as nice as pie, goody-goody and lovey-dovey. Like Hawthorne being such a blue-eyed darling, in life, and Longfellow and the rest such sucking-doves. Hawthorne's wife said she 'never saw him in time', which doesn't mean she saw him too late. But always in the 'frail effulgence of eternity'.

Serpents they were. Look at the inner meaning of their art and see what demons they were.

You *must* look through the surface of American art, and see the inner diabolism of the symbolic meaning. Otherwise it is all mere childishness.

That blue-eyed darling Nathaniel knew disagreeable things in his inner soul. He was careful to send them out in disguise.

Always the same. The deliberate consciousness of Americans so fair and smooth-spoken, and the under-consciousness so devilish. *Destroy! destroy! destroy!* hums the under-consciousness. *Love and produce! Love and produce!* cackles the upper consciousness. And the world hears only the Love-and-produce cackle. Refuses to hear the hum of destruction underneath. Until such time as it will *have* to hear.

The American has got to destroy. It is his destiny. It is his destiny to destroy the whole corpus of the white psyche, the white consciousness. And he's got to do it secretly. As the growing of a dragon-fly inside a chrysalis or cocoon destroys the larva grub, secretly.

Though many a dragon-fly never gets out of the chrysalis case: dies inside. As America might.

So the secret chrysalis of *The Scarlet Letter*, diabolically destroying the old psyche inside.

Be good! Be good! warbles Nathaniel. *Be good, and never sin! Be sure your sins will find you out.*

So convincingly that his wife never saw him 'as in time'.

Then listen to the diabolic undertone of *The Scarlet Letter*.

Man ate of the tree of knowledge, and became ashamed of himself.

Do you imagine Adam had never lived with Eve before that apple episode? Yes, he had. As a wild animal with his mate.

It didn't become 'sin' till the knowledge-poison entered. That apple of Sodom.

We are divided in ourselves, against ourselves. And that is the meaning of the cross symbol.

In the first place, Adam knew Eve as a wild animal knows its mate, momentaneously, but vitally, in blood-knowledge. Blood-knowledge, not mind-knowledge. Blood-knowledge, that seems utterly to forget, but doesn't. Blood-knowledge, instinct, intuition, all the vast vital flux of knowing that goes on in the dark, antecedent to the mind.

Then came that beastly apple, and the other sort of knowledge started.

Adam began to look at himself. 'My hat!' he said. 'What's this ? My Lord ! What the deuce !—And Eve ! I wonder about Eve.'

Thus starts KNOWING. Which shortly runs to UNDERSTANDING, when the devil gets his own.

When Adam went and took Eve, *after* the apple, he didn't do any more than he had done many a time before, in act. But in consciousness he did something very different. So did Eve. Each of them kept an eye on what they were doing, they watched what was happening to them. They wanted to KNOW. And that was the birth of sin. Not *doing* it, but KNOWING about it. Before the apple, they had shut their eyes and their minds had gone dark. Now, they peeped and pried and imagined. They watched themselves. And they felt uncomfortable after. They felt self-conscious. So they said, 'The act is sin. Let's hide. We've sinned.'

No wonder the Lord kicked them out of the Garden. Dirty hypocrites.

The sin was the self-watching, self-consciousness. The sin, and the doom. Dirty understanding.

Nowadays men do hate the idea of dualism. It's no good, dual we are. The cross. If we accept the symbol, then, virtually, we accept the fact. We are divided against ourselves.

For instance, the blood *hates* being KNOWN. Hence the profound instinct of privacy.

And on the other hand, the mind and the spiritual consciousness of man simply *hates* the dark potency of blood-acts: hates the genuine dark sensual orgasms, which do, for the time being, actually obliterate the mind and the spiritual consciousness, plunge them in a suffocating flood of darkness.

You can't get away from this.

Blood-consciousness overwhelms, obliterates, and annuls mind-consciousness.

Mind-consciousness extinguishes blood-consciousness, and consumes the blood.

We are all of us conscious in both ways. And the two ways are antagonistic in us.

They will always remain so.

That is our cross.

The antagonism is so obvious, and so far-reaching, that it extends to the smallest thing. The cultured, highly-conscious person of today *loathes* any form of physical, 'menial' work: such as washing dishes or sweeping a floor or chopping wood. This menial work is an insult to the spirit. 'When I see men carrying heavy loads, doing brutal work, it always makes me want to cry,' said a beautiful, cultured woman to me.

'When you say that, it makes me want to beat you,' said I, in reply. 'When I see you with your beautiful head pondering heavy thoughts, I just want to hit you. It outrages me.'

My father hated books, hated the sight of anyone reading or writing.

My mother hated the thought that any of her sons should be condemned to manual labour. Her sons must have something higher than that.

She won. But she died first.

He laughs longest who laughs last.

There is a basic hostility in all of us between the physical and the mental, the blood and the spirit. The mind is 'ashamed' of the blood. And the blood is destroyed by the mind, actually. Hence pale-faces.

At present the mind-consciousness and the so-called spirit triumphs. In America supremely. In America, nobody does anything from the blood. Always from the nerves, if not from the mind. The blood is chemically reduced by the nerves, in American activity.

When an Italian labourer labours, his mind and nerves sleep, his blood acts ponderously.

Americans, when they are *doing* things, never seem really to be doing them. They are 'busy about' it. They are always busy 'about' something. But truly *immersed* in *doing* something, with the deep blood-consciousness active, that they never are.

They *admire* the blood-conscious spontaneity. And they want to get it in their heads. 'Live from the body,' they shriek. It is their last mental shriek. *Co-ordinate.*

It is a further attempt still to rationalize the body and blood. 'Think about such and such a muscle,' they say, 'and relax there.'

And every time you 'conquer' the body with the mind (you can say 'heel' it, if you like) you cause a deeper, more dangerous complex or tension somewhere else.

Ghastly Americans, with their blood no longer blood. A yellow spiritual fluid.

The Fall.

There have been lots of Falls.

We *fell* into *knowledge* when Eve bit the apple. Self-conscious knowledge. For the first time the mind put up a fight against the blood. Wanting to UNDERSTAND. That is to intellectualize the blood.

The blood must be *shed*, says Jesus.

Shed on the cross of our own divided psyche.

Shed the blood, and you become mind-conscious. Eat the body and drink the blood, self-cannibalizing, and you become extremely conscious, like Americans and some Hindus. Devour yourself, and God knows what a lot you'll know, what a lot you'll be conscious of.

Mind you don't choke yourself.

For a long time men *believed* that they could be perfected through the mind, through the spirit. They believed, passionately. They had their ecstasy in pure consciousness. They *believed* in purity, chastity, and the wings of the spirit.

America soon plucked the bird of the spirit. America soon killed the *belief* in the spirit. But not the practice. The practice continued with a sarcastic vehemence. America, with a perfect inner contempt for the spirit and the consciousness of man, practices the same spirituality and universal love and KNOWING all the time, incessantly, like a drug habit. And inwardly gives not a fig for it. Only for the *sensation*. The pretty-pretty *sensation* of love, loving all the world. And the nice fluttering aeroplane *sensation* of knowing, knowing, knowing. Then the prettiest of all sensations, the sensation of UNDERSTANDING. Oh, what a lot they understand, the darlings! *So* good at the trick, they are. Just a trick of self-conceit.

The Scarlet Letter gives the show away.

You have your pure-pure young parson Dimmesdale.

You have the beautiful Puritan Hester at his feet.

And the first thing she does is to seduce him.

And the first thing he does is to be seduced.

And the second thing they do is to hug their sin in secret, and gloat over it, and try to understand.

Which is the myth of New England.

Deerslayer refused to be seduced by Judith Hutter. At least the Sodom apple of sin didn't fetch him

But Dimmesdale was seduced gloatingly. Oh, luscious Sin!

He was such a pure young man.

That he had to make a fool of purity.

The American psyche.

Of course, the best part of the game lay in keeping up pure appearances.

The greatest triumph a woman can have, especially an American woman, is the triumph of seducing a man: especially if he is pure.

And he gets the greatest thrill of all, in falling.—'Seduce me, Mrs Hercules.'

And the pair of them share the subtlest delight in keeping up pure appearances, when everybody knows all the while. But the power of pure appearances is something to exult in. All America gives in to it. *Look* pure!

To seduce a man. To have everybody know. To keep up appearances of purity. Pure!

This is the great triumph of woman.

A. The Scarlet Letter. Adulteress! The great Alpha. Alpha! Adulteress! The new Adam and Adama! American!

A. Adulteress! Stitched with gold thread, glittering upon the bosom. The proudest insignia.

Put her upon the scaffold and worship her there. Worship her there. The Woman, the Magna Mater. A. Adulteress! Abel!

Abel! Abel! Abel! Admirable!

It becomes a farce.

The fiery heart. A. Mary of the Bleeding Heart. Mater Adolerata! A. Capital A. Adulteress. Glittering with gold thread. Abel! Adultery. Admirable!

It is, perhaps, the most colossal satire ever penned. *The Scarlet Letter*. And by a blue-eyed darling of a Nathaniel.

Not Bumppo, however.

The human spirit, fixed in a lie, adhering to a lie, giving itself perpetually the lie.

All begins with *A*.

Adulteress. Alpha Abel, Adam. *A*. America.

The Scarlet Letter.

'Had there been a Papist among the crowd of Puritans, he might have seen in this beautiful woman, so picturesque in her attire and mien, and with the infant at her bosom, an object to remind him of the image of Divine Maternity, which so many illustrious painters have vied with one another to represent; something which should remind him, indeed, but only by contrast, of that sacred image of sinless Motherhood, whose infant was to redeem the world.'

Whose infant was to redeem the world indeed! It will be a startling redemption the world will get from the American infant.

Here was a taint of deepest sin in the most sacred quality of human life, working such effect that the world was only the darker for this woman's beauty, and more lost for the infant she had borne.

Just listen to the darling. Isn't he a master of apology?

Of symbols, too.

His pious blame is a chuckle of praise all the while.

Oh, Hester, you are a demon. A man must be pure, just so that you can seduce him to a fall. Because the greatest thrill in life is to bring down the Sacred Saint with a flop into the mud. Then when you've brought him down humbly wipe off the mud with your hair, another Magdalen. And then go home and dance a witch's jig of triumph, and stitch yourself a Scarlet Letter with gold thread, as duchesses used to stitch themselves coronets. And then stand meek on the scaffold and fool the world. Who will all be envying you your sin, and beating you because you've stolen an advantage over them.

Hester Prynne is the great nemesis of woman. She is the KNOWING Ligeia risen diabolic from the grave. Having her own back. UNDERSTANDING.

This time it is Mr Dimmesdale who dies. She lives on and is Abel.

His spiritual love was a lie. And prostituting the woman to his spiritual love, as popular clergymen do, in his preachings and loftiness, was a tall white lie. Which came flop.

We are so pure in spirit. Hi-tiddly-i-ty!

Till she tickled him in the right place, and he fell.

Flop.

Flop goes spiritual love.

But keep up the game. Keep up appearances. Pure are the pure. To the pure all things, etc.

Look out, Mister, for the Female Devotee. Whatever you do, don't let her start tickling you. She knows your weak spot. Mind your Purity.

When Hester Prynne seduced Arthur Dimmesdale it was the beginning of the end. But from the beginning of the end to the end of the end is a hundred years or two.

Mr Dimmesdale also wasn't at the end of his resources. Previously, he had lived by governing his body, ruling it, in the interests of his spirit. Now he has a good time all by himself torturing his body, whipping it, piercing it with thorns, macerating himself. It's a form of masturbation. He wants to get a mental grip on his body. And since he can't quite manage it with the mind, witness his fall—he will give it what for, with whips. His will shall lash his body. And he enjoys his pains. Wallows in them. To the pure all things are pure.

It is the old self-mutilation process, gone rotten. The mind wanting to get its teeth in the blood and flesh. The ego exulting in the tortures of the mutinous flesh. I, the ego, I *will* triumph over my own flesh. Lash! Lash! I am a grand free spirit. *Lash!* I am the master of my soul! *Lash! Lash!* I am the captain of my soul. *Lash!* Hurray! 'In the fell clutch of circumstance,' etc., etc.

Good-bye Arthur. He depended on women for his Spiritual Devotees, spiritual brides. So, the woman just touched him in his weak spot, his Achilles Heel of the flesh. Look out for the spiritual bride. She's after the weak spot.

It is the battle of wills.

'For the will therein lieth, which dieth not—'

The Scarlet Woman becomes a Sister of Mercy. Didn't she just, in the late war. Oh, Prophet Nathaniel!

Hester urges Dimmesdale to go away with her, to a new country, to a new life. He isn't having any.

He knows there is no new country, no new life on the globe today. It is the same old thing, in different degrees, everywhere. *Plus ça change, plus c'est la meme chose.* Hester thinks, with Dimmesdale for her husband, and Pearl for her child, in Australia, maybe, she'd have been perfect.

But she wouldn't. Dimmesdale had already fallen from his integrity as a minister of the Gospel of the Spirit. He had lost his manliness. He didn't see the point of just leaving himself between the hands of a woman and going away to a 'new country', to be her thing entirely. She'd only have despised him more, as every woman despises a man who has 'fallen' to her; despises him with her tenderest lust.

He stood for nothing any more. So let him stay where he was and dree out his weird.

She had dished him and his spirituality, so he hated her. As Angel Clare was dished, and hated Tess. As Jude in the end hated Sue: or should have done. The women make fools of them, the spiritual men. And when, as men, they've gone flop in their spirituality, they can't pick themselves up whole any more. So they just crawl, and die detesting the female, or the females, who made them fall.

The saintly minister gets a bit of his own back, at the last minute, by making public confession from the very scaffold where he was exposed. Then he dodges into death. But he's had a bit of his own back, on everybody.

'Shall we not meet again?' whispered she, bending her face down close to him. 'Shall we not spend our immortal life together ? Surely, surely, we have ransomed one another with all this woe! Thou lookest far into eternity with those bright dying eyes. Tell me what thou seest!' 'Hush, Hester—hush,' said he, with tremulous solemnity. 'The law we broke!—the sin here so awfully revealed! Let these alone be in thy thoughts. I fear! I fear!'

So he dies, throwing the 'sin' in her teeth, and escaping into death.

The law we broke, indeed. You bet.

Whose law!

But it is truly a law, that man must either stick to the belief he has grounded himself on, and obey the laws of that belief, or he must admit the belief itself to be inadequate, and prepare himself for a new thing.

There was no change in belief, either in Hester or in Dimmesdale or in Hawthorne or in America. The same old treacherous belief, which was really cunning disbelief, in the Spirit, in Purity, in Selfless Love, and in Pure Consciousness. They would go on following this belief, for the sake of the sensation of it. But they would make a fool of it all the time. Like Woodrow Wilson, and the rest of modern Believers. The rest of modern Saviours.

If you meet a Saviour, today, be sure he is trying to make an innermost fool of you. Especially if the saviour be an UNDERSTANDING WOMAN, offering her love.

Hester lives on, pious as pie, being a public nurse. She becomes at last an acknowledged saint, Abel of the Scarlet Letter.

She would, being a woman. She has had her triumph over the individual man, so she quite loves subscribing to the whole spiritual life of society. She will make herself as false as hell, for society's sake, once she's had her real triumph over Saint Arthur.

Blossoms out into a Sister-of-Mercy Saint.

But it's a long time before she really takes anybody in. People kept on thinking her a witch, which she was.

As a matter of fact, unless a woman is held, by man, safe within the bounds of belief, she becomes inevitably a destructive force. She can't help herself. A woman is almost always vulnerable to pity. She can't bear to see anything physical hurt. But let a woman loose from the bounds and restraints of man's fierce belief, in his gods and in himself, and she becomes a gentle devil. She becomes subtly diabolic. The colossal evil of the united spirit of Woman. WOMAN, German woman or American woman, or every other sort of woman, in the last war, was something frightening. As every man knows.

Woman becomes a helpless, would-be-loving demon. She is helpless. Her very love is subtle poison.

Unless a man believes in himself and his gods, *genuinely*: unless he fiercely obeys his own Holy Ghost; his woman will destroy him. Woman is the nemesis of doubting man. She can't help it.

And with Hester, after Ligeia, woman becomes a nemesis to man. She bolsters him up from the outside, she destroys him from the inside. And he dies hating her, as Dimmesdale did.

Dimmesdale's spirituality had gone on too long, too far. It had become a false thing. He found his nemesis in woman. And he was done for.

Woman is a strange and rather terrible phenomenon, to man. When the subconscious soul of woman recoils from its creative union with man, it becomes a destructive force. It exerts, willy-nilly, an invisible destructive influence. The woman herself may be as nice as milk, to all appearance, like Ligeia. But she is sending out waves of silent destruction of the faltering spirit in men, all the same. She doesn't know it. She can't even help it. But she does it. The devil is in her.

The very women who are most busy saving the bodies of men, and saving the children: these women-doctors, these nurses, these educationalists, these public-spirited women these female saviours: they are all, from the inside, sending out waves of destructive malevolence which eat out the inner life of a man, like a cancer. It is so, it will be so, till men realize it and react to save themselves.

God won't save us. The women are so devilish godly. Men must save themselves in this strait, and by no sugary means either.

A woman can use her sex in sheer malevolence and poison, while she is *behaving* as meek and good as gold. Dear darling, she is really snow-white in her blamelessness. And all the while she is using her sex as a she-devil, for the endless hurt of her man. She doesn't know it. She will never believe it if you tell her. And if you give her a slap in the face for her fiendishness, she will rush to the first magistrate, in indignation. She is so *absolutey* blameless, the she-devil, the dear, dutiful creature.

Give her the great slap, just the same, just when she is being most angelic. Just when she is bearing her cross most meekly.

Oh, woman out of bounds is a devil. But it is man's fault. Woman never *asked*, in the first place, to be cast out of her bit of an Eden of belief and trust. It is man's business to bear the responsibility of belief. If he becomes a spiritual fornicator and liar, like Ligeia's husband and Arthur Dimmesdale, how *can* a woman believe in him? Belief doesn't go by choice. And if a woman doesn't believe in a *man*, she believes, essentially, in nothing. She becomes, willy-nilly, a devil.

A devil she is, and a devil she will be. And most men will succumb to her devilishness.

Hester Prynne was a devil. Even when she was so meekly going round as a sick-nurse. Poor Hester. Part of her wanted to be saved from her own devilishness. And another part wanted to go on and on in devilishness, for revenge. Revenge! REVENGE! It is this that fills the unconscious spirit of woman today. Revenge against man, and against the spirit of man which has betrayed her into unbelief. Even when she is most sweet and a salvationist, she is her most devilish, is woman. She gives her man the sugar-plum of her own submissive sweetness. And when he's taken this sugar-plum in his mouth, a scorpion comes out of it. After he's taken this Eve to his bosom, oh, so loving, she destroys him inch by inch. Woman and her revenge! She will have it, and go on having it, for decades and decades, unless she's stopped. And to stop her you've got to believe in yourself and your gods, your own Holy Ghost, Sir Man; and then you've got to fight her, and never give in. She's a devil. But in the long run she is conquerable. And just a tiny bit of her wants to be conquered. You've got to fight three-quarters of her, in absolute hell, to get at the final quarter of her that wants a release, at last, from the hell of her own revenge. But it's a long last. And not yet.

'She had in her nature a rich, voluptuous, oriental characteristic—a taste for the gorgeously beautiful.' This is Hester. This is American. But she repressed her nature in the above direction. She would not even allow herself the luxury of labouring at fine, delicate stitching. Only she dressed her little sin-child Pearl vividly, and the scarlet letter was gorgeously embroidered. Her Hecate and Astarte insignia.

'A voluptuous, oriental characteristic—' That lies waiting in American women. It is probable that the Mormons are the forerunners of the coming real America. It is probable that men will have more than one wife, in the coming America. That you will have again a half-oriental womanhood, and a polygamy.

The grey nurse, Hester. The Hecate, the hell-cat. The slowly-evolving voluptuous female of the new era, with a whole new submissiveness to the dark, phallic principle.

But it takes time. Generation after generation of nurses and political women and salvationists. And in the end, the dark erection of the images of sex-worship once more, and the newly submissive women. That kind of depth. Deep women in that respect. When we have at last broken this insanity of mental-spiritual consciousness. And the women *choose* to experience again the great submission.

'The poor, whom she sought out to be the objects of her bounty, often reviled the hand that was stretched to succour them.'

Naturally. The poor hate a salvationist. They smell the devil underneath.

'She was patient—a martyr indeed—but she forebore to pray for her enemies, lest, in spite of her forgiving aspirations, the words of the blessing should stubbornly twist themselves into a curse.'

So much honesty, at least. No wonder the old witch-lady Mistress Hibbins claimed her for another witch.

'She grew to have a dread of children; for they had imbibed from their parents a vague idea of something horrible in this dreary woman gliding silently through the town, with never any companion but only one child.'

'A vague idea!' Can't you see her 'gliding silently'? It's not a question of a vague idea imbibed, but a definite feeling directly received.

But sometimes, once in many days, or perchance in many months, she felt an eye—a human eye—upon the ignominious brand, that seemed to give a momentary relief, as if half her agony were shared. The next instant, back it all rushed again, with a still deeper throb of pain; for in that brief interval she had sinned again. Had Hester sinned alone?

Of course not. As for sinning again, she would go on all her life silently, changelessly 'sinning'. She never repented. Not she. Why should she? She had brought down Arthur Dimmesdale, that too-too snow-white bird, and that was her life-work.

As for sinning again when she met two dark eyes in a crowd, why, of course. Somebody who understood as she understood.

I always remember meeting the eyes of a gipsy woman, for one moment, in a crowd, in England. She knew, and I knew. What did we know! I was not able to make out. But we knew.

Probably the same fathomless hate of this spiritual conscious society in which the outcast woman and I both roamed like meek-looking wolves. Tame wolves waiting to shake off their tameness. Never able to.

And again, that 'voluptuous, oriental' characteristic that knows the mystery of the ithyphallic gods. She would not betray the ithyphallic gods to this white, leprous-white society of 'lovers'. Neither will I, if I can help it. These leprous-white, seducing, spiritual women, who 'understand' so much. One has been too often seduced, and 'understood'. 'I can read him like a book,' said my first lover of me. The book is in several volumes, dear. And more and more comes back to me the gulf of dark hate and *other* understanding, in the eyes of the gipsy woman. So different from the hateful white light of understanding which floats like scum on the eyes of white, oh, so white English and American women, with their understanding voices and their deep, sad words, and their profound, *good* spirits. Pfui!

Hester was scared only of one result of her sin: Pearl. Pearl, the scarlet letter incarnate. The little girl. When women bear children, they produce either devils or sons with gods in them. And it is an evolutionary process. The devil in Hester produced a purer devil in Pearl. And the devil in Pearl will produce—she married an Italian Count—a piece of purer devilishness still.

And so from hour to hour we ripe and ripe.

And then from hour to hour we rot and rot.

There was that in the child 'which often impelled Hester to ask in bitterness of heart, whether it were for good or ill that the poor little creature had been born at all'.

For ill, Hester. But don't worry. Ill is as necessary as good. Malevolence is as necessary as benevolence. If you have brought forth, spawned, a young malevolence, be sure there is a rampant falseness in the world against which this malevolence must be turned. Falseness has to be bitten and bitten, till it is bitten to death. Hence Pearl.

Pearl. Her own mother compares her to the demon of plague, or scarlet fever, in her red dress. But then, plague is necessary to destroy a rotten false humanity.

Pearl, the devilish girl-child, who can be so tender and loving and *understanding*, and then, when she has understood, will give you a hit across the mouth, and turn on you with a grin of sheer diabolic jeering.

Serves you right, you shouldn't be *understood*. That is your vice. You shouldn't want to be loved, and then you'd not get hit across the mouth. Pearl will love you: marvellously. And she'll hit you across the mouth: oh, so neatly. And serves you right.

Pearl is perhaps the most modern child in all literature.

Old-fashioned Nathaniel, with his little-boy charm, he'll tell you what's what. But he'll cover it with smarm.

Hester simply *hates* her child, from one part of herself. And from another, she cherishes her child as her one precious treasure. For Pearl is the continuing of her female revenge on life. But female revenge hits both ways. Hits back at its own mother. The female revenge in Pearl hits back at Hester, the mother, and Hester is simply livid with fury and 'sadness', which is rather amusing.

The child could not be made amenable to rules. In giving her existence a great law had been broken; and the result was a being whose elements were perhaps beautiful and brilliant, but all in disorder, or with an order peculiar to themselves, amidst which the point of variety and arrangement was difficult or impossible to discover.

Of course, the order is peculiar to themselves. But the point of variety is this: 'Draw out the loving, sweet soul, draw it out with marvellous understanding; and then spit in its eye.'

Hester, of course, didn't at all like it when her sweet child drew out her motherly soul, with yearning and deep understanding: and then spit in the motherly eye, with a grin. But it was a process the mother had started.

Pearl had a peculiar look in her eyes: 'a look so intelligent yet so inexplicable, so perverse, sometimes so malicious, but generally accompanied by a wild flow of spirits, that Hester could not help questioning at such moments whether Pearl was a human child.'

A little demon! But her mother, and the saintly Dimmesdale, had borne her. And Pearl, by the very openness of her perversity, was more straightforward than her parents. She flatly refuses any Heavenly Father, seeing the earthly one such a fraud. And she has the pietistic Dimmesdale on toast, spits right in his eye: in both his eyes.

Poor, brave, tormented little soul, always in a state of recoil, she'll be a devil to men when she grows up. But the men deserve it. If they'll let themselves be 'drawn', by her loving understanding, they deserve that she shall slap them across the mouth the moment they *are* drawn. The chickens! Drawn and trussed.

Poor little phenomenon of a modern child, she'll grow up into the devil of a modern woman. The nemesis of weak-kneed modern men, craving to be love-drawn.

The third person in the diabolic trinity, or triangle, of the Scarlet Letter, is Hester's first husband, Roger Chillingworth. He is an old Elizabethan physician, with a grey beard and a long-furred coat and a twisted shoulder. Another healer. But something of an alchemist, a magician. He is a magician on the verge of modern science, like Francis Bacon.

Roger Chillingworth is of the old order of intellect, in direct line from the medieval Roger Bacon alchemists. He has an old, intellectual belief in the dark sciences, the flermetic philosophies. He is no Christian, no selfless aspirer. He is not an aspirer. He is the old authoritarian in man. The old male authority. But without passional belief. Only intellectual belief in himself and his male authority.

Shakespeare's whole tragic wail is because of the downfall of the true male authority, the ithyphallic authority and masterhood. It fell with Elizabeth. It was trodden underfoot with Victoria.

But Chillingworth keeps on the *intellectual* tradition. He hates the new spiritual aspirers, like Dimmesdale, with a black, crippled hate. He is the old male authority, in intellectual tradition.

You can't keep a wife by force of an intellectual tradition. So Hester took to seducing Dimmesdale.

Yet her only marriage, and her last oath, is with the old Roger. He and she are accomplices in pulling down the spiritual saint.

'Why dost thou smile so at me—' she says to her old, vengeful husband. 'Art thou not like the Black Man that haunts the forest around us? Hast thou not enticed me into a bond which will prove the ruin of my soul?'

'Not thy soul!' he answered with another smile. 'No, not thy soul!'

It is the soul of the pure preacher, that false thing, which they are after. And the crippled physician—this other healer—blackly vengeful in his old, distorted male authority, and the 'loving' woman, they bring down the saint between them.

A black and complementary hatred, akin to love, is what Chillingworth feels for the young, saintly parson. And Dimmesdale responds, in a hideous kind of love. Slowly the saint's life is poisoned. But the black old physician smiles, and tries to keep him alive. Dimmesdale goes in for self-torture, self-lashing his own white, thin, spiritual saviour's body. The dark Chillingworth listens outside the door and laughs, and prepares another medicine, so that the game can go on longer. And the saint's very soul goes rotten. Which is the supreme triumph. Yet he keeps up appearances still.

The black, vengeful soul of the crippled, masterful male, still dark in his authority: and the white ghastliness of the fallen saint! The two halves of manhood mutually destroying one another.

Dimmesdale has a 'coup' in the very end. He gives the whole show away by confessing publicly on the scaffold, and dodging into death, leaving Hester dished, and Roger as it were, doubly cuckolded. It is a neat last revenge.

Down comes the curtain, as in Ligeia's poem.

But the child Pearl will be on in the next act, with her Italian Count and a new brood of vipers. And Hester greyly Abelling, in the shadows, after her rebelling.

It is a marvellous allegory. It is to me one of the greatest allegories in all literature. *The Scarlet Letter*. Its marvellous under-meaning! And its perfect duplicity.

The absolute duplicity of that blue-eyed *Wunderkind* of a Nathaniel. The American wonder-child, with his magical allegorical insight.

But even wonder-children have to grow up in a generation or two.

And even SIN becomes stale.

—D.H. Lawrence, "Nathaniel Hawthorne and
The Scarlet Letter," *Studies in Classic American Literature,*
New York, 1923, pp. 83–99

THE HOUSE OF THE SEVEN GABLES

Following the success of *The Scarlet Letter*, *The House of the Seven Gables* was greatly anticipated. Its comparison to the preceding novel was inevitable, and *The House of the Seven Gables* seems to have fared well in that process. The poet Lowell—a keen custodian of New England folk-ways and history—valued the novel for its historic faithfulness and its ability to invest the past with relevance to Hawthorne's present. Lowell notices how ably Hawthorne "reconcile[s] the present with the past," an aspect of the novel repeatedly distinguished for praise. Such a successful fusion also occurs in Hawthorne's admixture of the humorous and the grave, that "skilful blending of the tragic and the comic" heralded by the unsigned reviewer for *Harper's Monthly*. While *The Scarlet Letter* had the humorous "Custom House" preface, the story proper was "tragic almost to ghastliness." This, E.P. Whipple argues, was *The Scarlet Letter's* "error," resolved in the subsequent novel.

This lightening of tone was not universally esteemed, however. While Whipple proclaims this to be Hawthorne's greatest work, he finds it flags after the first hundred pages (and the first edition had 344 pages). Toward the work's conclusion, "the author's mind betrays a slight fitfulness" and "somewhat departs from the integrity of the original conception." The story's ending divides opinion (Hawthorne's wife was delighted by it) and the novel remains an enigma for critics for this reason. Mark Twain's *Huckleberry Finn* similarly has confounded readers with its ill-fitting closing tone. E.P Whipple dismisses the love between Holgrave and Phoebe as implausible, while Henry Tuckerman finds it "remarkably natural." Henry James found the novel fragmentary, hinting at a larger story than the one that it recounted.

SOPHIA PEABODY HAWTHORNE (1851)

In this private letter, Hawthorne's wife, Sophia—perhaps his most influen-tial reader—addresses what is, for many critics, the novel's main problem: Holgrave's apparent ideological about-face, leading to the novel's slightly incongruous happy conclusion.

Unlike many critics, Sophia welcomed this turnaround. She had been inconsolable and had retired to bed with a "grievous headache" when Hawthorne first read *The Scarlet Letter* to her. *The House of the Seven*

Gables placated her, and she much preferred it. Students interested in the novel's varying reception will be illuminated by Sophia's response.

———— ———— ————

The House of the Seven Gables was finished yesterday. Mr. Hawthorne read me the close, last evening. There is unspeakable grace and beauty in the conclusion, throwing back upon the sterner tragedy of the commencement an ethereal light, and a dear home-loveliness and satisfaction. How you will enjoy the book,—its depth of wisdom, its high tone, the flowers of Paradise scattered over all the dark places, the sweet wall-flower scent of Phoebe's character, the wonderful pathos and charm of old Uncle Venner. I only wish you could have heard the Poet sing his own song, as I did; but yet the book needs no adventitious aid,—it makes its own music, for I read it all over again to myself yesterday, except the last three chapters.

> —Sophia Peabody Hawthorne, Letter (January 27, 1851),
> cited in Julian Hawthorne, *Nathaniel Hawthorne
> and His Wife,* 1884, Vol. 1, p. 383

NATHANIEL HAWTHORNE (1851)

The *House of the Seven Gables,* in my opinion, is better than *The Scarlet Letter;* but I should not wonder if I had refined upon the principal character a little too much for popular appreciation; nor if the romance of the book should be found somewhat at odds with the humble and familiar scenery in which I invest it. But I feel that portions of it are as good as anything I can hope to write, and the publisher speaks encouragingly of its success.

> —Nathaniel Hawthorne, Letter to Horatio Bridge
> (March 15, 1851), cited in Horatio Bridge,
> *Personal Recollections of Nathaniel Hawthorne,* 1893, p. 125

JAMES RUSSELL LOWELL (1851)

I have been so delighted with *The House of the Seven Gables* that I cannot help sitting down to tell you so. I thought I could not forgive you if you wrote anything better than *The Scarlet Letter;* but I cannot help believing it a great triumph that you should have been able to deepen and widen the impression made by such a book as that. It seems to me that the "House" is the most valuable contribution to New England history that has been made. It is with the highest art that you have typified (in the revived likeness of Judge Pyncheon to his ancestor the Colonel) that intimate relationship between the Present and the Past in the way of ancestry and descent, which historians so carefully overlook. Yesterday is commonly looked upon and written about as of no kin to To-day, though the one is legitimate child of the other, and has its veins filled with the same blood. And the chapter about Alice and the Carpenter,—Salem, which would not even allow you so much as Scotland gave Burns, will build you a monument yet for having shown that she did not hang her witches for nothing. I suppose the true office of the historian is to reconcile the present with the past.

—James Russell Lowell, Letter to Nathaniel Hawthorne
(April 24, 1851), cited in Julian Hawthorne,
Nathaniel Hawthorne and His Wife, 1884, Vol. 1, pp. 390–91

ANONYMOUS (1851)

Ticknor, Reed, and Fields have issued *The House of the Seven Gables*, a Romance, by NATHANIEL HAWTHORNE, which is strongly marked with the bold and unique characteristics that have given its author such a brilliant position among American novelists. The scene, which is laid in the old Puritanic town of Salem, extends from the period of the witchcraft excitement to the present time, connecting the legends of the ancient superstition with the recent marvels of animal magnetism, and affording full scope for the indulgence of the most weird and sombre fancies. Destitute of the high-wrought manifestations of passion which distinguished *The Scarlet Letter*, it is more terrific in its conception, and not less intense in its execution, but exquisitely relieved by charming portraitures of character, and quaint and comic descriptions of social eccentricities. A deep vein of reflection underlies the whole narrative, often rising naturally to the surface, and revealing the strength of the foundation on which the subtle, aerial inventions of the author are erected. His frequent dashes of humor gracefully blend with the monotone of the story, and soften the harsher colors in which he delights to clothe his portentous conceptions. In no former production of his pen, are his unrivalled powers of description displayed to better advantage. The rusty wooden house in Pyncheon-street, with its seven sharp-pointed gables, and its huge clustered chimney—the old elm tree before the door—the grassy yard seen through the lattice fence, with its enormous fertility of burdocks—and the green moss on the slopes of the roof, with the flowers growing aloft in the air in the nook between two of the gables—present a picture to the eye as distinct as if our childhood had been passed in the shadow of the old weather-beaten edifice. Nor are the characters of the story drawn with less sharp and vigorous perspective. They stand out from the canvas as living realities. In spite of the supernatural drapery in which they are enveloped, they have such a genuine expression of flesh and blood, that we can not doubt we have known them all our days. They have the air of old acquaintance—only we wonder how the artist got them to sit for their likenesses. The grouping of these persons is managed with admirable artistic skill. Old Maid Pyncheon, concealing under her verjuice scowl the unutterable tenderness of a sister—her woman-hearted brother, on whose sensitive nature had fallen such a strange blight—sweet and beautiful Phoebe, the noble village-maiden, whose presence is always like that of some shining angel—the dreamy, romantic descendant of the legendary wizard—the bold, bad man of the world, reproduced at intervals in the bloody Colonel, and the unscrupulous judge—wise old Uncle Venner—and inappeasable Ned Higgins—are all made to occupy the place on the canvas which shows the lights and shades of their character in the most impressive contrast, and contributes to the wonderful vividness and harmony of the grand historical picture. On the whole, we regard *The House of the Seven Gables*, though it exhibits no single scenes that may not be matched in depth and pathos by some of Mr Hawthorne's previous creations, as unsurpassed by any thing he has yet written, in exquisite beauty of finish, in the skillful blending of the tragic and comic, and in the singular life-like reality with which the wildest traditions of the Puritanic age are combined with the everyday incidents of modern society.

—Anonymous, *Harper's New Monthly Magazine*, II,
May 1851, pp. 855–56

E.P. WHIPPLE (1851)

Whipple praises the novel for its combination of "humor and pathos," but finds the balance slips in the latter two-thirds of the book. He laments the discord between the character development and the sequence of events; "dramatic unity" is forfeited. While Whipple finds some of the characterizations among Hawthorne's strongest (particularly Hepzibah and Phoebe), the delineation of the character Holgrave is a failure. The reader cannot like him, thus Phoebe's love for him is unfathomable and so "the love scenes accordingly lack love." Students exploring Hawthorne's characterization and its shortcomings will find rich material here.

'The wrong-doing of one generation lives into the successive ones, and, divesting itself of every temporary advantage, becomes a pure and uncontrollable mischief;' this is the leading idea of Hawthorne's new romance, and it is developed with even more than his usual power. The error in *The Scarlet Letter*, proceeded from the divorce of its humor from its pathos—the introduction being as genial as Goldsmith or Lamb, and the story which followed being tragic even to ghastliness. In *The House of the Seven Gables*, the humor and the pathos are combined, and the whole work is stamped with the individuality of the author's genius, in all its variety of power. The first hundred pages of the volume are masterly in conception and execution, and can challenge comparison, in the singular depth and sweetness of their imaginative humor, with the best writing of the kind in literature. The other portions of the book have not the same force, precision, and certainty of handling, and the insight into character especially, seems at times to follow the processes of clairvoyance more than those of the waking imagination. The consequence is that the movement of the author's mind betrays a slight fitfulness toward the conclusion, and, splendid as is the supernaturally grotesque element which this ideal impatience introduces, it still somewhat departs from the integrity of the original conception, and interferes with the strict unity of the work. The mental nerve which characterizes the first part, slips occasionally into mental nervousness as the author proceeds.

We have been particular in indicating this fault, because the work is of so high a character that it demands, as a right, to be judged by the most exacting requirements of art. Taken as a whole, it is Hawthorne's greatest work, and is equally sure of immediate popularity and permanent fame. Considered as a romance, it does not so much interest as fasten and fascinate attention; and this attractiveness in the story is the result of the rare mental powers and moods out of which the story creatively proceeds. Every chapter proves the author to be, not only a master of narrative, a creator of character, an observer of life, and richly gifted with the powers of vital conception and combination, but it also exhibits him as a profound thinker and skillful metaphysician. We do not know but that his eye is more certain in detecting remote spiritual laws and their relations, than in the sure grasp of individual character; and if he ever loses his hold upon persons it is owing to that intensely meditative cast of his mind by which he views persons in their relations to the general laws whose action they illustrate. There is some discord in the present work in the development of character and sequence of events; the dramatic unity is therefore not perfectly preserved; but this cannot be affirmed of the unity of the law. That is always sustained, and if it had been thoroughly embodied, identified, and harmonized with the concrete events and characters, we have little hesitation in asserting that the present volume would be the deepest work of imagination ever produced on the American continent.

Before venturing upon any comments on the characters, we cannot resist the temptation to call the attention of our readers to the striking thoughts profusely scattered over the volume. These are generally quietly introduced, and spring so naturally out of the narrative of incidents, that their depth may not be at first appreciated. Expediency is the god whom most men really worship and obey, and few realize the pernicious consequences and poisonous vitality of bad deeds performed to meet an immediate difficulty. Hawthorne hits the law itself in this remark:

> The act of the present generation is the germ which may and must produce good or evil fruit, in a far distant time; for, together with the seed of the merely temporary crop, which mortals term expediency, they inevitably sow the acorns of a more enduring growth, which may darkly overshadow their posterity.

In speaking of the legal murder of old Matthew Maule for witchcraft, he says that Matthew

> was one of the martyrs to that terrible delusion, which should teach us, among its other morals, that the influential classes, and those who take upon themselves to be leaders of the people, are fully liable to all the passionate error that had ever characterized the maddest mob.

In reference to the hereditary transmission of individual qualities, it is said of Colonel Pyncheon's descendants, that 'his character might be traced all the way down, as distinctly *as if the colonel himself, a little diluted, had been gifted with a sort of intermittent immortality on earth.*' In a deeper vein is the account of the working of the popular imagination on the occasion of Col. Pyncheon's death. This afflicting event was ascribed by physicians to apoplexy; by the people to strangulation. The colonel had caused the death of a reputed wizard; and the fable ran that the lieutenant-governor, as he advanced into the room where the colonel sat dead in his chair, *saw a skeleton hand* at the colonel's throat, which vanished away as he came near him. Such touches as these are visible all over the volume, and few romances have more quotable felicities of thought and description.

The characters of the romance are among the best of Hawthorne's individualizations, and Miss Hepzibah and Phoebe are perhaps his masterpieces of characterization, in the felicity of their conception, their contrast, and their inter-action. Miss Hepzibah Pyncheon, the inhabitant of the gabled house, is compelled at the age of sixty to stoop from her aristocratic isolation from the world, and open a little cent shop, in order that she may provide for the subsistence of an unfortunate brother. The chapters entitled 'The Little Shop-Window,' 'The First Customer,' and a 'Day Behind the Counter,' in which her ludicrous humiliations are described, may be placed beside the best works of the most genial humorists, for their rapid alterations of smiles and tears, and the perfect April weather they make in the heart. The description of the little articles at the shop-window, the bars of soap, the leaden dragoons, the split peas, and the fantastic Jim Crow, 'executing his world-renowned dance in gingerbread;' the attempts of the elderly maiden to arrange her articles aright, and the sad destruction she makes among them, crowned by upsetting that tumbler of marbles, 'all of which roll different ways, and each individual marble, devil-directed, into the most difficult obscurity it can find;' the nervous irritation of her deportment as she puts her shop in order, the twitches of pride which agonize her breast, as stealing on tiptoe to the window, 'as cautiously as if she conceived some bloody-minded villain to be watching behind the elm-tree, with intent to take her life,' she stretches out her long, lank arm to put a paper of pearl-buttons, a Jew's harp, or what not, in its destined place, and then straitway vanishing back into the dusk, 'as if the world need never hope for another glimpse of her;' the 'ugly and spiteful little din' of the door-bell, announcing her first penny customer; all these, and many more minute details, are instinct with the life of humor, and cheerily illustrate that 'entanglement of something mean and trivial with whatever is noblest in joy and sorrow,' which it is the office of the humorist to represent and idealize.

The character of Phoebe makes the sunshine of the book, and by connecting her so intimately with Miss Hepzibah, a quaint sweetness is added to the native graces of her mind and disposition. The 'homely witchcraft' with which she brings out the hidden capabilities of every thing, is exquisitely exhibited, and poor Uncle Venner's praise of her touches the real secret of her fascination. 'I've seen,' says that cherry mendicant,

> a great deal of the world, not only in people's kitchens and back-yards, but at the street corners, and on the wharves, and in other places where my business calls me; but I'm free to say that I never knew a human creature do her work so much like one of God's angels as this child Phoebe does!

Holgrave, the young gentleman who carries off this pearl of womanhood, appears to us a failure. It is impossible for the reader to like him, and one finds it difficult to conceive how Phoebe herself can like him. The love scenes accordingly lack love, and a kind of magnetic influence is substituted for affection. The character of Clifford is elaborately drawn, and sustained with much subtle still, but he occupies perhaps too much space, and lures the author too much into metaphysical analysis and didactic disquisition. Judge Pyncheon is powerfully delineated, and the account of his death is a masterpiece of fantastic description. It is needless, perhaps, to say that the characters of the book have, like those in *The Scarlet Letter*, a vital relation to each other, and are developed not successively and separately, but mutually, each implying the other by a kind of artistic necessity.

The imagination in the *House of Seven Gables*, is perhaps most strikingly exhibited in the power with which the house itself is pervaded with thought, so that every room and gable has a sort of human interest communicated to it, and seems to symbolize the whole life of the Pyncheon family, from the grim colonel, who built it, to that delicate Alice, 'the fragrance of whose rich and delightful character lingered about the place where she lived, as a dried rose-bud scents the drawer where it has withered and perished.' In conclusion, we hope to have the pleasure of reviewing a new romance by Hawthorne twice a year at least. We could also hope that if Holgrave continues his contributions to the magazines, that he would send Graham some such a story as 'Alice Pyncheon,' which he tells so charmingly to Phoebe. *The Scarlet Letter*, and *The House of Seven Gables*, contain mental qualities which insensibly lead some readers to compare the author to other cherished literary names. Thus we have seen Hawthorne likened for this quality to Goldsmith, and for that to Irving, and for still another to Dickens; and some critics have given him the preference over all whom he seems to resemble. But the real cause for congratulation in the appearance of an original genius like Hawthorne, is not that he dethrones any established prince in literature, but that he founds a new principality of his own.

—E.P. Whipple, *Graham's Magazine*, XXXVIII,
May 1851, pp. 467–68

Henry T. Tuckerman
"Nathaniel Hawthorne" (1851)

Thus narrowly, yet with reverence, does Hawthorne analyze the delicate traits of human sentiment and character, and open vistas into that beautiful and unexplored world of love and thought, that exists in every human being, though overshadowed by material circumstance and technical duty. This, as we have before said, is his great service; digressing every now and then, from the main drift of his story, he takes evident delight in expatiating on phases of character and general traits of life, or in bringing into strong; relief the more latent facts of consciousness. Perhaps the union of the philosophic tendency with the poetic instinct is the great charm of his genius. It is common for American critics to estimate the interest of all writings by their comparative glow, vivacity and rapidity of action: somewhat of the restless temperament and enterprising life of the nation infects its taste: such terms as 'quiet,' 'gentle' and 'tasteful,' are equivocal when applied in this country, to a book; and yet they may envelope the rarest energy of thought and depth of insight as well as earnestness of feeling: these qualities, in reflective minds, are too real to find melo-dramatic development: they move as calmly as summer haves, or glow as noiselessly as the firmament; but not the less grand and mighty is their essence: to realize it, the spirit of contemplation, and the recipient mood of sympathy, must be evoked, for it is not external but moral excitement that is proposed; and we deem one of Hawthorne's most felicitous merits—that of so patiently educing artistic beauty and moral interest from life and nature, without the least sacrifice of intellectual dignity.

The healthy spring of life is typified in Phoebe so freshly as to magnetize the feelings as well as engage the perceptions of the reader: its intellectual phase finds expression in Holgrave, while the state of Clifford, when relieved of the nightmare that oppressed his sensitive temperament, the author justly compares to an Indian-summer of the soul. Across the path of these beings of genuine flesh and blood, who constantly appeal to our most humane sympathies, or rather around their consciousness and history, flits the pale, mystic figure of Alice—whose invisible music and legendary fate overflow with a graceful and attractive superstition—yielding an Ariel-like melody to the more solemn and cheery strains of the whole composition. Among the apt though incidental touches of the picture, the idea of making the music-grinder's monkey an epitome of avarice, the daguerreotype a test of latent character, and the love of the reformer Holgrave for the genially practical Phoebe, win him to conservatism, strike us as remarkably natural yet quite as ingenuous and charming as philosophical. We may add that the same pure, even, unexaggerated and perspicuous style of diction that we have recognized in his previous writing, is maintained in this.

As earth and sky appear to blend at the horizon though we cannot define the point of contact, things seen and unseen, the actual and the spiritual, mind and matter, what is within and what is without our consciousness, have a line of union, and, like the colour of the iris, are lost in each other. About this equator of life the genius of Hawthorne delights to hover as its appropriate sphere, whether indulging a vein of Spenserian allegory, Hogarth sketching, Goldsmith domesticity, or Godwin metaphysics, it is around the boundary of the possible that he most freely expatiates; the realities and the mysteries of life to his vision are scarcely ever apart; they act and re-act as to yield dramatic hints or vistas of sentiment. Time broods with touching solemnity over his imagination; the function of conscience awes while it occupies his mind; the delicate and the profound in love, and the awful beauty of death transfuse his meditation; and these supernal he loves to link with terrestrial influences—to hallow a graphic description by a sacred association or to brighten a commonplace occasion with the scintillations of humour—thus vivifying or chastening the 'light of common day.'

—Henry T. Tuckerman, "Nathaniel Hawthorne,"
Southern Literary Messenger, XVII, June 1851, pp. 344–49

HERMAN MELVILLE (1851)

The contents of this book do not belie its clustering romantic title. With great enjoyment we spent almost an hour in each separate gable. This book is like a fine old chamber, abundantly but still judiciously furnished with precisely that sort of furniture best fitted to furnish it. There are rich hangings, whereon are braided scenes from tragedies. There is old china with rare devices, set about on the carved beaufet; there are long and indolent lounges to throw yourself upon; there is an admirable sideboard, plentifully stored with good viands; there is a smell of old wine in the pantry; and finally, in one corner, there is a dark little black-letter volume in golden clasps, entitled *Hawthorne: A Problem*.

We think the book for pleasantness of running interest surpasses the other work of the author. The curtains are now drawn; the sun comes in more; genialities peep out more. Were we to particularize what has most struck us in the deeper passages, we should point out the scene where Clifford, for a minute, would fain throw himself from the window, to join the procession; or the scene where the Judge is left seated in his ancestral chair.

Clifford is full of an awful truth throughout. He is conceived in the finest, truest spirit. He is no caricature. He is Clifford. And here we would say, that did the circumstances permit, we should like nothing better than to devote an elaborate and careful paper to the full consideration and analysis of the purpose and significance of what so strongly characterizes all of this author's writing. There is a certain tragic phase of humanity, which, in our opinion, was never more powerfully embodied than by Hawthorne: we mean the tragicalness of human thought in its own unbiased, native, and profound workings. We think that into no recorded mind has the intense feeling of the whole truth ever entered more deeply than into this man's. By whole truth, we mean the apprehension of the absolute condition of present things as they strike the eye of the man who fears them not, though they do their worst to him.

> —Herman Melville, Letter to Nathaniel Hawthorne
> (1851), cited in George Parsons Lathrop,
> *A Study of Hawthorne*, 1876, pp. 230–31

EMILY DICKINSON (1851)

In this private letter, the American poetess and Massachusetts recluse Emily Dickinson identifies (after a fashion) with Hepzibah Pyncheon, the elderly stalwart in Hawthorne's novel. This semi-recognition (as well as Dickinson's slightly squeamish disavowal of it) will interest students discussing the character of Hepzibah. Readers might speculate on the degree to which (beyond the "relative sense") the identification is relevant, and what Dickinson's "reading" suggests about Hepzibah.

How lonely it was last night when the chilly wind went down, and the clear, cold moon was shining—it seemed to me I could pack this little earthly bundle, and bidding the world Goodbye, fly away and away, and never come back to be so lonely here, and then I thought of "Hepzibah" how sorrowful she was, and how she longed to sleep, because the grave was peaceful, yet for affection's sake, and for the sake of "Clifford" she wearied on, and bye and bye, kind angels took both of them home, and it seemed almost a lesson, given us to learn. I dont mean that you are *him*, or that Hepzibah's *me* except in a relative sense, only I was reminded.

> —Emily Dickinson, Letter to her brother Austin Dickinson,
> November 11, 1851, in Thomas H. Johnson (ed.),
> *The Letters of Emily Dickinson*, Cambridge, MA:
> Harvard University Press, 1958, p. 135

Washington Irving (1852)

Accept my most cordial thanks for the little volume you have had the kindness to send me. I prize it as the right hand of fellowship extended to me by one whose friendship I am proud and happy to make, and whose writings I have regarded with admiration as among the very best that have ever issued from the American press.

> —Washington Irving, Letter to Nathaniel Hawthorne
> (1852), cited in Julian Hawthorne,
> *Nathaniel Hawthorne and His Wife*, 1884, Vol. 1, p. 440

Henry James (1879)

Like many critics, James praises *The House of the Seven Gables* highly while questioning its completeness. He finds the novel fragmentary and less rounded than *The Scarlet Letter,* a "magnificent fragment" that is "more like a prologue to a great novel than a great novel itself." Hawthorne's purposes seem to exceed the novel, and James senses an "expansive quality which never wholly fructifies." Students researching Hawthorne's structural strategy and aims will find James's perspectives salient.

This novel portrays Hawthorne's contemporary world more than his other American novels, but he is by no means a realist. Hawthorne "never attempted to render exactly or closely the actual facts of the society that surrounded him." Rather, the contemporary, the local, and the national qualities lurk "between the lines" and in the "*indirect* testimony of his tone." Nevertheless, this novel contains the most "literal actuality" in any of Hawthorne's novels. Students exploring questions of Hawthorne's relation to his times, his native qualities, or the extent of his use of realism should turn to James.

Regarding Hawthorne's characterization, which is variously praised or challenged by other critics, James proposes that Hawthorne employs figures rather than characters, pictures rather than persons. This serves Hawthorne's purpose, the figures being "types . . . of something general" concerning families and history. Students evaluating Hawthorne's characterization might find relevant material here.

The *House of the Seven Gables* comes nearer being a picture of contemporary American life than either of its companions; but on this ground it would be a mistake to make a large claim for it. It cannot be too often repeated that

Hawthorne was not a realist. He had a high sense of reality—his *Note-Books* superabundantly testify to it; and fond as he was of jotting down the items that make it up, he never attempted to render exactly or closely the actual facts of the society that surrounded him. I have said—I began by saying—that his pages were full of its spirit, and of a certain reflected light that springs from it; but I was careful to add that the reader must look for his local and national quality between the lines of his writing and in the indirect testimony of his tone, his accent, his temper, of his very omissions and suppressions. *The House of the Seven Gables* has, however, more literal actuality than the others, and if it were not too fanciful an account of it, I should say that it renders, to an initiated reader, the impression of a summer afternoon in an elm-shadowed New England town. It leaves upon the mind a vague correspondence to some such reminiscence, and in stirring up the association it renders it delightful. The comparison is to the honour of the New England town, which gains in it more than it bestows. The shadows of the elms, in *The House of the Seven Gables*, are exceptionally dense and cool; the summer afternoon is peculiarly still and beautiful; the atmosphere has a delicious warmth, and the long daylight seems to pause and rest. But the mild provincial quality is there, the mixture of shabbiness and freshness, the paucity of ingredients. The end of an old race—this is the situation that Hawthorne has depicted, and he has been admirably inspired in the choice of the figures in whom he seeks to interest us. They are all figures rather than characters—they are all pictures rather than persons. But if their reality is light and vague, it is sufficient, and it is in harmony with the low relief and dimness of outline of the objects that surround them. They are all types, to the author's mind, of something general, of something that is bound up with the history, at large, of families and individuals, and each of them is the centre of a cluster of those ingenious and meditative musings, rather melancholy, as a general thing, than joyous, which melt into the current and texture of the story and give it a kind of moral richness. A grotesque old spinster, simple, childish, penniless, very humble at heart, but rigidly conscious of her pedigree; an amiable bachelor, of an epicurean temperament and an enfeebled intellect, who has passed twenty years of his life in penal confinement for a crime of which he was unjustly pronounced guilty; a sweet-natured and bright-faced young girl from the country, a poor relation of these two ancient decrepitudes, with whose moral mustiness her modern freshness and soundness are contrasted; a young man still more modern, holding the latest opinions, who has sought his fortune up and down the world, and, though he has not found it, takes a genial and enthusiastic view of the future: these, with two or three remarkable accessory figures, are the persons concerned in the little drama. The drama is a small one, but as Hawthorne does not put it before us for its own superficial sake, for the dry facts of the case, but for something in it which he holds to be symbolic and of large application, something that points a moral and that it behooves us to remember, the scenes in the rusty wooden house whose gables give its name to the story, have something of the dignity both of history and of tragedy.

—Henry James, *Hawthorne*, London, 1879, pp. 1–14

THE BLITHEDALE ROMANCE

Critics of *The Blithedale Romance* singled out the character of Zenobia as of supreme importance. For some, this was because of her suspicious resemblance to Margaret Fuller. For others, such as George S. Hillard, it was on account of Hawthorne's portrayal of a "ripe and rich woman." Hillard wished there were more of such women in the literature of his day. Whatever Hawthorne's motives, and opinions vary, he was introducing a new type into fiction—a radical feminist.

Reading *The Blithedale Romance* prompts any number of questions. Hawthorne's smirking assurance in the preface that the characters in the novel were "creatures of his brain" and "entirely fictitious" was not believed by many. Questions of models for his fiction would plague Hawthorne after the publication of this novel. Even as far away as England, the real-life models who suggested the characters in this roman à clef seemed common knowledge: "Margaret Fuller seems to have suggested the idea of Zenobia, as Hollingsworth may be a fancy sketch of Elihu Burritt."

Also debatable is Hawthorne's political position regarding radical reform. The conservative critic writing in the *Southern Quarterly Review* objects to Hawthorne's making Zenobia a suicide; he should have "converted her, by marriage—the best remedy for such a case" and "left her, a mother, with good prospects of a numerous progeny." Hawthorne's martyrdom of Zenobia unsettled the conservatives almost as much as his beatification of Hester Prynne did.

Other readers take *The Blithedale Romance* for a withering satire and critique by a confirmed conservative. The earnest reviewer for the English *Westminster Review* (George Eliot, most likely) finds Hawthorne hostile to the socialist cause and guilty of political complacency. His sacrifice of Zenobia is an example of this moral feebleness: "Socialism is apparently made responsible for consequences which it utterly condemned." The reviewer challenges Hawthorne's whimsical art-for-art's-sake position, invoking the decidedly unwhimsical issue of slavery. Hawthorne's attitude to slavery would become an increasing problem for the author, his audience, and even his friends. Students inquiring into Hawthorne's politics should consult the critic for the *Westminster Review*.

Questions of the degree to which Hawthorne identified with the narrator confound easy resolution. Charles Hale finds Miles Coverdale in turns "lurid" and "glaring," so that the reader can "scarcely see at all, except to see dark shadows," which only render Coverdale's smiles "ghastly." Students interested in Hawthorne's identification with his narrator, and his use of an unreliable narrator, may find Hale's observations of value.

Anonymous (1852)

The anonymous reviewer for the English magazine *The Spectator* rehashes the comments that proliferated in reviews of *Mosses from an Old Manse*, regarding Hawthorne's excellence and his lack of commensurate popular recognition—this time in England. "The generality," the reviewer writes, "have not taste, skill, or patience to relish minutiae of execution." Students interested in the various ways Hawthorne's work was viewed and received will find this account noteworthy.

The Spectator reviewer also repeats the comparison (previously made with *The Scarlet Letter*) of Hawthorne's novels to "the so-called classical drama." Hawthorne's story or plotline is as simple as a drama; the merit lies in "the manner in which the details are worked up."

The "lessons" learned from the novel are "the danger of a woman deviating . . . from the received usages of society; though this lesson is by no means new." Additionally Hawthorne warns of the danger of "earnest philanthropy swallowing up every other feeling." The reviewer equates Hollingsworth with abolitionism. *The Spectator* reviewer confidently assures the reader that "Mr. Hawthorne is not a disciple of that school of human perfectibility."

Nathaniel Hawthorne is an American writer of considerable repute in his own country, and of high though limited estimation here. Extensive *popularity* he is not perhaps likely to achieve, because his great merit lies rather in execution than in structure—in finish than in breadth. 'Materiem superabat opus': but the matter in a large sense is what strikes the generality, who have not taste, skill, or patience to relish minutiae of execution, even if those minutiae are combined into a complete whole, as is the case with Nathaniel Hawthorne.

Although Hawthorne undoubtedly belongs to the class of novelists, his novels are of a peculiar kind. A story there is, and in its principal characters and catastrophe generally a striking though singular one; but its conduct partakes more of the simplicity of the so-called classical drama than of the rapid narrative, the various incidents, and the mutations of fortune which distinguish the romantic school. So far as *story* is concerned, the effect is probably as good in an abridgment as in the work itself, the great merit of the writer arising from the manner in which the details are worked up, as with some of Washington Irving's sketches. This manner might probably run into tediousness, and the singularity verge upon plagiarism, were the themes European and hackneyed. But Mr Hawthorne, by taking his subjects from the actual life or traditions of America, gives to his detailed pictures an attraction of novelty to English readers, while the just delineation and easy elegance of his pen impart an air of vivid truthfulness to his reflections and elaborate descriptions.

The framework of *The Blithedale Romance* is founded on a Communist attempt of some enthusiasts at Blithedale farm, rather after the fashion of Godwin and other admirers of the principles of the first French Revolution than after modern Socialist schemes. At the head of this party, though hardly belonging to it, is Hollingsworth, a quondam blacksmith, of great heart and natural powers, whose whole soul is embarked in a project for reforming criminals. A woman called Zenobia, of full rich beauty, independent spirit, and high intellectual power, is also a principal; and represents the advocate of the 'rights of women,' chafing at the control which convention and the real or assumed superiority of man enforce upon the sex. There is also another conspicuous female, Priscilla, who exhibits the clinging, devoted, feminine character, seeing nothing but the person she loves. The real story turns upon the passion of Zenobia for Hollingsworth, his preference for Priscilla, and the suicide of the proud, passionate, ill-regulated, queenly Zenobia. The story, however, is expanded by many matters, and some mysteries not thoroughly cleared up; including a mesmerist adventurer, Westervelt, a veiled lady, a connexion between Westervelt and Zenobia, and some use of magnetism. The preface distinctly repudiates all idea of sketching the actors in a real project of philanthropy, which Blithedale was: but Margaret Fuller seems to have suggested the idea of Zenobia, as Hollingsworth may be a fancy sketch of Elihu Burritt.

One lesson impressed by the book is the danger of a woman, no matter what her gifts, deviating ever so little from the received usages of society; though this lesson is by no means new, and it had been done as conclusively already. Another, a newer and a more important moral, is the danger of earnest philanthropy swallowing up every other feeling, till your genuine philanthropist becomes as hard, as selfish, and as indifferent to the individual results of his conduct, if it forward his end, as the most adamantine conqueror or statesman. This feeling, the more extreme and engrossing in proportion to the comprehension of the philanthropist's nature and consciousness, without any sort of regard to the feasibility or importance of its project, is not perhaps so much illustrated by the catastrophe as noted by passing occurrences. It is a moral, however, that cannot be too strongly impressed; for it actuates classes as well as individuals, and with a less sense of responsibility. If the reader wishes an instance, he may see it in the ruin of the British West Indies, and, in some cases, the aggravated miseries of the African race. The Anti-Slavery body and the individuals composing it were types of Hollingsworth, without his conscience or his punishment. Years after the death of Zenobia, Miles Coverdale, the friend of all parties, went in search of Hollingsworth and Priscilla, with some feeling about Zenobia's death yet rankling at his heart.

> I learned that he inhabited a small cottage; that his way of life was exceedingly retired; and that my only chance of encountering him or Priscilla was to meet them in a secluded lane, where, in the latter part of the afternoon, they were accustomed to walk. . .
>
> 1 see in Hollingsworth an exemplification of the most awful truth in Bunyan's book of such; from the very gate of heaven there is a by-way to the pit.

Mr Hawthorne is not a disciple of that school of human perfectibility which has given rise to plans of pantisocracy and similar Arcadias. Of course, so fair a subject for satire as the equality and non-competitiveness of Blithedale is not lost sight of, in gentle but pungent touches. This was their first tea-drinking.

> We all sat down—grisly Silas Foster, his rotund helpmate, and the two bouncing handmaidens, included—and looked at one another in a friendly but rather awkward way. . . . It was while I sat beside him on his cobbler's bench, or clinked my hoe against his

own in the corn-field, or broke the same crust of bread, my earth-grimed hand to his, at our noontide lunch. The poor proud man should look at both sides of sympathy like this.

The following was the first proof of how the practical mingles in real life, ever dashing its romance.

Stout Silas Foster mingled little in our conversation; but when he did speak it was very much to some practical purpose. . . .
Constituting so pitiful a minority as now, we were inevitably estranged from the rest of mankind in pretty fair proportion with the strictness of our mutual bond among ourselves.

—Anonymous, *The Spectator*, XXV, July 3, 1852, pp. 637–38

Charles Hale (1852)

Hale was a politician and a journalist who founded *To-Day: A Boston Literary Journal*. Hale confesses confusion at Coverdale's narrative—it is "shrouded with doubt, by being told by one who is a spectator, and not an actor." Coverdale is an unreliable narrator, and his "supposed ignorance" lends the story an "unnatural light" that distorts the recounting of events.

While the novel is ostensibly about a community seeking to improve the world by setting a better example, Hale finds that the characters simply reaffirm "the conventionalities of life [and] society as it is." Hale questions Coverdale's (or is it Hawthorne's?) motives. He finds it hard to avoid the impression that "a covert sneer" at both spheres (the conventional, wider world and the utopian society of the experimental community) "imbues every chapter." This excerpt will be of particular interest to students examining Hawthorne's narrative strategy in *The Blithedale Romance*.

This book is marked with all the beauties and all the faults which Mr. Hawthorne's genius strews over his works. It is full of graceful description, dancing humor, delicate appreciation of character, and contemplative views of the relations of individuals to each other in confined societies. It has also the mysticism which adds a charm, and that which carries a gloom, to many of his writings. The story upon which the series of pictures and conversations is centred is shrouded with doubt, by being told by one who is a spectator, and not an actor; and a sort of supernatural glow is given to its results, by the ignorance in which the reader has been kept by the supposed ignorance of the narrator. Hawthorne does not give us his pictures or his battles covered by a fog; but there is an unnatural light, now so lurid that we cannot see distinctly by it, and now so glaring that we can scarcely see at all, except to recognize dark shadows, which makes even his smiles ghastly, and his mildest incidents catastrophes.

The scene is laid at 'Brook Farm,' the locality in this neighborhood of a 'community' now separated; but the author disavows having taken either character or incident from the parties who were actually there assembled. It is a romance supposed to be founded upon the life of persons gathered together with the purpose of first avoiding, but eventually improving, the world. In fact, however, the whole incident and action of the story is based upon the conventionalities of life, and the passions recognized as those most fostered by society as it is. We can hardly avoid the feeling that a covert sneer at that which is considered good by those who live 'in the world,' and also at those who would try to live above the things of the world, imbues every chapter.

Some parts of the book suggest unconscious imitations of *Wilhelm Meister*; but its close, and perhaps its tenor, belong more to the Hoffman school. It cannot be read without pleasure, although the pleasure is constantly subdued by the presence of a constructed fatalism, which, though not incorrect perhaps in any instance, shadows and gives a sombre tone to the picture. If it were to rest pleasantly, as a whole, in the memory, the last sixty or seventy pages, with all their melodrama,—deeply studied and highly wrought, but melodrama still,—should be torn off. With all this, we feel that Mr. Hawthorne has added a new laurel to his crown by this book. We have dwelt more upon what strikes us as its faults, than we should, did we not know that its beauties and its power would be recognized by every intelligent reader, and that no word of ours will dim the justly earned reputation of the author.

—Charles Hale, *To-Day* II, July 17, 1852, p. 42

George S. Hillard (1852)

George S. Hillard was one of Hawthorne's closest friends. They met through the Peabody sisters before Hawthorne and Sophia Peabody married. Hillard became Hawthorne's lawyer, facilitating the unpleasant lawsuit against Brook Farm to recover money Hawthorne had invested in the enterprise. It is unsurprising, then, that Hillard "heartily approves" of Hawthorne's portrayal of the reform movement. Hillard significantly, and with some justification, allies the legitimate reform movement with "spiritual rappings" (the then-popular practice of supposedly contacting the dead through mediums). In the novel, Hawthorne likewise connects the high-thinking political reform movement with such sensational arts as mesmerism and animal magnetism. Students investigating the extent of Hawthorne's radicalism (or equally, his conservatism) should attend to Hillard's comments.

———————

It is enough for me that you have put another rose into your chaplet, and I will not ask whether it outblooms or outswells its sister flowers. Zenobia is a splendid creature, and I wish there were more such rich and ripe women about. I wish, too, you could have wound up your story without killing her, or that at least you had given her a drier and handsomer death. Priscilla is an exquisite sketch. I don't know whether you have quite explained Hollingsworth's power over two such diverse natures. Your views about reform and reformers and spiritual rappings are such as I heartily approve. Reformers need the enchantment of distance. Your sketches of things visible, detached observations, and style generally, are exquisite as ever. May you live a thousand years, and write a book every year!

—George S. Hillard, Letter to Nathaniel Hawthorne
(July 27, 1852), cited in Julian Hawthorne,
Nathaniel Hawthorne and His Wife, 1884, Vol. 1, p. 448

ANONYMOUS "HAWTHORNE'S *BLITHEDALE*" (1852)

We are inclined to think this very pretty story quite as successful, as a work of art, as any of the preceding volumes of our author. It has all their defects, and these defects are such as seem inseparable from the writer's mind. These lie chiefly in the shaping and conception of the work, and in the inadequate employment of his characters. Their results do not co-operate with their natures; and the events are not always accommodated to the moral of the personage. The catastrophe rarely satisfies the reader, and seldom accords with poetical propriety. Instead of Zenobia committing suicide, an action equally shocking and unnecessary, he should have converted her, by marriage—the best remedy for such a case—from the error of her ways, and left her, a mother, with good prospects of a numerous progeny. Apart from faults such as this, the book is full of beauties. The character of Hollingsworth is admirably drawn in most respects.

—Anonymous, "Hawthorne's *Blithedale*,"
Southern Quarterly Review, n.s. 6, October 1852, p. 543

Attributed to George Eliot "Contemporary Literature of America" (1852)

This unsigned critique from the English publication the *Westminster Review* has been tentatively ascribed to the novelist George Eliot (Mary Ann Evans, the author of novels including *Middlemarch* and *Daniel Deronda*) as well as to the Reverend Rufus Griswold.

The author frames the review by referring to the English success of Harriet Beecher Stowe's *Uncle Tom's Cabin*, and predicting a less bright future for the novel under current consideration. Students investigating Hawthorne's English reception will find useful background material here.

The reviewer finds the story told in *The Blithedale Romance* negligible; Hawthorne's signature is in the manner of its telling (a view echoing the *Spectator* reviewer). "Hawthorne's *forte* is the analysis of character, and not the dramatic arrangement of events. . . . The main tendency is toward isolation." There is a fault in this, however; the character analyses are so exacting that any "dramatic co-operation" is smothered. The actors are "simply contemporaries, obliged, somehow, to be on familiar terms with one another." It is fortunate, in the reviewer's eyes, that the cast of characters is limited to four people, since any more "would have been fatal to their united action and combined effect."

As has been the case with reviewers of earlier works, this critic is struck by Hawthorne's penchant for morbid characters, "plunging, orbitless, into the abyss of despair." Each is a wandering star, tracing an eddy towards "disaster" and a "wretched end." The reviewer notably reads Coverdale's purpose and Hawthorne's as identical, and she—or he—goes on to note that Coverdale (Hawthorne) "falls into a moral scepticism more desolate than death." Students investigating the pessimism of Hawthorne, his philosophy, and the way his works anticipated existentialism would do well to look here.

The reviewer finds Hawthorne's manner of dramatizing his "moral or social truths" unartistic, evidence of "weak moral power" and "feebleness of moral purpose." Art's purpose, the critic attests, is "the development of beauty—not merely sensuous beauty, but moral and spiritual beauty." Art should administer pleasure and mercy. Hawthorne's "new path in art" does the opposite. This "anatomist" cuts and hacks his subjects, developing a "beauty of deformity" and a "poetry of the dissecting-room." Reality intervenes too harshly into the novel for this reviewer; it should "only be so far introduced as to give effect to the bright ideal which Hope pictures in the future." Students examining Hawthorne's use of realism and the grotesque should consult this review for dissenting attitudes.

The author of the review also conducts a rigorous and sensitive ethical critique of Hawthorne's novel that anticipates Lawrence's later charges of diabolism (Hawthorne "is a Mephistopheles"). Coverdale's ("Hawthorne's") bantering tenor is read as a burlesque and as "manic levity." Zenobia is deemed the one character "worthy to be the Trustee of Human Right, and the Representation of Human Destiny." She alone should have prospered; that she did not is an "outrage on the decorum of art." The strong should not be conquered by the weak, as happens when Priscilla prevails over Zenobia.

The reviewer then discourses on the probable use of Margaret Fuller as a model for Zenobia. With his poetic insight, Hawthorne could have served Brook Farm as a worthier chronicler than its actual historians. Again Hawthorne disappoints, though, "through his lack of moral earnestness."

Hawthorne's political complacency and hostility to the reform enterprise is also lambasted. A powerful and apt analogy is made, when the reviewer asks: "Would [Hawthorne] paint an ideal slave-plantation merely for the beauty of the thing, without pretending to 'elicit a conclusion favorable or otherwise' to slavery?" Students inquiring into Hawthorne's political position and his attitudes to slavery and to reform should undoubtedly read this review.

———

From fact we pass to fiction, and to the examination of Hawthorne's last production, in order to which we must brush aside the whole brood of negro tales now swarming amongst us. 'Uncle Tom' has become a notoriety; and the success of the book is the great literary fact of the day. Sir Walter Scott and Charles Dickens never addressed as many readers, in the same space of time, as Harriet Beecher Stowe. The extraordinary sale in England, however, is due, first of all, to the *price*, secondly to the *subject*, and finally to the *novelty* of the thing. Meanwhile it is a hopeful omen for the slave, that a universal sympathy has been excited in his behalf. *The Blithedale Romance* will never attain the popularity which is vouchsafed (to borrow a pulpit vocable) to some of its contemporaries, but it is unmistakably the finest production of genius in either hemisphere, for this quarter at least—to keep our enthusiasm within limits so far. Of its literary merits we wish to speak, at the outset, in the highest terms, inasmuch as we intend to take objection to it in other respects.

'Blithedale' is an idealization of Brook Farm, where, about ten years ago, a few young and hearty enthusiasts, tired of moving on so slowly toward the millennium, took Destiny into their own hands, and set up 'Paradise

Regained', not by writing verses or romances, but by the more prosaic method of planting their own potatoes, baking their own bread, and cobbling their own shoes, as in the days before the Flood, when every man was his own master and his own servant, and political economy had not yet brought social death into the world, 'and all our woe.' How this modern Arcadia originated, how it thrived, and why it was abandoned, we do not know; but it may be taken for granted that hoeing turnips, feeding pigs, and milking cows, turned out less romantic than was anticipated. Its denizens accordingly went back to the old ways of the world, most of them having since become conspicuous, in various walks of literature, and all of them the better for an experience so well paid for.

Of this experience Hawthorne, who was one of them, has availed himself, in writing this romance. With our limited space, we cannot pretend to give even a faint outline of a tale which depends for its interest altogether upon the way of telling it. Hawthorne's *forte* is the analysis of character, and not the dramatic arrangement of events. 'To live in other lives, and to endeavour—by generous sympathies, by delicate intuitions, by taking note of things too slight for record, and by bringing his spirit into manifold acquaintance with the companions whom God assigned him—to learn the secret which was hidden even from themselves,'—this, which is the estimate formed of Miles Coverdale, has its original in the author himself. The adoption of the autobiographical form (now so common in fictions) is, perhaps, the most suitable for the exercise of such peculiar powers. Not more than six or seven characters are introduced, and only four of them are prominent figures. They have, therefore, ample room for displaying their individuality, and establishing each an independent interest in the reader's regards. But this is not without disadvantages, which become more apparent towards the close. The analysis of the characters is so minute, that they are too thoroughly individualized for dramatic co-operation, or for that graduated subordination to each other which tends to give a harmonious swell to the narrative, unity to the plot, and concentrated force to the issue. They are simply contemporaries, obliged, somehow, to be on familiar terms with each other, and, even when coming into the closest relationship, seeming rather driven thereto by destiny, than drawn by sympathy. It is well that the *dramatis personae* are so few. They are a manageable number, and are always upon the stage; but had there been more of them, they would only have presented themselves there in turns, which, with Hawthorne's slow movement, would have been fatal to their united action and combined effect. Even with a consecutive narrative, and a concentration of interest, the current flows with an eddying motion, which tends to keep them apart, unless, as happens once or twice, it dash over a precipice, and then it both makes up for lost time, and brings matters to a point rather abruptly. But the main tendency is toward isolation—for the ruling faculty is analytic. It is ever hunting out the anomalous; it discovers more points of repulsion than of attraction; and the creatures of its fancy are all morbid beings—all 'wandering stars,' plunging, orbitless, into the abyss of despair—confluent but not commingling streams, winding along to the ocean of disaster and death; for all have a wretched end—Zenobia and Priscilla, Hollingsworth and Coverdale—the whole go to wreck. The queenly Zenobia drowns herself in a pool; her ghost haunts Hollingsworth through life; and, as for Coverdale, he falls into a moral scepticism more desolating than death. Hear him at middle age:

> As regards human progress, let them believe in it who can, and aid in it who choose. If I could earnestly do either, it would be all the better for my comfort.

Is this the moral of the tale? It is but too appropriate. Poor Miles Coverdale! so genial, so penetrative, so candid—he begins by mocking others, and he ends with mocking himself! Hollingsworth's life teaches a solemn lesson to traffickers in humanity, and with due solemnity is it enforced. Priscilla's life is too shadowy and colourless to convey any lesson. She is a mere straw upon the current. And what of Zenobia? It is difficult to say what we may gather from her life—so many lives were in her! She discusses it herself with Coverdale (quite characteristic) on the eve of her fall. It is a wise point to settle, but she makes it out thus:—

> A moral? Why this: that in the battle-fields of life, the downright stroke that would fall only on a man's steel head-piece, is sure to light upon a woman's heart, over which she wears no breastplate, and whose wisdom it is, therefore, to keep out of the conflict. Or thus: that the whole universe, her own sex and yours, and Providence or destiny to boot, make common cause against the woman who swerves one hair's breadth out of the beaten track. Yes; and add (for I may as well own it now) that, with that one hair's breadth, she goes all astray, and never sees the world in its true aspect afterwards.

There is something very unartistic in such formal applications of moral or social truths, reminding us of the old homiletic fashion of making a 'practical improvement' of a discourse to saints, sinners, and all sorts of folk. It indicates imperfection in the construction and colouring of the picture. So many morals—one a-piece for Coverdale and Hollingsworth, and two and a-half for Zenobia—are symptomatic of weak moral power, arising from feebleness of moral purpose. Hawthorne has a rich perception of the beautiful, but he is sadly deficient in moral depth and earnestness. His moral faculty is morbid as well as weak; all his characters partake of the same infirmity. Hollingsworth's project of a penitentiary at Blithedale is here carried out in imagination. Hawthorne walks abroad always at night, and at best it is a moonlight glimmering which you catch of reality. He lives in the region and shadow of death, and never sees the deep glow of moral health anywhere. He looks mechanically (it is a habit) at Nature and at man through a coloured glass, which imparts to the whole view a pallid, monotonous aspect, painful to behold. And it is only because Hawthorne can see beauty in everything, and will look at nothing but beauty in anything, that he can either endure the picture himself, or win for it the admiration of others. The object of art is the development of beauty—not merely sensuous beauty, but moral and spiritual beauty. Its ministry should be one of pleasure, not of pain; but our anatomist, who removes his subjects to Blithedale, that he may cut and hack at them without interference, clears out for himself a new path in art, by developing the beauty of deformity! He would give you the poetry of the hospital, or the poetry of the dissecting-room; but we would rather not have it. Art has a moral purpose to fulfil; its mission is one of mercy, not of misery. Reality should only be so far introduced as to give effect to the bright ideal which Hope pictures in the future. In fact, a poet is nothing unless also a prophet. Hawthorne is the former; but few poets could be less of the latter. He draws his inspiration from Fate, not from Faith. He is not even a Jeremiah, weeping amid the ruins of a fallen temple, and mourning over the miseries of a captive people. He is a Mephistopheles, doubtful whether to weep or laugh; but either way it would be in mockery. 'It is genuine tragedy, is it not?' said Zenobia (referring to the fatal blow which laid her hopes prostrate), at the same time coming out 'with *a sharp, light laugh.*' Verily, a tragedy!—burlesqued by much of the same maniac levity. That 'Blithedale' itself should end in smoke, was, perhaps, fit matter for mirth; that Hollingsworth's huge tower of selfishness should be shattered to pieces was poetically just; but that the imperial Zenobia should be vanquished, was to give the victory to Despair. Zenobia is the only one in the group worthy to be the Trustee of Human Right, and the Representative of Human Destiny; and she, at least, should have come out of all her struggles in regal triumph. But, after the first real trial of her strength with adversity, and when there was resolution yet left for a thousand conflicts, to throw her into that dirty pool, and not even to leave her there, but to send her base-hearted deceiver, and that lout of a fellow, Silas Foster, to haul her out, and to let the one poke up the corpse with a boat-hook, and the other tumble it about in the simplicity of his desire to make it look more decent—these, and many other things in the closing scene, are an outrage upon the decorum of art, as well as a violation of its purpose. That such things do happen, is no reason why they should be idealized; for the Ideal seeks not to imitate Reality, but to perfect it. The use it makes of that which *is* true, is to develope that which *ought* to be true: and it ought *never* to be true that the strong should be conquered by the weak, as Zenobia was by Priscilla; or, that the most buoyant spirit should sink soonest in the struggle of life, as did Zenobia, who was the first that found a grave in 'Blithedale;' or, that *all* should be wrecked that sail on troubled waters, as were all who figure in this romance. It is a hard saying to proclaim to a fallen world, that the first false step is a fatal one. There was more truth in the words, and more beauty in the picture, of the man standing by the outcast, telling her to go and sin no more. From thence let Hawthorne draw his inspiration. Let him study that benignant attitude, and endeavour to realize it in himself toward a similar subject, and he might yet write with a prophet's power, and accomplish a saviour's mission.

We are cautioned, in the preface, against the notion (otherwise very liable to be entertained) that this is a history of Brook Farm under a fictitious disguise.

> He begs it to be understood, that he has considered the institution itself as not less fairly the subject of fictitious handling than the imaginary personages whom he has introduced there. It is an ideal, not a real picture. It is what Brook Farm became in his own fancy, and, considering what that fancy is, there is no need for supposing that he has drawn largely upon his recollection. It would indeed (considering how few amiable qualities he distributes among his imaginary progeny) be a most grievous wrong to his former excellent associates, were the author to allow it to be supposed that he had been sketching any of their likenesses.

Imaginary as the characters are, however, the supposition that Zenobia is an apograph of Margaret Fuller, may not be so far wrong. That extraordinary woman could not have been absent from the mind of the novelist—nay, must have inspired his pencil, whilst sketching 'the high-spirited woman bruising herself against the narrow limitations of her sex.' And, in so far as it is the embodiment of this sentiment or relation, we may have in the career of Zenobia (not in its details, but in its essential features), a missing chapter in Margaret Fuller's life—unwritten hitherto, because never sufficiently palpable to come under the cognizance of the biographer, and only capable of being unveiled by the novelist, whose function it is to discern the intents of the heart, and to describe things that are not as though they were. We may, at least, venture to say that the study of Zenobia will form an excellent introduction to the study of her supposed prototype. There are problems both in biography and in history which imagination only can solve; and in this respect, *Blithedale*, as a whole, may tell a truer tale with its fictions than Brook Farm with its facts. Hence it is that our author, while expressing an earnest wish that the world may have the benefit of the latter, felt that it belonged to him to furnish it with the former. A poetic soul sees more in history than it can reproduce in a historical form, and must, therefore, create a symbolism for itself, less inexorable in its conditions, and more expressive of his latest thought. The historical result of the experiment at Brook Farm, and its direct didactic value, may have been inconsiderable enough, but its reproductive capacity in a fruitful mind might have issued in a work which would have rendered that bubble a permanent landmark in the progress of humanity.

But here, again, Hawthorne disappoints us, and again through his lack of moral earnestness. Everybody will naturally regard this story, whether fact or fiction, as a socialistic drama, and will expect its chief interest as such to be of a moral kind. 'Blithedale,' whatever may be its relation to Brook Farm, is itself a socialistic settlement, with its corresponding phases of life, and therefore involves points both of moral and material interest, the practical operation of which should have been exhibited so as to bring out the good and evil of the system. But this task Hawthorne declines, and does not 'put forward the slightest pretensions to illustrate a theory, or elicit a conclusion favourable or otherwise to Socialism.' He confines himself to the delineation of its picturesque phases, as a 'thing of beauty,' and either has no particular convictions respecting its deeper relations, or hesitates to express them. It was not necessary for him to pass judgment upon the theories of Fourier or Robert Owen. He had nothing to do with it as a theory; but as a phase of life it demanded appropriate colouring. Would he paint an ideal slave-plantation merely for the beauty of the thing, without pretending to 'elicit a conclusion favourable or otherwise' to slavery? Could he forget the moral relations of this system, or drop them out of his picture, 'merely to establish a theatre a little removed from the highway of ordinary travel, where the creatures of his brain may play their phantasmagorical antics without exposing them to too close a comparison with the actual events of real life?' In respect of involving moral relations, the two cases are analogous, and the one may be rendered morally colourless with no more propriety than the other. 'Blithedale,' then, as a socialistic community, is merely used here as a scaffolding—a very huge one—in the construction of an edifice considerably smaller than itself! And then, the artist leaves the scaffolding standing! Socialism, in this romance, is prominent enough to fill the book, but it has so little business in it, that it does not even grow into an organic part of the story, and contributes nothing whatever toward the final catastrophe. It is a theatre—and, as such, it should have a neutral tint; but it should also be made of neutral stuff; and its erection, moreover, should not be contemporaneous with the performance of the play. But the incongruity becomes more apparent when we consider the kind of play acted in it. Take the moral of Zenobia's history, and you will find that Socialism is apparently made responsible for consequences which it utterly condemned, and tried, at least, to remedy. We say, apparently, for it is really not made responsible for anything, good, bad, or indifferent. It forms a circumference of circumstances, which neither mould the characters, nor influence the destinies, of the individuals so equivocally situated,—forms, in short, not an essential part of the picture, but an enormous fancy border, not very suitable for the purpose for which it was designed. Zenobia's life would have been exhibited with more propriety, and its moral brought home with more effect, in the 'theatre' of the world, out of which it really grew, and of which it would have formed a vital and harmonious part. Zenobia and Socialism should have been acted in the ready-made theatre of ordinary humanity, to see how it would fare with them there. Having occupied the ground, Hawthorne owed it to truth, and to a fit opportunity, so to dramatize his experience and observation of Communistic life, as to make them of practical value for the world at large.

—Anonymous (attributed to George Eliot),
"Contemporary Literature of America,"
Westminster Review, October 1852, p. 591–98

JOHN NICHOL (1882)

Nichol reduces the novel to a series of useful sayings and epithets, such as: "half the work of the wise is to counteract the mischief done by the good." To Nichol, Miles Coverdale is the one wise man in the novel. Hawthorne's mastery of antithesis is prominent, Nichol notes, listing the pairing of Coverdale with Hollingsworth, Zenobia with Priscilla, and old Moodie with Westervelt. Wholesome and honest farm life finds its antithesis in the artificial and mendacious mesmerist shows in the lyceum. Readers studying either doubling or antithesis in Hawthorne's work will find this review useful.

———————— ⸙⸙⸙ ———— ⸙⸙⸙ ———— ⸙⸙⸙ ————

The Blithedale Romance is no bundle of biographies: it has been more properly described as "a humanitarian ballet danced by four figures, who quarrel and dance out of tune." The central idea is, in this case, almost too obvious: the proposition to be proved is that the exaggeration of right may turn to wrong—*Summum jus, summa injuria.* It is *Measure for Measure* without the treason in Angelo's blood, though Hollingsworth is, in the result, as cruel as Angelo meant to be. Much of the work is a comment on the melancholy truth that "half the work of the wise is to counteract the mischief done by the good;" but the only wise man on the stage is Coverdale, and he is not strong enough: all he has to tell us in the end is, by his own confession, "Nothing, nothing, nothing!" Silas Foster interrupting the regenerators of society with the question, "Which man among you is the best judge of swine?" and the discovery, soon made by the masquerading Arcadians, that "intellectual activity is incompatible with any large amount of bodily exercise," point to the foregone conclusion. The descriptive skill displayed in the book is beyond praise. Nowhere has the author more successfully availed himself of his favourite trick of antithesis. The man whose life is ruined by too much, and the man whose life is an emptiness from too little, purpose; the magnificent Zenobia,—the most Titian-like figure on Hawthorne's canvas,—pulsing in every vein with passionate life, and the veiled lady, the pale "anemone," whose appearance in the drama is like the sigh of a flute in a rich orchestra;—these are not more strikingly contrasted than old Moodie, the frail shadow of Fauntleroy, and Westervelt, charlatan and "salamander"—people who seem to have walked entire out of some unwritten novel of Balzac. The variety in the scenery is similarly enhanced by juxtaposition, as of the Hermitage and the Hotel, Elliot's Pulpit and the Boarding-house; just as the healthy atmosphere of the fields is set off by the miasmas of Mesmerism and Spiritualism, which, in this instance, represent the inevitable element of superstition. *The Blithedale Romance* has attracted an unusual amount of attention from French critics, owing to the interest taken by their countrymen in the social problem—a problem which it, however, suggests and sets aside rather than discusses, the references to Fourierism, etc., being mere interpolations cut short by Hollingsworth's dogmatism. The only point made plain is the baleful and blighting effect of the philanthropy that overrides private personal claims. The book is the tragedy of which Dickens' Mrs. Jellaby is the comedy; and it is the most dismal ever written by the author, the only rays of light being the rustic scenes, and the impressive emancipation of Priscilla in the village hall. The finding of Zenobia's body is, perhaps, the most ghastly description in literature: it is aggravated to a climax by the horrible cynicism of Coverdale's remark, that had she foreseen "how ill it would become her, she would no more have committed the dreadful act than have exhibited herself in public in a badly-fitting garment." Time passes, and the impartial torturer meets the philanthropic bird of prey with the question, "Up to this moment, how many criminals have you reformed?" "No one," said Hollingsworth, with his eyes still fixed on the ground. "Ever since we parted, I have been busy with a single murderer." It is a fit close to the wreck of idealisms and the holocaust of aspirations, that leaves us with a deeper sense of the mockery of life, of more utter hopelessness than any other English work of fiction, excepting perhaps *Middlemarch*.

—John Nichol, *American Literature*, 1882, pp. 345–47

THE MARBLE FAUN

Hawthorne's intentions remain veiled—at least to certain critics—in his last novel. The ambiguities (or, as Katharine Lee Bates terms them, the "misleading suggestions and tricksy hypotheses") of *The Marble Faun* were such that the reviewer for the *Atlantic Monthly* groused that "the suggestive faculty is tormented rather than genially excited and in the end is left a prey to doubts." Readers were either confounded or enchanted by Hawthorne's "misty ways." The historian John Lothrop Motley was infuriated only by the prevailing bemusement among the novel's wider readers. "I suppose that nothing less than illustrated edition, with a large gallows on the last page, with Donatello in the most pensile of attitudes . . . would be satisfactory," he rails in defense of Hawthorne.

The Marble Faun has the distinction of being Hawthorne's only non-American novel. While anxieties regarding a national, independent idiom and literature were less pronounced in 1860 than they had been at the start of Hawthorne's career, there is still a certain uneasiness among some critics that Hawthorne chose Italy as his setting. This sentiment possibly emerges from the recurring criticism that with this novel Hawthorne lapsed from storytelling into travel writing. William Ellery Channing notes this, but in the fashion of the *literati* of the time, he adds dreamily that Italy is the subject that best justifies such a lapse.

John Lothrop Motley (1860)

Motley was the New England writer whose major work was a multivolume history of the Netherlands. He writes to Hawthorne taking issue with popular criticism of the novel. Again, Hawthorne's defenders lament the failure of the public to detect and embrace Hawthorne's subtler charms. The critics lack imagination, Lothrop insists, and would require a laboriously blatant illustrated edition to clarify Hawthorne's ambiguities.

I have said a dozen times that nobody can write English but you. With regard to the story, which has been somewhat criticised, I can only say that to me it is quite satisfactory. I like those shadowy, weird, fantastic, Hawthornesque shapes flitting through the golden gloom, which is the atmosphere of the book. I like the misty way in which the story is indicated rather than revealed; the outlines are quite definite enough from the beginning to the end to those who have imagination enough to follow you in your airy flights; and to those who complain, I suppose that nothing less than an illustrated edition, with a large gallows on the last page, with Donatello in the most pensile of attitudes,—his ears revealed through a white nightcap,—would be satisfactory. I beg your pardon for such profanation, but it really moves my spleen that people should wish to bring down the volatile figures of your romance to the level of an every-day romance. The way in which the two victims dance through the Carnival on the last day is very striking. It is like a Greek tragedy in its effect, without being in the least Greek.

—John Lothrop Motley, Letter to Nathaniel Hawthorne
(March 29, 1860), cited in George Parsons Lathrop,
A Study of Hawthorne, 1876, pp. 262–63

Anonymous "Nathaniel Hawthorne" (1860)

While this reviewer for the *Atlantic Monthly* praises *The Marble Faun* in its capacity as a travelogue, he finds the book's conclusion "unsatisfactory." It resembles an "unsolved puzzle," even to the "tolerant and interpretative 'gentle reader.'" Like Motley, the reviewer finds the novel mired in mist. Unlike Motley, he views this as a problem. In Hawthorne's conclusion, "nothing is really concluded." Hawthorne's tortuous logic loses the reader in a "labyrinth of guesses."

When it comes to characterization, such vagueness serves to subvert the story. Miriam's persecutor—that is, Donatello's victim—is "deprived of all human attributes," and so Donatello's crime lacks the requisite veneer of sin.

Students interested in Hawthorne's use (or abuse) of ambiguity should consult this review, alongside the preceding John Lothrop Motley entry.

———————

The romance of *The Marble Faun* will be widely welcomed, not only for its intrinsic merits, but because it is a sign that its writer, after a silence of seven or eight years, has determined to resume his place in the ranks of authorship. In his preface he tells us, that in each of his previous publications he had unconsciously one person in his eye, whom he styles his 'gentle reader.' He meant it

> for that one congenial friend, more comprehensive of his purposes, more appreciative of his success, more indulgent of his short-comings, and, in all respects, closer and kinder than a brother,—that all-sympathizing critic, in short, whom an author never actually meets, but to whom he implicitly makes his appeal, whenever he is conscious of having done his best.

He believes that this reader did once exist for him, and duly received the scrolls he flung 'upon whatever wind was blowing, in the faith that they would find him out.' 'But,' he questions,

> is he extant now? In these many years since he last heard from me, may he not have deemed his earthly task accomplished, and have withdrawn to the paradise of gentle readers, wherever it may be, to the enjoyments of which his kindly charity on my behalf must surely have entitled him?

As we feel assured that Hawthorne's reputation has been steadily growing with the lapse of time, he has no cause to fear that the longevity of his gentle reader will not equal his own. As long as he writes, there will be readers enough to admire and appreciate. . . .

Eight years have passed since *The Blithedale Romance* was written, and during nearly the whole of this period Hawthorne has resided abroad. *The Marble Faun*, which must, on the whole, be considered the greatest of his works, proves that his genius has widened and deepened in this interval, without any alteration or modification of its characteristic merits and characteristic defects. The most obvious excellence of the work is the vivid truthfulness of its descriptions of Italian life, manners, and scenery; and, considered merely as a record of a tour in Italy, it is of great interest and attractiveness. The opinions on Art, and the special criticisms on the masterpieces of architecture, sculpture, and painting, also possess a value of their own. The story might have been told, and the characters fully represented, in one-third of the space devoted to them, yet description and narration are so artfully combined that each assists to give interest to the other. Hawthorne is one of those true observers who concentrate in observation every power of their minds. He has accurate sight and piercing insight. When he modifies either the form or the spirit of the objects he describes, he does it either by viewing them through the medium of an imagined mind or by obeying associations which they themselves suggest. We might quote from the descriptive portions of the work a hundred pages, at least, which would demonstrate how closely accurate observation is connected with the highest powers of the intellect and imagination.

The style of the book is perfect of its kind, and, if Hawthorne had written nothing else, would entitle him to rank among the great masters of English composition. Walter Savage Landor is reported to have said of an author whom he knew in his youth, 'My friend wrote excellent English, a language now obsolete.' Had *The Marble Faun* appeared before he uttered this sarcasm, the wit of the remark would have been pointless. Hawthorne not only writes English, but the sweetest, simplest, and clearest English that ever has been made the vehicle of equal depth, variety, and subtilty of thought and emotion. His mind is reflected in his style as a face is reflected in a mirror; and the latter does not give back its image with less appearance of effort than the former. His excellence consists not so much in using common words as in making common words express uncommon things. Swift, Addison, Goldsmith, not to mention others, wrote with as much simplicity; but the style of neither embodies an individuality so complex, passions so strange and intense, sentiments so fantastic and preternatural, thoughts so profound and delicate, and imaginations so remote from the recognized limits of the ideal, as find an orderly outlet in the pure English of Hawthorne. He has hardly a word to which Mrs. Trimmer would primly object, hardly a sentence which would call forth the frosty anathema of Blair, Hurd, Kames, or Whately, and yet he contrives to embody in his simple style qualities which would almost excuse the verbal extravagances of Carlyle.

In regard to the characterization and plot of *The Marble Faun*, there is room for widely varying opinions. Hilda, Miriam, and Donatello will be generally received as superior in power and depth to any of Hawthorne's previous creations of character; Donatello, especially, must be considered one of the most original and exquisite conceptions in the whole range of romance; but the story in which they appear will seem to many an unsolved puzzle, and even the tolerant and interpretative 'gentle reader' will be troubled with the unsatisfactory conclusion. It is justifiable for a romancer to sting the curiosity of his readers with a mystery, only on the implied obligation to explain it at last; but this story begins in mystery only to end in mist. The suggestive faculty is tormented rather than genially excited, and in the end is left a prey to doubts. The central idea of the story, the necessity of sin to convert such a creature as Donatello into a moral being, is also not happily illustrated in the leading event. When Donatello kills the wretch who malignantly dogs the steps of Miriam, all readers think that Donatello committed no sin at all; and the reason is, that Hawthorne has deprived the persecutor of Miriam of all human attributes, made him an allegorical representation of one of the most fiendish forms of unmixed evil, so that we welcome his destruction with something of the same feeling with which, in following the allegory of Spenser or Bunyan, we rejoice in the hero's victory over the Blatant Beast or Giant Despair. Conceding, however, that Donatello's act was murder, and not 'justifiable homicide,' we are still not sure that the author's conception of his nature and of the change caused in his nature by that act, are carried out with a felicity corresponding to the original conception.

In the first volume, and in the early part of the second, the author's hold on his design is comparatively firm, but it somewhat relaxes as he proceeds, and in the end it seems almost to escape from his grasp. Few can be satisfied with the concluding chapters, for the reason that nothing is really concluded. We are willing to follow the ingenious processes of Calhoun's deductive logic, because we are sure, that, however severely they task the faculty of attention, they will lead to some positive result; but Hawthorne's logic of events leaves us in the end bewildered in a labyrinth of guesses. The book is, on the whole, such a great book, that its defects are felt with all the more force.

In this rapid glance at some of the peculiarities of Hawthorne's genius, we have not, of course, been able to do full justice to the special merits of the works we have passed in review; but we trust that we have said nothing which would convey the impression that we do not place them among the most remarkable romances produced in an age in which romance-writing has called forth some of the highest powers of the human mind. In intellect and imagination, in the faculty of discerning spirits and detecting laws, we doubt if any living novelist is his equal; but his genius, in its creative action, has been heretofore attracted to the dark rather than the bright side of the interior life of humanity, and the geniality which evidently is in him has rarely found adequate expression. In the many works which he may still be expected to write, it is to be hoped that his mind will lose some of its sadness of tone without losing any of its subtilty and depth; but, in any event, it would be unjust to deny that he has already done enough to insure him a commanding position in American literature as long as American literature has an existence.

—Anonymous, "Nathaniel Hawthorne,"
Atlantic Monthly, V, May 1860, pp. 614–22

HENRY BRIGHT (1860)

Henry Bright was an English businessman and literary reviewer from Liverpool who met Hawthorne during a pilgrimage to Concord. He became one of Hawthorne's closest friends when the novelist assumed his consulship in Liverpool. Despite this intimacy, Bright was outraged by Hawthorne's "cruelty" in *The Marble Faun*. Bright accuses Hawthorne of deliberately—maliciously, even—withholding necessary information.

I've finished *the* book, and am, I think, more angry at your tantalizing cruelty than either *Athenaeum* or *Saturday Review*. I want to know a hundred things you do not tell me,—who Miriam was, what was the crime in which she was concerned and of which all Europe knew, what was in the packet, what became of Hilda, whether Miriam married Donatello, whether Donatello got his head cut off, etc. Of course you'll say I ought to *guess*; well, if I do guess, it is but a guess, and I want to *know*. Yesterday I wrote a review of you in the *Examiner*, and in spite of my natural indignation, I hope you will not altogether dislike what I have said. In other respects I admire *Monte Beni* more than I can tell you; and I suppose no one now will visit Rome without a copy of it in his hand. Nowhere are descriptions to be found so beautiful, so true, and so pathetic. And there are little bits of *you* in the book which are best of all,—half moralizing, half thinking aloud. There is a bit about *women sewing* which Harriet raves about. There are bits about Catholicism and love and sin, which are marvellously thought and gloriously written.

—Henry Bright, Letter to Nathaniel Hawthorne (1860),
cited in Julian Hawthorne, *Nathaniel Hawthorne
and His Wife*, 1884, Vol. 2, p. 240

NATHANIEL HAWTHORNE (1860)

Smith and Elder certainly do take strange liberties with the titles of books. I wanted to call it *The Marble Faun,* but they insisted upon *Transformation,* which will lead the reader to anticipate a sort of pantomime. They wrote me some days ago that the edition was nearly all sold, and that they are going to print another; to which I mean to append a few pages, in the shape of a conversation between Kenyon, Hilda, and the author, throwing some further light on matters which seem to have been left too much in the dark. For my own part, however, I should prefer the book as it now stands.

> —Nathaniel Hawthorne, Letter to Henry Bright (1860),
> cited in Julian Hawthorne, *Nathaniel Hawthorne*
> *and His Wife,* 1884, Vol. 2, p. 241

WILLIAM ELLERY CHANNING (1860)

Channing was the nephew of the elder (and more notable) William Ellery Channing, a prominent radical cleric and anticipator of transcendentalism. The nephew, meanwhile, was a minor poet, best remembered as the close confidant and sauntering companion of Henry David Thoreau. Channing wrote cloying odes to Hawthorne's genius. In this letter, Channing reiterates the difficulty in seizing the novel's "thread," and also returns to another recurring observation: the prominence of the "Italian criticism." Hawthorne was straying into travel writing. There is a danger in mixing the didactic with the dramatic, Channing cautions; yet if ever there was a deserving subject, he coos, "it should be Italy." Readers interested in *The Marble Faun*'s structure and focus might compare Channing's view with Leslie Stephen's objection to Hawthorne's description of an Italian loaf of bread.

I was greatly pleased with the success of your last book, *The Marble Faun.* It seemed to me at first, until I got well a-going, a little difficult to seize the thread; but when I once found it, I went rapidly forward unto the end. I always consider the rapidity with which I can read a story the test of its merit, at least for me. Many others have spoken to me of its effect on them. I greatly enjoyed the Italian criticism. As a matter of art, there is possibly always a certain danger in combining didactic and dramatic situations; but if any field is open to this, it should be Italy. "Corinne," I think, deals in character rather than criticism. I should be ashamed to tell you how often I have read *The Marble Faun*.

—William Ellery Channing, Letter to Nathaniel Hawthorne
(September 3, 1860), cited in Julian Hawthorne,
Nathaniel Hawthorne and His Wife, 1884, Vol. 2, p. 265

James Russell Lowell
"Swinburne's Tragedies" (1866)

Marble Faun, whether consciously or not, illustrates that invasion of the aesthetic by the moral which has confused art by dividing its allegiance, and dethroned the old dynasty without as yet firmly establishing the new in an acknowledged legitimacy.

—James Russell Lowell, "Swinburne's Tragedies" (1866),
Works, Riverside ed., Vol. 2, pp. 125–26

George Parsons Lathrop (1876)

In all we may find our way to some mystic monument of eternal law, or pluck garlands from some new-budded bough of moral truth. The romance is like a portal of ebony inlaid with ivory,—another gate of dreams,—swinging softly open into regions of illimitable wisdom. But some pause on the threshold, unused to such large liberty; and these cry out, in the words of a well-known critic, "It begins in mystery, and ends in mist."

Though the book was very successful, few readers grasped the profounder portions. It is a vast exemplar of the author's consummate charm as a simple storyteller, however, that he exercised a brilliant fascination over all readers, notwithstanding the heavy burden of uncomprehended truths which they were obliged to carry with them. Some critics complain of the extent to which Roman scenery and the artistic life in Rome have been introduced; but, to my mind, there is scarcely a word wasted in the two volumes. The "vague sense of ponderous remembrances" pressing down and crowding out the present moment till "our individual affairs are but half as real here as elsewhere," is essential to the perspective of the whole; and nothing but this rich picturesqueness and variety could avail to balance the depth of tragedy which has to be encountered; so that the nicety of art is unquestionable. It is strange, indeed, that this great modern religious romance should thus have become also the ideal representative of ruined Rome—the home of ruined religions—in its aesthetic aspects.

—George Parsons Lathrop,
A *Study of Hawthorne*, 1876, pp. 260-61

ARTHUR SHERBURNE HARDY
"HAWTHORNE'S ITALIAN ROMANCE" (1889)

Hardy was a nineteenth-century American mathematician, engineer, academic, and journalist. In this review—of a later illustrated edition of the novel—he defends Hawthorne against the many criticisms that accused the author of morbidity. Conceding Hawthorne's darkness, Hardy argues that the fire in Hawthorne's crucible is "a purifying flame." As a realist Hawthorne scoured at "the sky above our heads as well as the mud under our feet." Hardy's defense will serve any reader researching a question regarding Hawthorne's pessimism and use of dark themes.

Of *The Marble Faun*, Hardy allows that Hawthorne strayed into the realm of the guidebook. However, since this story, unlike Hawthorne's others, is "withdrawn from the realm of the imagination," it is fitting and right that the edition being considered here, published in 1889, should contain fifty photogravures. Students interested in perceptions of the novel and differing presentations of Hawthorne's works can compare Hardy's take on this illustrated edition with John Lothrop Motley's letter of 1860 to Hawthorne, sarcastically imagining such an edition as being necessary for unimaginative readers. Readers comparing *The Marble Faun* with Hawthorne's earlier novels should also attend to Hardy's words.

The shadow of a Miriam's guilt dims the purity of a Hilda's innocence. But in painting life as it is, it is always possible to paint it as it ought to be. When it is said that Hawthorne makes us familiar with sin and suffering, it must be remembered that there is a familiarity which degrades and another which ennobles. Out of this sombre background Hawthorne evokes the greatness of human nature. The radiance of a spiritual sky falls upon his darkest picture. From the standpoint of the philosopher or the theologian, every writer will always be subject to criticism, for the reason that the standpoints are many. An early critic complained that Hawthorne was morbid because he evinced "so little conception of the remedial system which God has provided for the sins and sorrows of mankind." Granting the fact set forth in this narrow arraignment, it remains true that without avowing distinctly any ethical purpose Hawthorne is ever revealing the sublimity of life, the grandeur of human nature. The fire of his crucible is a purifying flame. However realistic the woes or littlenesses he portrays, they neither crush nor disgust. His vision was too all-embracing, his purpose too deep for this. He is the thinker interpreting to us the world of reality, not the mirror reflecting it. Even as the realist he reflected the sky above our heads as well as the mud under our feet. . . .

I may mention one delicious quality in the melancholy of Hawthorne for which we are always grateful—its impersonality. His eye looks outward. There is analysis, but not self-analysis, no introspection. He shows us suffering humanity, not the suffering Hawthorne. His is no Byronic literature of personal griefs, with its littlenesses, self-infatuations, and idolatry. There is, of course, the melancholy of the temperament, the constitutional tendency of the individual, but no autobiography of a bitter personal experience. He is summing up greater than individual issues. It is infinitely refreshing to be free from this oppressive sense of subjective suffering, the single accidental experience, so insignificant when compared with the general law and so fatal to dispassionate analysis.

I may mention one impression derived from a last re-reading of *The Marble Faun* which is perhaps wholly personal, but which has lessened its first effect as a work of art. The local color and descriptive passages of Hawthorne's earlier works impart the information necessary to the setting of the story, and no more. What may be called the decorative elements are so intimately associated with the constructive plan that each heightens the effect of the other. I cannot recall a writer more successful in this union of ornamental detail and organic structure. It is like the pediment end of the Doric order, whose beauty is not applied but wrought in. Whenever this is true, a style, whether in literature or architecture, painting or sculpture, gains immensely in dignity and unity. I do not say that it is not true of *The Marble Faun,* nor that its local color is less natural than that of Hawthorne's New England novels; but that mingled with what is strictly necessary to the scenic effect is a great deal of information which belongs to the guide-book rather than the work of art. Hawthorne's analysis of a painting or interpretation of a statue is often vital to the story, and has a value apart from its relation to it; but there is much of description and history which belongs rather to a work like Irving's *Alhambra* than to a romance.

For this very reason, however, the illustration of *The Marble Faun* is withdrawn from the realm of imagination. We would have no other

Donatello than that of Praxiteles, desire no Hilda's Tower but that of the Via Portoghese. The present edition, glorious in red and gold, yet exquisitely tasteful, with its fifty photogravures, is a gem in bookmaking. Remembering that this work was received with so little favor that Hawthorne used to say of it, "The thing is a failure," it makes one wish he might see this last effort to array it in the beauty it deserves.

—Arthur Sherburne Hardy, "Hawthorne's Italian Romance,"
Book Buyer, November 1889, pp. 427–28

KATHARINE LEE BATES (1897)

Katharine Lee Bates was a Massachusetts poet, notably the author of the poem that became the anthem "America the Beautiful." She also taught and wrote on American literature at Wellesley College. She returns to the subject of Hawthorne's obscurity of intention in *The Marble Faun*, with the new suggestion that Hawthorne was not being willful, but that "perhaps he hardly knew the actual fate of Miriam and Donatello." Bates's thesis (anticipating the tide of late-twentieth-century literary theory) removes the authority from Hawthorne. Any students exploring questions of writerly authority in Hawthorne's work should consider this account.

In *The Marble Faun* his pure and tranquil grace of style is at its best. The economy of incident is not so strict as in the statuesque simplicity of the *Scarlet Letter* groupings, nor is the dramatic intensity so keen; but there is Hawthorne's own rich, subdued, autumnal coloring, with the first soft shadows deepening into sable. Emerson, whom Hawthorne's Concord journal once noted as coming to call "'with a sunbeam in his face," unwittingly returned the compliment by saying that Hawthorne "rides well his horse of the night." Gloom has its own enchantment, and so has mystery, but the issues of this romance were left in an uncertainty that its readers found hard to bear. Hawthorne would not help them. He was fertile in misleading suggestions and tricksy hypotheses, but perhaps he hardly knew the actual fate of Miriam and Donatello. Such a "cloudy veil" as he found stretched over "the abyss" of his own nature may have been interposed between himself and the innermost secrets of his characters. Supernatural forces, too, entered in, as in life, amid the personages of his tales and played their inscrutable parts beside them. Among the baffling questions is one suggested by Hawthorne's younger daughter, who, with her husband, George Parsons Lathrop, poet and novelist, has embraced the Roman faith. Mrs. Lathrop claims that *The Marble Faun,* if closely studied, shows in the treatment of sin and atonement a significant divergence from the Puritan romances.

—Katharine Lee Bates, *American Literature,*
1897, pp. 314–15

Chronology

‒ᴧᴧᴧ‒ ‒ᴧᴧᴧ‒ ‒ᴧᴧᴧ‒

1804 Nathaniel Hawthorn (later Hawthorne) born July 4 in Salem, Massachusetts. Both parents are descended from prominent New England families.

1808 Father dies of yellow fever in New Guinea.

1821–25 Attends Bowdoin College. Longfellow and Franklin Pierce are among his classmates. Writes first fiction.

1828 Publishes *Fanshawe: A Tale* anonymously and at his own expense. He later destroys the manuscript, which is not republished until after his death.

1830 Begins to publish many sketches and tales anonymously or using a pseudonym.

1837 Publishes the first edition of *Twice-Told Tales,* a collection of previously published stories.

1839 Engaged to Sophia Peabody.

1839–41 Works as a measurer of salt and coal at the Boston Customs House.

1841 In April, joins and invests in Brook Farm community in West Roxbury, Massachusetts, but withdraws by the end of the year.

1842 Marries Sophia Peabody and moves to the Old Manse, Concord, Massachusetts. Neighbors include Emerson, Thoreau, and Margaret Fuller.

1844 Daughter Una is born.

1846 Publishes *Mosses from an Old Manse,* a collection of previously published stories and sketches with an introductory essay. Son Julian is born. Works as a surveyor at the Salem Custom House.

1847 Rents house in Salem.

1850 *The Scarlet Letter* is published. Hawthorne moves to a farm near Lenox, Massachusetts, where he lives until the following year.

1851 Publishes *The House of the Seven Gables, The Snow-Image*. Daughter Rose is born. Moves to West Newton, Massachusetts.

1852 Purchases and lives at Wayside in Concord, Massachusetts. Publishes *The Blithedale Romance, A Wonder-Book for Girls and Boys,* and a campaign biography of Franklin Pierce.

1853–57 Appointed by President Pierce, Hawthorne serves as U.S. consul in Liverpool, England.

1857–59 Lives in Italy, in Rome and then Florence.

1860 Publishes *The Marble Faun*. Returns with family to Wayside.

1863 Publishes *Our Old Home*.

1864 Nathaniel Hawthorne dies on May 19 in Plymouth, New Hampshire. He is buried at Sleepy Hollow Cemetery, Concord, Massachusetts.

Index

DATE DUE

Nathaniel Hawthorne

APR   2008